MIND THE GAP

TEXTUAL EXPLORATIONS

General editors:

MICK SHORT Lancaster University
ELENA SEMINO Lancaster University

Books published in this series:

Language and World Creation in Poems and other Texts
ELENA SEMINO

Text Worlds: Representing Conceptual Space in Discourse
PAUL WERTH

Mind the Gap: Ellipsis and Stylistic Variation in Spoken and Written English
PETER WILSON

The Poetics of Science Fiction
PETER STOCKWELL

MIND THE GAP

ELLIPSIS AND STYLISTIC
VARIATION IN SPOKEN
AND WRITTEN ENGLISH

PETER WILSON

An imprint of **Pearson Education**

Harlow, England · London · New York · Reading, Massachusetts · San Francisco
Toronto · Don Mills, Ontario · Sydney · Tokyo · Singapore · Hong Kong · Seoul
Taipei · Cape Town · Madrid · Mexico City · Amsterdam · Munich · Paris · Milan

Pearson Education Limited
Edinburgh Gate
Harlow
Essex CM20 2JE
England

and Associated Companies throughout the world

Visit us on the World Wide Web at:
www.pearsoneduc.com

─────────

First published 2000

ISBN 0–582–35680–6 CSD
ISBN 0–582–35679–2 PPR

British Library Cataloguing-in-Publication Data

A catalogue record for this book is available from the British Library

Library of Congress Cataloging-in-Publication Data

Wilson, Peter, 1945–
     Mind the gap : ellipsis and stylistic variation in spoken and written English / Peter Wilson.
         p.   cm. — (Textual explorations)
     ISBN 0–582–35680–6 — ISBN 0–582–35679–2 (pbk.)
     Includes bibliographical references (p.   ) and index.
     1. English language—Ellipsis.   2. English language—Spoken English.
   3. English language—Written English.   4. English language—Variation.
   5. English language—Style.   I. Title.   II. Series.

PE1369.W55   2000
425—dc21   99–059042

Set in 11/13pt Bembo by 35
Produced by Addison Wesley Longman Singapore (Pte) Ltd.
Printed in Singapore

CONTENTS

Author's Acknowledgements	*ix*
Publisher's Acknowledgements	*xi*
Introduction	*1*

PART ONE: THE FORMS OF ELLIPSIS — 5

CHAPTER 1: WHAT IS ELLIPSIS? — 7

Some preliminary considerations	7
A sample of dialogue	10
Compressed language	14
Defining ellipsis	17

CHAPTER 2: WHAT ISN'T ELLIPSIS — 22

Lapses in performance	22
Nonrealization	27
Inferential gaps	31

CHAPTER 3: THE LINGUISTIC CONTEXT — 38

Intrasentential ellipsis: subordination reduction	41
Intersentential ellipsis: contextual rejoinders	45

CHAPTER 4: THE SITUATIONAL CONTEXT — 55

Sentence-initial ellipsis	55
Situational ellipsis	62

CHAPTER 5: TELEGRAPHIC ELLIPSIS   69

Headlinese   71

Lists, headings and things   73

Telegraphic speech, telegraphic thought   76

Notices and signs   78

CHAPTER 6: COORDINATION REDUCTION   85

Levels of coordination   86

Categories of coordination reduction   92

Leftmost coordination reduction   92

Rightmost coordination reduction   94

Central coordination reduction   97

CHAPTER 7: THE ROUGH GUIDE TO GAPS   104

PART TWO: THE STYLISTIC EFFECTS OF ELLIPSIS   115

CHAPTER 8: STYLE AND STYLISTICS   117

Form —— Formal   119

Function —— Functional   122

Individuation —— Authorial   125

Act of listening or reading —— Affective   127

CHAPTER 9: SPEECH STYLES AND ELLIPSIS   136

Levels of spontaneity   138

Number of participant speakers   142

CHAPTER 10: SPORTS COMMENTARY   149

Two types of commentary   149

Football commentary   152

Horse race commentary   156

CHAPTER 11: DRAMATIZING DIALOGUE 163

Stage directions 163

Dramatizing conversation 166

Dramatic monologue 171

CHAPTER 12: THE CONATIVE TURN 178

Telling language 179

Selling language 183

Persuasion without conation 188

CHAPTER 13: NARRATIVE VOICES, NARRATIVE GAPS 194

Narrative voices 195

Mimesis and diegesis 199

The ambiguous voice: free indirect speech and thought 204

CHAPTER 14: ELLIPSIS AND COMPRESSION IN POETRY 210

Expansiveness versus compression 210

The compression of imagism 215

Compression in translation 219

Conclusion 226

Bibliography 229

Index 235

AUTHOR'S ACKNOWLEDGEMENTS

I would like to thank the Faculty of Humanities and Education of the University of North London for granting me sabbatical leave without which the first draft of this book would have been much more difficult, if not impossible, to complete.

My appreciation also goes to Professor Mick Short for his painstaking editorial work without which subsequent drafts would not have arrived at this final form.

Errors and infelicities remain, of course, my own.

Peter Wilson

PUBLISHER'S ACKNOWLEDGEMENTS

We are grateful to the following for permission to reproduce copyright material:

Figure 12.1, advertisement for Ssang Yong Korando, reproduced with permission of I. M. Group Limited; Figure 12.2, advertisement for Panasonic NV EX1B, reproduced with approval of Panasonic; Figures 12.3 and 12.4, advertisements for Minolta Vectis 300, reproduced with permission of Jack Bankhead and Wood Burdon; BBC for extracts from transcripts of '1998 British Open Golf Championship' commentary on *Radio 5* 17.7.98 and '1998 World CupFinal' on *BBC Radio 5 Live* 12.7.98; BBC Rights Archive for an extracts from transcripts of a radio 'phone-in' programme on *Radio 5* 24.9.98, transcripts of interviews with Elton, Bell & McKellen in BBC's *Face to Face* programmes, and brief extracts from *Question time* BBC TV 10.12.98; Dorling Kindersley Ltd for an extract from *Children's Quick and Easy Cookbook* by A. Wilkes © 1997 Dorling Kindersley Ltd, London; Faber & Faber Limited/ Harcourt Brace Inc for an extracts from the poems 'The Wasteland' and 'Portrait of a Lady' from *Collected Poems* 1963 by T. S. Eliot; Faber & Faber Ltd/New Directions Publishing Corporation for poem 'The Return' by Ezra Pound from *Selected Poems* 1975/*Personea*, Copyright © 1926 by Ezra Pound; Guardian Newspapers Ltd for extracts from *The Guardian Guide* 18–24.4.98, and 'And What's More' in *Observer Review* 27.9.98; HarperCollins Publishers for an extract from *Halliwell's Film Guide* 1997 edited by J. Walker; Pan Macmillan Ltd for an extract from *Walkers Britain* 1982; TSL Education Ltd for the headline 'Citizenship Heads for Secondary Schools' © Times Supplements Limited and Waltham Abbey Guardian for the headline 'Cannabis man jailed for one year' in *Waltham Abbey Guardian* 9.10.98.

We have been unable to trace the copyright holder of the poem 'Picket' by R. Arlington and would appreciate any information that would enable us to do so.

INTRODUCTION

Gaps are everywhere. At least, it seems essentially human to recognize gaps, to note the spaces between things as well as the things there are spaces between, to register when the things themselves are incomplete, lacking some potential element in the wholeness we expect of them. Our sense of the incomplete is probably twofold. We can look upon gaps as structural facts, taking into account such things as the size and nature of the missing element. We can also respond to the perceptual or aesthetic effect a gap creates. As you would expect of a book in the *Textual Explorations* series, the topic here is the gaps that occur in language. Definitions of ellipsis, the most common technical term for linguistic gaps, usually reflect these twin aspects. For example, the *Chambers English Dictionary* defines ellipsis as: 'a figure of syntax by which a word or words are left out and implied', emphasizing the structural aspect. The dictionary goes on to define the adjectival derivation 'elliptical' as: 'having a part understood, concise, compendious, obscure, dubious', picking up on various perceived stylistic effects (1992: 459).

The treatment of ellipsis presented here also takes a twofold approach, investigating facts of linguistic structure and exploring their stylistic effects. Such an approach to some extent makes for a book of two halves. Accordingly, Part One, The Forms of Ellipsis, deals more directly with issues of definition and categorization. Part Two, The Stylistic Effects of Ellipsis, focuses on stylistic variation in spoken and written English. However, in the spirit of textual exploration, I have tried to allow the approaches to interact and overlap by, for example, using literary text as data to support my discussion of linguistic arguments concerning ellipsis. Linguistics, in its most generally agreed meaning, is the systematic study of language. As such, the linguistic element in this book attempts to present a systematic account of ellipsis within the framework of descriptive language study. 'Style' and 'stylistics' are rather more problematical terms. In general, style relates to a distinctive manner of using language. Stylistics is the study and explanation of such

1

language variation. Problematically though, stylistics is often used more narrowly to mean the linguistic analysis of exclusively literary language. In broad terms, the textual exploration presented here does not compartmentalize literary and non-literary stylistics. There are some chapters which are exclusively about literature and some which deal mainly with non-literary texts, but the aim of many chapters is to bring out the common ground between literary and non-literary uses of language. In this respect the relation between speech and writing is an important one and the notion of textual exploration is very much inclusive of the way the two main mediums of language operate.

The significance of ellipsis as a phenomenon of more or less everyday awareness was recently brought home to me by its occurrence in two very different contexts. The Department for Education and Employment's guidelines concerning *The National Literacy Strategy* (1998) require that pupils in English primary schools should be taught: 'to experiment with deleting words in sentences to see which are essential to retain meaning and which are not' (p. 35); 'to explore ambiguities that arise from sentence contractions, e.g. through signs and headlines' (p. 47). Although the document does not require the term 'ellipsis' to be taught to pupils, it is given the following entry in the glossary for teachers:

> ellipsis (. . .) this signifies a place where something has been omitted, or there is a pause or interruption. It is often marked by dots (. . .). These dots are also called ellipsis.
>
> Writers and speakers may use ellipsis for purposes of economy or style. For instance in the exchange: '*Where are you going?*' '*To town*', the second speaker has missed out '*I am going*'. She/he assumes that the reader will understand the omission; this saves boring repetition.
>
> Ellipsis is found in writing: *While her parents were away she threw a party. The party of the year.* The writer assumes that the reader will understand that *it was* is operating in the second sentence. (p. 79)

Primary school teachers, then, need to know about ellipsis and their pupils should be aware of, and understand the effects of, elliptical structures. Whether this is a reasonable expectation for children under the age of eleven or not, it is nevertheless official: ellipsis is part of the English National Curriculum.

The other context was this brief assessment of a recommended novel in the *The Observer* newspaper: 'Elliptical prose and oblique plotting add up to a contemporary novel of supreme importance' (27.9.98: 16). Whether the prose is elliptical in the linguistic sense, by virtue of having words left out and implied, or whether it is stylistically elliptical, say concise or obscure, I have no way of knowing, since I have not yet studied the novel referred to. Nevertheless, the newspaper assumes its readers understand the notion of ellipsis in general. The novel in question could, of course, be elliptical in both the indicated senses, a reasonable hypothesis on which to end this introduction. To what extent a figure of syntax can realize a stylistic quality is central to the textual exploration of this book.

PART ONE

THE FORMS OF ELLIPSIS

CHAPTER 1

WHAT IS ELLIPSIS?

Some gaps can be dangerous things, like those between platform and train. Public warnings tell us to mind them, that is, pay attention and avoid. Other gaps may be beneficial, like the one in the hedge that gives access to the footpath that leads to the park. We mind such gaps in a quite different way, by seeking them out and using them. Whether they are structurally necessary or part of some environmental plan, these gaps probably have one overriding thing in common: they are easily overlooked. Commuters need constantly reminding of the dangerous gap. Walkers can be guaranteed to stroll right past the gap they are looking for. The title of this book implies an analogy between these physical gaps and those that occur in language. When examined closely, language is very gappy. However, these linguistic gaps are also easily overlooked in the relatively unexamined routines of language in use and one of the main aims of this book is to identify the different types of gap and how they operate within the linguistic system as a whole.

Some preliminary considerations

The most widespread term for many of the gaps that occur in language is 'ellipsis'. Although the term is defined and used in slightly different ways by different linguists, I am taking it as generic for the purposes of this book. The main aim just mentioned can accordingly be expressed as a simple question: what is ellipsis? As is often the case with apparently simple questions, the answer proves to be less than straightforward. On the basis that exemplification is a good starting point for explanation, here is a clear-cut example of ellipsis in everyday language, similar to one cited in the English National Curriculum document I referred to in the Introduction:

> A: What is the capital of England?
> B: London [ ].

In most conversational question-and-answer sequences, or contextual rejoinders as they are often referred to, we do not bother to encode information that can be understood from the linguistic context. This creates a gap, which I have indicated by an empty set of square brackets. In this case we know that B's reply 'means' that 'London [is the capital of England]'. The gap has been filled with material recoverable from the linguistic context, a process I most often refer to as expansion. Not all instances of ellipsis are as simple and easily expanded as this one, however, and part of the aim of this book is to explore the range and complexity of the various types of gap identified.

The status of ellipsis as a linguistic phenomenon, its scope and range as a generic term, continues to be a matter of some debate within various branches of linguistics. Accordingly, this first part of the book provides a broad outline of ellipsis according to various formal, contextual and situational criteria. The overall aim of this classification is descriptive adequacy, though relevant theoretical issues will be taken into account. The rationale for this study of ellipsis is not, however, purely taxonomic. Elliptical features contribute to stylistic variation across a wide range of spoken and written genres. Therefore, another major aim of this book is to investigate how ellipsis manifests itself as an exponent of various styles of speech and writing. Accordingly, Part Two looks at how different types of ellipsis interact within texts to produce different stylistic effects. The range here is broad. Verbal artistry is reflected in linguistic choice, and the incidence of ellipsis is one of the ways in which the styles of particular writers, groups of writers and types of text can vary. For example, what, if any, relationship is there between linguistically elliptical features and the stylistic characterization elliptical, in the sense of obliquely expressed or coyly compressed? But, besides such literary concerns, these chapters also explore the way speakers and writers employ ellipsis in other, non-literary, categories of language in use, such as sports commentary or advertisements.

It is appropriate to note here that most of the examples discussed in this book are derived from actual language events: for speech, transcriptions of spontaneous conversation and media broadcasts; for writing, anything from newspapers and magazines to poems, plays and novels. The selectivity of these examples reflects at least preference, if not contrivance, on my part. It follows that any insights of a more general nature carry an implicit proviso about their wider applicability and significance, though I would hope the range of examples is sufficiently wide to justify some generalization. Some examples, particularly in the earlier chapters, are not from actual language events. They may have been generated by other linguists for the purpose of testing a hypothesis or illustrating a marginal case. Occasionally, examples of this kind are of my own devising.

The linguistic and stylistic properties of ellipsis are worthy objects of study in their own right. Within a largely descriptive approach it is unrealistic to aim for a unified theory of ellipsis, though some analytical principles, working hypotheses and contributions to theory are concomitant with a study of this kind. However, resulting insights from such study can contribute to wider aspects of language awareness, attitudes to linguistic correctness, textual analysis and critical 'readings' of language events as well as pedagogy related to these aspects. Take, for example, those primary school exercises that require answers to be given in complete sentences. By this token, my earlier example 'What is the capital of England?' would need to be answered by 'London is the capital of England', belying the naturally communicative answer 'London', that takes contextual information as understood. The requirement for answers in complete sentences probably reflects an unexamined equation between completeness and correctness that takes no account of the syntactic and contextual factors which make elliptical answers both more economical and stylistically attractive. It is also the case, however, that many teachers are aware of the need for children to assimilate complete syntactic structures into their written repertoire and this too prompts the call for complete sentences. Trivial though this particular example is, it illustrates how an awareness of ellipsis can inform pedagogic debate. *The National Literacy Strategy* entry for 'ellipsis', which I quoted in my introduction, suggests that a shift in awareness is being recorded and promoted in this respect.

At the other end of the spectrum of application the concept of ellipsis can help us to explain the impact of a poetic line in terms of its formal properties. Take, for example, the opening lines of Basil Bunting's *Chomei at Toyama*:

> Swirl sleeping in the waterfall!
> On motionless pools scum appearing
> disappearing!

> (Bunting 1978: 63)

These seemingly unfathomable lines challenge the reader to make sense of their bizarre exclamations. Is the first line an exhortation to swirl while asleep in the waterfall? In this unlikely case, how does such an imperative relate to the lines that follow? At this stage the reader might decide to accept the lines as vivid images with no precise meaning and that would be fair enough. An alternative approach is to reconstruct, however tentatively, a more fully realized text by expanding perceived gaps:

> [A] Swirl [is] sleeping in the waterfall!
> On motionless pools scum [is] appearing
> [scum is] disappearing!

Here 'Swirl' is the subject noun phrase of the opening exclamatory statement, which may be taken to mean that a powerful eddy lurks beneath the surface of the water. If so, the next lines begin to make sense: the swirl is repeatedly releasing and swallowing the scum, accounting for its appearance and disappearance on an apparently calm surface. The key to this reconstruction is the restoration of the finite verbal elements which disambiguate the syntactic structures in which they occur. Bunting, of course, deliberately maintains this ambiguity and the non-finite quality of the participles by creating the gaps in structure that he does. My reconstruction at least makes possible an interpretation of these opening lines as a metaphor for the sinking and surfacing memories of the poem's protagonist, who some lines later says: 'I have been noting events forty years'.

Ellipsis could well be defined as language's faculty for incompleteness. How we acquire and use that faculty, appreciate and interpret it as listeners and readers, manipulate it as speakers and writers, are interesting and important issues at whatever level we are operating, from beginning reader to literary critic. When we listen, read, speak or write, we are always minding the gaps, whether we are aware of it or not, and it is the overriding aim of what follows to make them a more explicit object of our linguistic and critical awareness. The rest of this chapter explores some further examples of ellipsis as a way of introducing structures and processes that need to be taken into account and raising some of the issues that will need to be resolved in the chapters that follow.

A sample of dialogue

We began with a single contextual rejoinder. This next example is a rather more sustained piece of dialogue:

CONSTABLE: Millions of years ago, Martians landed on earth. And found apes. They doctored the apes, and made 'em think.

SLAUGHTER: Why did they doctor the apes, and make 'em think?

CONSTABLE: What did you say?

SLAUGHTER: Why did they doctor the apes, and make 'em think?

CONSTABLE: Well . . . they doctored the apes, and made 'em think, as an experiment.

SLAUGHTER: That was a pretty cruel experiment.

CONSTABLE: Martians have got a higher sense of morality than us.

SLAUGHTER: They must have got a higher sense of morality than us.

CONSTABLE: They stuck bits of their own minds in the poor apes' heads. And those apes, they're us.

Much of this dialogue will strike you as absurdly repetitious. If you do not recognize its origins, you might wonder if it is a parody of an absurdist script. Like most dialogue it consists of contextually linked questions, answers, statements and comments. As I noted above, we tend not to encode those elements that can be understood from the linguistic context. We can do so for special emphasis, but to do so at every opportunity, which is what I have done here, creates dialogue that is absurd or probably just tedious. Playwrights and other writers who 'have an ear for dialogue' are sensitive to the structural gaps that are typical of conversation. Although they would hardly couch it in these terms, they are aware that they need to reflect the fact that 'it is part of the language competence of a speaker of a language (if not his linguistic competence in the narrower sense) that he should be able to produce grammatically incomplete, but contextually appropriate and interpretable, sentence-fragments' (Lyons 1977: 589). The playwright Howard Brenton, dialogue from whose play, *Magnificence*, I expanded to create the above example, naturally built into his characters' speech the kind of contextually appropriate gaps that make his playscripts so convincing, as the following original version shows:

CONSTABLE: Millions of years ago, Martians landed on earth. And found apes. They doctored the apes, and made 'em think.

SLAUGHTER: Why?

CONSTABLE: What?

SLAUGHTER: Why?

CONSTABLE: Well . . . As an experiment.

SLAUGHTER: Pretty cruel.

CONSTABLE: Martians have got a higher sense of morality than us.

SLAUGHTER: They must have.

CONSTABLE: Stuck bits of their own minds in the poor apes' heads. And those apes, they're us. (Brenton 1986: 51)

Most of the ellipses that I expanded here were recoverable from the linguistic context, just like my earlier example of a contextual rejoinder. For example, when Slaughter asks 'Why?', we can assume he is asking about the Martians' actions. Based on the immediately preceding context, his question can be expanded accordingly: 'Why [did they doctor the apes, and make 'em think]?' The standard explanation is that the elliptical 'Why?' refers back to the antecedent sentence: it is, in standard terminology, anaphoric. The important role of anaphoric reference in the linguistic context of ellipsis is given further consideration at the beginning of Chapter 3. Just how this apparently backward-acting thread of discourse operates in actual conversation or when readers are following dialogue on the page is still something of a mystery. At least one researcher has suggested that, as a mental operation or cognitive process, anaphoric reference is 'forward-oriented', in that language users make mental representations of recently mentioned information in anticipation of more inexplicit references, such as ellipsis (Emmott 1997: 221–35). Theories of this kind are both intrinsically interesting and important to our understanding of the cognitive processing of language. However, within my rather more restricted focus on ellipsis as a textual feature, standard theories of anaphoric reference as backward acting provide a reasonably adequate analytical framework and, if nothing else, terminological continuity. As Emmott herself notes: 'The expression "refer back" is still very common even since mental representations have been included in models of reference, in linguistics, psychology, and artificial intelligence' (p. 222). The idea that Slaughter's 'Why?' refers back to the antecedent sentence provides us with a way of mapping our own understanding of the text as well as how the characters understand each other. Constable's eventual reply, 'Well . . . As an experiment', is also best understood as an elliptical anaphoric reference whose expansion,

'Well [they doctored the apes, and made 'em think] . . . As an experiment', traces the thread of discourse through the text.

Not all the gaps in this dialogue can be filled by recovering material from the immediate linguistic context. For example, Slaughter's remark, 'Pretty cruel', cannot be expanded with any certainty. My expansion, '[That was a] Pretty cruel [experiment]' represents a possible response to the preceding linguistic context, not an anaphorically exact recovery. Constable's 'What?' is even more of a problem. The character may be asking for a repeat of the question, as my expansion suggests, or he could be expressing exasperation. The latter meaning is probably best explained as a conversational implicature, an inferential gap of the kind I discuss in the third section of the next chapter. My expansion, 'What [did you say]?' is, then, only one possibility for mapping our understanding of the text. Some treatments of ellipsis actually exclude incomplete and fragmentary elements of this kind, because they are not fully recoverable from the linguistic context. In their comprehensive description of English grammar Quirk *et al.* (1985) strike a compromise. They invoke the principle of 'verbatim recoverability' whereby the actual material implied by an elliptical gap must be recoverable word for word, but they go on to say: '. . . like those of so many other grammatical categories, the boundaries of ellipsis are unclear, and it is best to recognize different degrees of "strength" in the identification of examples of ellipsis' (Quirk *et al.* 1985: 884).

A category of 'strict ellipsis' is then differentiated against such concepts as 'weak ellipsis' and 'quasi-ellipsis'. The examples I have discussed do suggest that there are different types of ellipsis depending on the degree to which linguistic context supports expansion. Compare, for example, the recoverability of 'Why [did they doctor the apes, and make 'em think]?' with the more indeterminate '[That was a] Pretty cruel [experiment]'. Subsequent chapters in Part One of the book will look at these categories in more detail with respect to structural, contextual and situational factors.

Exercise 1.1

In the following screenplay extract from Peter Greenaway's *Drowning by Numbers* I have expanded all the ellipsis sites in the dialogue to create a more or less non-elliptical text. Try to reconstitute the original by omitting what you consider to be my added material. Compare my expanded version with your revision. Note any problems you have in deciding where ellipsis sites occurred and what elements needed to be omitted. What kinds of contextual clues supported your decisions?

CISSIE 1:	(*Looking up*) What's he doing?
MADGETT:	He's counting the leaves.
CISSIE 2:	Whatever is he counting the leaves for?
MADGETT:	Haven't you ever wondered how many leaves there were on a tree?
CISSIE 2:	I've never wondered how many leaves there were on a tree.
MADGETT:	Or haven't you ever wondered how many hairs there were on your head?
CISSIES 2 and 3:	(*Together*) No, we haven't ever wondered how many hairs there were on our heads.
MADGETT:	Or haven't you ever wondered how many fish there were in the sea?
CISSIES 1, 2 and 3:	(*Together*) No, we haven't ever wondered how many fish there were in the sea.
CISSIE 1:	On Saturday, we'll put the ashes in the sea – or rather we'll put the ashes in the river. You, Madgett, can be our witness.
MADGETT:	What do you want a witness for?
CISSIE 1:	We want a witness to make sure we do it correctly, of course.
MADGETT:	Isn't it illegal?
SMUTT:	(*Shouting down from the tree*) NO IT ISN'T ILLEGAL!

(Greenaway 1988: 97)

Compressed language

Incomplete sentences, sentence fragments and structural gaps are not just features of spoken conversation or its representation in written dialogue. There are many other instances of language in use where omitted items need to be understood in some way or other. Fluent speakers of a language are usually able to expand such fragments or elaborate upon them in a way that makes their meaning more explicit. As we have already seen, in some cases the context is unable to support the specification of uniquely recoverable items and there may well also be some level of grammatical indeterminacy. Relevance rather than structural exactitude is likely to be the overriding factor in expanding such elliptical language in use, particularly where the sentence fragments are not part of some textually supportive discourse.

One form of discourse which makes quite heavy demands on the reader's ability to expand upon contextually unsupported ellipses and abbreviated expressions is the personal column entry in newspapers and magazines. The following example is fairly typical of such advertisements in both the local and national press:

> Laughing Eyes
> Warm, attract F, mid-40s, loves travel, arts, city life & countryside. WLTM sim M. Ldn.
> (The Guardian, 18–24.4.98: 65)

The main problem for the reader unfamiliar with such entries is that they are written in a kind of abbreviatory code which Sinclair (1988) calls 'compressed'. There are truncated words: 'attract' for 'attractive', 'sim' for 'similar'. There are straightforward initial letter abbreviations: 'WLTM' for 'would like to meet' and 'M' for 'male'. The abbreviation 'Ldn' for 'London' constitutes a written parallel to spoken elision. Recall Constable's opening lines in the playscript extract: 'They doctored the apes, and made 'em think'. Here the word 'them' is spelt to indicate a more colloquial pronunciation which elides the first sound of the word. In running speech most speakers tend to reduce some words in this way. The abbreviatory device used for London also omits letters, though it is not meant to indicate a particular pronunciation, but to save typespace. These features of abbreviatory code, even though they create interesting gaps, do not need to be taken into account in our treatment of ellipsis, since they are not syntactic in origin or subject to an explanation that is based on a syntactic analysis. Their incidence in the personal column entry nevertheless contributes strongly to the impression of the text as compressed language. In the following version, I have filled out the abbreviatory devices:

> [ ] Laughing Eyes
> [ ] Warm, attractive female, [ ] mid-40s, [ ] loves travel, arts, city life & countryside. [ ] Would like to meet similar male.
> [ ] London.

Even with all the abbreviatory devices filled out, the structure of this text is still truncated in some respects, as I have indicated with possible ellipsis site markers. By filling in these gaps, it is possible to suggest an expansion to a potential complete text-sentence that makes its meaning explicit:

> [ ] Laughing Eyes
> A warm, attractive female in her mid-40s, who loves travel, the arts, city life & the countryside, would like to meet a male with similar interests in London.

As this expansion reveals, the missing elements are supplied on the basis of the syntax of the potential sentence and the structure of its constituent phrases, though they are not strictly recoverable from the linguistic context as such. At least one expansion, 'a male with similar interests' is more of a gloss on implied meaning, since the strict expansion 'a similar male' is anomalous.

Another uncertainty is the status of the entry's title, which I have indicated with a gap marker. In a paper on the status of 'non-sentences', Stainton makes a convincing defence of the thesis that, 'Ordinary words and phrases can be used in isolation to make assertions' (1994: 269). We can suggest that the ordinary phrase 'Laughing Eyes' asserts something along the lines of 'The title of this entry is "Laughing Eyes"'. How titles, headings and other isolated phrases might be accommodated within a quasi-elliptical framework is discussed further in Chapter 5, which examines telegraphic ellipsis.

Exercise 1.2

The following is an entry in *Halliwell's Film and Video Guide*. Some of the abbreviatory devices are comparable with those in the personal column advertisement, such as truncated words and initial letters, which give the text a compressed quality. Write an expanded version of the entry, filling in any gaps that you consider to be elliptical. Make a note of the basis for your expansions in terms of the syntax of the potential sentences, the structure of their constituent phrases and the support of the linguistic context.

> Shock Corridor ★★
> US 1963 101m bw (colour sequence)
> A journalist gets himself admitted to a mental asylum to solve the murder of an inmate.

Sensational melodrama, a cinematic equivalent of the yellow
press, and on that level quite lively.
wd Samuel Fuller ph Stanley Cortez m Paul Dunlap
★ Peter Breck, Constance Towers, Gene Evans, James Best,
Hari Rhodes, Philip Ahn
'A minor masterpiece' – Derek Malcolm, Guardian

(J. Walker 1997: 675)

Defining ellipsis

Subsequent chapters of this book will attempt to clarify with further
examples and more detailed analysis the types of ellipsis indicated here
along with many others on the continuum of linguistic gaps. Given the
wide range of phenomena this includes, it is probably impossible to
achieve a satisfactory unitary definition of ellipsis. The one provided
by *The National Literacy Strategy*, quoted in my introduction, usefully
signals 'a place where something has been omitted', but overgeneralizes
to pauses and interruptions. Thomas's scholarly definition builds in a
clear syntactic framework: 'the omission from the overt manifestation
of the sentence of meanings that are syntagmatically required by what is
overtly manifested and which are available in the context of the sentence
in question' (1987: 1). However, his formula also seems to confine ellipsis
to gaps which are strictly recoverable, ruling out the looser forms that
Quirk *et al.* (1985) refer to as quasi-ellipsis. Carter and McCarthy are
more succinct and cast a wider net: 'the omission of elements otherwise
considered required in a structure' (1995: 145). This is less restrictive
because structural elements do not need to be uniquely recoverable to
be otherwise considered required.

In respect of a major investigation into the challenges of speech-to-
speech machine translation, with specific reference to English and Spanish, Selders (1995: node7.html) defines ellipted information as that 'which
the speaker intentionally expressed implicitly'. He elaborates on the
problems associated with this definition and notes:

we do assume that acts of 'expressing something implicitly'
are clear from various types of incompleteness in the form of
the expression uttered in contrast with its interpretation and
that, to be interpreted, the information implicitly expressed
must be recoverable from the context of the utterance.

This discussion is particularly interesting because it relates imprecise notions of implicitness to structural incompleteness. It is also clear from further exemplification of the project that 'context of the utterance' here includes both linguistic and situational factors.

Prompted by these definitions and taking into account the very limited amount of data surveyed so far, my own working definition of ellipsis is as follows: structural gaps that can be related to (a) omitted elements recoverable from the linguistic context, (b) other potential syntactic forms, (c) the situational context. This definition places the contextually recoverable aspect of ellipsis first, since many ellipses, such as contextual rejoinders, come into that category. Other gaps, as we have already seen, are not recoverable in this way, but can be related to a potential sentence that makes their meaning more explicit. The importance of situational context is also built into this definition. The context of situation may be specific to a particular gap, as in public notices, for example, but in a wider sense situational factors figure in our understanding of most language in use and this discourse dimension of ellipsis needs to be taken into account.

Definitions of ellipsis also have implications of a psycholinguistic nature. The idea that a gap may involve omission from what is 'otherwise considered required' or expansion to what I have called potential forms inevitably implies a related mental operation. As I noted earlier, that implication is of great interest to cognitive theories of language and language processing. My own use of terms like 'omission' and 'expansion' is meant to be neutral with regard to such processes, a way of labelling practical strategies for analysing and describing particular forms of ellipsis. Even so, the psycholinguistic reality of our productive and receptive minding of the gaps is an implicit aspect of subsequent discussion.

This chapter has demonstrated that even when consciously addressing the first, linguistic, aspect of my question, 'what is ellipsis?', it is more or less impossible to avoid the second, stylistic, aspect. This is quite encouraging, since it suggests that a holistic approach to language and style is possible. The notion of style is rather general and imprecise. For many commentators, style is a matter of choice, a concern with 'how' rather than 'what'. Where conscious choice reflects verbal artistry, we have the literary style of individual writers and the quality of literary texts. Some of my chapters, particularly in Part Two, will be trying to characterize the way ellipsis contributes to these literary effects. However, I am also very much concerned with the way speakers and writers employ ellipsis in much less rarefied categories of language use. Style, in this respect, is closely related to function and is often used synonymously with terms like 'register' or 'situational variety'. Chapter 8, at the outset of Part Two, attempts to tease out some of these problems of definition and delineation. Whatever the communicative context, literary or non-literary, I work from the premise that language functions by utilizing the possibility of incompleteness in a fairly systematic way. This produces gaps that are worth minding for the insight they give about how language works and how we work with language.

Discussion of Exercises

Exercise 1.1

This extract from Greenaway's screenplay is odd enough in its own right without the additional burden created by my expansion of all possible ellipsis sites. Once these have been removed again, the dialogue's fairly tight structure can be seen to rely on carrying presupposed material through segments of the discourse by means of ellipsis. The following discussion reproduces Greenaway's script, though I have inserted ellipsis site markers to show where I added material. It will be useful for you to compare your own attempts to reconstitute the original with the actual screenplay revealed in the following discussion. The first segment of discourse is as follows:

> CISSIE 1: (*Looking up*) What's he doing?
> MADGETT: [ ] Counting the leaves.
> CISSIE 2: Whatever [ ] for?

Madgett's truncated reply is straightforwardly typical of contextual rejoinders, but Cissie 2's question is more problematical. Clearly, it queries Smutt's leaf-counting, but the full expansion, based on the principle of verbatim recoverability outlined from Quirk *et al.* (1985) earlier in the chapter, is clumsy. 'Whatever for?' is a kind of formula, for which the category 'quasi-ellipsis' may be more appropriate.

The next segment consists of Madgett's series of bizarre questions and the Cissies' monosyllabic answers:

> MADGETT: Haven't you ever wondered how many leaves there were on a tree?
> CISSIE 2: [ ] Never [ ].

19

MADGETT:	Or [ ] hairs [ ] on your head?
CISSIES 2 and 3:	(*Together*) No [ ].
MADGETT:	Or [ ] fish [ ] in the sea?
CISSIES 1, 2 and 3:	(*Together*) No [ ].

The Cissies' contextual rejoinders are unproblematic, since, typically of such negatives, they relate to the whole of the preceding question. Because Madgett's initial question is complex, however, his subsequent truncated versions are rather more awkward to reconstitute. Two ellipsis sites have to be recognized, making the overall structure discontinuous. Nevertheless, this piece of dialogue is a very good example of how ellipsis sustains the thread of discourse across a series of contextual rejoinders.

The final segment of this extract again has elliptical rejoinders in response to questions:

CISSIE 1:	On Saturday, we'll put the ashes in the sea – or rather we'll put the ashes in the river. You, Madgett, can be our witness.
MADGETT:	What do you want a witness for?
CISSIE 1:	[ ] To make sure we do it correctly, of course.
MADGETT:	Isn't it illegal?
SMUTT:	(*Shouting down from the tree*) NO [ ]!

Cissie 1's answer here relies on the presupposition embodied in Madgett's question. The structure is typical of replies which take the form of a subordinate clause that omits the main clause, 'we want a witness', on which it is dependent. With Smutt's shouted 'No', we are back to verbatim recoverability again, though the word order adjustment reminds us that expansion is not a purely replicative mechanism.

Exercise 1.2

Texts which serve a specialist purpose, like personal column advertisements or film guide entries, are likely to have very distinctive characteristics. These typifying features are known as text conventions, something I discuss further in Chapter 8. For the moment, it is useful to note that the abbreviatory devices and layout, as well as the elliptical syntax of the film guide entry, are all aspects of this example's text conventions. If you are not familiar with this particular film guide, then some of the conventions might be puzzling. For example, the two stars beside the title indicate the film's rating, whereas the single star later on merely signals the cast list of actors. Other abbreviations include: 'bw: black and white', 'wd: written and directed by', 'ph: photography by', 'm: music by'. As with the personal column advertisement, these and other abbreviatory devices provide a conventional setting for structural ellipses.

These abbreviatory features are a 'main peripheral device' in Sinclair's treatment of 'compressed English'. However, he also notes finite verbs, particularly forms of BE, as a 'main missing feature' (Sinclair 1988: 132–3). The film guide entries tend to be made up largely of strings of phrases. One way of accounting for these is to see them as sentence fragments that relate to the omission of finite elements and other functional markers, as the following expansions indicate: '[There is a] colour sequence', '[This is a] Sensational melodrama, a cinematic equivalent of the yellow press, and on that level [it is] quite lively', '[This is] A minor masterpiece' – [wrote] Derek Malcolm, [in the] Guardian'. This lack of functional elements is typical of telegraphic ellipsis, a category described in more detail in Chapter 5. It is worth noting that the only fully realized sentence without abbreviations is the brief plot summary: 'A journalist gets himself admitted to a mental asylum to solve the murder of an inmate.' The text conventions of the film guide can lead to puzzlement and misunderstanding on the part of the unfamiliar reader, something the compilers are no doubt aware of. Accordingly, at this point they are making sure that there is no uncertainty about the basic storyline of the film.

CHAPTER 2

WHAT ISN'T ELLIPSIS

Our preliminary look at ellipsis in Chapter 1 suggested that the absence of structurally potential linguistic elements is a pervasive feature of language. Language allows, indeed facilitates, gaps that speakers use and interpret, mostly in the relatively unexamined give and take of everyday communication, but sometimes for more deliberate effect. We saw that a wide range of seemingly different features figure in this general notion of ellipsis, while noting that some missing elements, in abbreviations, contracted forms and the like, could hardly count as ellipsis at all. Such elements are of minor significance, but they prompt a more interesting line of enquiry, that has both theoretical and practical implications, as to what kinds of gaps are best treated as ellipsis and what, if any, can be discounted. The main aim of this chapter, therefore, will be to illustrate certain kinds of linguistic omission and absence that have something superficially in common with ellipsis, but which can be explained more satisfactorily in other ways. Some may be considered accidental in the sense that they are syntactically and/or situationally unmotivated. Others are semantic in origin or related to the contextually motivated inferences of language in use. All these features are interesting and significant in their own right, so my aim in discounting them is not to belittle their importance as properties of discourse, but rather to suggest some necessary delimitations to the range of features that are best treated within a framework of ellipsis as I have defined it. These discountable gaps are discussed under the following headings: lapses in performance, nonrealization, inferential gaps.

Lapses in performance

In a well-known pronouncement that set parameters for a particularly influential branch of linguistic enquiry Chomsky suggested that a theory of linguistic competence has to discount certain features that stem from 'such grammatically irrelevant conditions as memory limitations, dis-tractions, shifts of attention and interest, and errors (random or charac-teristic) in applying knowledge of the language in actual performance' (Chomsky 1965: 3). Chomsky himself did not give any examples of these performance errors, but most stretches of spoken English contain features we can safely assume to be instances of what he was referring to. Take the following extract from a conversation between two friends practising some music together:

A: I wondered if we, er, aren't, like, taking it a bit slow
B: Erm
A: Or is that [ ], would it help [ ]
B: I think we were taking it a bit slow, but, er, I think I'd find it easier if we did it a bit faster
A: Yeah, right
B: Because the, erm [ ]
A: Yeah they're quite long-breathed lines aren't they?
B: Yeah they are and they're all quite long notes and, er, I found myself several times [ ]
A: Yeah, right, well I, I don't mind, it's [ ], we could easily speed that up, erm, a bit . . .

There are several features here which are typical of spontaneous dialogue. Tag questions like 'aren't they' are a systematically patterned syntactic feature, while casual markers of agreement like 'yeah' and 'right' may be loosely accounted for as contextual rejoinders. Other features, like pauses and pause fillers such as 'er', and overlaps and interruptions between the speakers, seem rather more random. Overlaps and interruptions often result in abandoned utterances that create gaps: 'would it help [ ]', 'because the, erm [ ]' 'I found myself several times [ ]'. But even when they aren't interrupted, speakers create gaps resulting from an uncom-pleted embarkation on a new syntactic structure, a so-called false start: 'or is that [ ]', 'I don't mind, it's [ ]'. Just how random such features are is open to debate. They are almost always relevant to the context and a potential syntactic structure can often be discerned. Insofar as they result from distractions and shifts in attention, they are often said to be unin-tentional, but it is also the case that speakers use false starts, especially with accompanying pauses, to buy verbal planning time. The authors of one authoritative survey of what they call 'speech errors' suggest three main sources: cognitive difficulty, situational anxiety and social reasons (Clark and Clark 1977: 271–3). In the first case, topics that are conceptually more demanding to talk about are likely to generate more lapses in performance. Secondly, when people are anxious, their speech errors increase. Clark and Clark comment:

> One possibility is that anxiety disrupts the planning and execution processes generally. Speakers become tense, and their planning and execution become less efficient. Another possibility is that what people talk about when they are anxious is simply more difficult cognitively. (p. 272)

Furthermore, the incidence of such features varies according to social factors: for example, we are more likely to use hesitations, pauses, fillers and false starts when conversation is highly interactive or competitive.

Commenting on lapses in performance from a very different perspective, Kress notes that: 'very few people are aware of these things when they hear spoken language, particularly when they are themselves engaged in conversation: we have to "distance" ourselves from the conversation quite self-consciously before such features of language impinge on our awareness' (Kress 1979: 48). The most common way of achieving that distance is, of course, by the process of transcription. Only by transcribing the above dialogue was I able to scrutinize its lapses in performance with any precision. To the extent that most listeners are not involved in that process, there is some truth in Kress's point, then. Even so, ordinary language users may become more consciously aware of these features in some cases. The hesitations and false starts of impromptu speech are often called 'normal non-fluency', emphasizing their naturalness. But such features can be more characteristic of some speakers than others. They can even become recognized as part of someone's idiolect or individual manner of using language and, as such, subject to overt comment, parody or exaggeration.

The fact that transcription misleadingly highlights the apparently messy syntactic organization of spoken language has prompted some linguists to oppose the syntactic norm of the written sentence as a measure for the structure of speech. Halliday, for example, argues that transcription is comparable to presenting the roughest drafts of writing with all their mistakes and alterations, in part basing his critique of 'the myth of structureless speech' upon such misleading representations (1994: 62–3). Because much of the writing we see is in its final edited form, we rarely encounter what Halliday claims to be the written equivalent of transcribed speech. He draws a parallel between spontaneous speech and the rough drafts of maturely competent writers with their crossed-out false starts, reorderings and lacunae. While these may well be a reasonable meta-phor for the cognitive processes of spoken language, a more realistic parallel is likely to be found in unedited spontaneous written commun-ications. One source of such writing is the e-mail. As Nash and Stacey note: 'You write quickly on e-mail as you might in a diary. Errors of spelling and sentence construction and mechanics are not always regarded as cardinal sins by writers on the Internet' (1997: 158). Here are two examples from my own e-mail correspondence of the kinds of thing Nash and Stacey are referring to:

> There's something I'd like to rectify for 1999–200 [ ].
> Other people apparently [ ] an e-mail address wit [ ] their name.

The gaps indicated here are only weakly parallel to lapses in spoken per-formance. Two of them omit elements at the orthographic level, '1999–200 [0]', 'wit [h]', resulting in what can be called 'transcription errors'. The other gap omits a word such as 'have' or 'own' from an otherwise complete structure. Another source of written lapses in performance is the writing of less mature writers. Here is the opening paragraph of a piece of writing by a twelve-year-old girl:

> Is pop better today than in the 50s to 60s? Well it depends on
> [ ] you think. Are the lyrics or words of a song more import-
> ant? This [ ] what I will write about in my next paragraph.

It is worth noting that the writer herself pointed out the gaps to me on a read through and suggested possible completions: 'it depends on what you think', 'this is what I will write'. So the errors were not due to some fundamental lack of grammatical knowledge. As lapses in performance, however, they are different from the conversational false start, since they do not result from the abandonment of one syntactic structure in favour of another. Rather they are failures to realize in concrete form elements required by otherwise well-formed structures. Gaps of this kind in adult e-mails and children's writing reveal a genuine difference in medium between the demands of spoken language and those of spontan-eous, unedited writing. Such differences are likely to be minimized at the most interactively 'chatty' end of the e-mail spectrum, where writ-ing comes closer to something it usually isn't: speech written down.

It is with some irony that Chomsky and Halliday, with their very different agendas for linguistics, are both dismissive of lapses in perform-ance. Chomsky discounts them because such messy instances of spoken language in use are not relevant to the kind of rule-governed syntax he wishes to elaborate, while Halliday is wary because such draft features, when transcribed, actually disguise the previously underrated orderliness of speech. Both, however, give support to the idea that gaps resulting from lapses in performance are deviations, in that they are not predictable or generated by syntactic rule. Halliday is more positive about accounting for them systematically, 'if we had a grammar that took into account the specifically "spoken" resources of the linguistic system' (1994: 65). Whatever that might mean, it is a big 'if', and at this stage it is fair to say that lapses of performance are not describable within even the least strict definition of ellipsis.

Exercise 2.1

In the following extract from a radio phone-in programme, speaker A is a caller, B is the show's host and C is a studio guest. Identify those gaps created by lapses in performance and comment on any differences you discern between speakers A and C in respect of such lapses.

> A: I'd like to just address the comment to, to the teacher that you have in the office, er, in the radio sta, the studio today.
>
> B: Yeah.
>
> A: Erm people who, who eat too much, and I'm overweight myself, people who
>
> B: How much overweight?
>
> A: I'm probably about a stone and a half overweight, I'd say, but er, I mean that's because I don't exercise, er and probably because I eat too many fatty foods and fast foods, but I mean it's my choice. Why should I, why should I exercise er and and eat low fat grits and er rice cakes and lettuce er just to please you?
>
> C: You don't have to eat lettuce. I mean people always take sort of the extreme, I'm not expecting you to do that. All I'm saying is if you're slightly overweight, then there's nothing to worry about. All I'm saying is a lot of people are very much overweight, you don't fall into that category. Why are they overweight? They're overweight because they eat far too much and don't do enough exercise, it's just common sense.
>
> B: Oh yawn yawn. (BBC *Radio Five Live*, 24.9.98)

Nonrealization

It is commonplace to suggest that meaning is often conveyed as much by what is *not* said as by what is. Since ellipsis results in things not being said, it is worth exploring whether all significant lack of expression, an important aspect of discourse, needs to be classified as a type of ellipsis. At a syntactic level not all potentially expressible constituents are always realized. Again, this raises an interesting theoretical issue with practical implications: should such apparent gaps be treated as a kind of indefinite ellipsis?

A useful exemplification of the issue arises when we consider verbs that can be both transitive and intransitive. An obvious example is 'read':

Suraiya reads pulp fiction for pleasure.   (transitive)
Suraiya reads for pleasure.   (intransitive)

Both sentences are perfectly acceptable. The most common explanation is that 'read' is sometimes a transitive verb, requiring the overt expression of a direct object, and sometimes an intransitive verb that does not need a direct object. However, a theory of indefinite ellipsis proposes that the second sentence above results from the deletion of an indefinitely specified direct object:

Suraiya reads [some x] for pleasure.

If we accept such a theory, the implications for what counts as ellipsis are large. While the number of verbs that are both transitive and intransitive may be relatively few, the theory would also apply quite indiscriminately to other instances of nonrealization of which there are many. Take, for example, verbs which are only transitive and always require their direct objects to be expressed. If they are not, the result is an unacceptable sentence, as the following examples for the verb 'receive' show:

The Terence Higgins Trust received many donations last year.
★The Terence Higgins Trust received last year.

Since the nonrealization of the direct object cannot occur without resulting ungrammaticality, its occurrence is rare and stylistically marked, as in the example I discuss below. However, transitive verbs may be seen to carry other constituents which may or may not be realized. In the case of 'receive' one such constituent could be the 'source' of the donation. In that case the above sentence would have to be seen as an ellipsis of:

The Terence Higgins Trust received many donations [from some x] last year.

Most verbs, intransitive as well as transitive, could be allocated at least one constituent of this type which is not always required to be expressed: 'place' and 'time' are obvious candidates. A theory of ellipsis which took into account such potential constituents would be unnecessarily inflated. For example, for the verb 'arrive' it would be necessary to suggest that:

The train arrived about six o'clock.

is an elliptical form of:

The train arrived [at place x] about six o'clock.

This line of reasoning can be extended to the level of phrasal constituents in order to demonstrate the practical difficulties involved in such a theory. Take the following sentence:

The victim suffered multiple injuries.

It would be logical to suggest that the subject NP lacked a postmodifying element by indefinite ellipsis, for example, 'the victim [of event x]'. Once this analysis is conceded, then further unrealized constituents can be suggested, for example, [at time y] or [at place z]. This logical strategy could be applied to more or less all phrasal structures without any principled cut-off point.

The examples so far show that English sentences vary in the degree of explicitness they provide over and against what is potentially expressible. This facility can be explained in terms of the semantic structure of verbs and other linguistic elements of sentences and the extent to which they allow for the nonrealization of predicate arguments and other constituents. In general, an elliptical theory of such nonrealization is unhelpful because it cannot be given a sufficiently precise definition which would exclude a wide range of vaguely inexplicit expressions. Crystal's caveat is worth quoting in this respect: 'Unless one wishes to include a general and uncontrollable notion of "being understood" into one's analysis, it is essential to introduce specific constraints onto the notion of ellipsis' (1980: 157). This is not to deny either the theoretical import-ance of nonrealization, particularly within generative accounts of lin-guistic structure, or its stylistic interest. This is best illustrated by one of the most famous uses of nonrealization as a literary device, in William Faulkner's *The Sound and the Fury*:

> Through the fence, between the curling flower spaces, I could see them hitting. They were coming toward where the flag was and I went along the fence. Luster was hunting in the grass by the flower tree. They took the flag out, and they were hitting. Then they put the flag back and they went to the table, and he hit and the other hit. (1929: 1)

I noted above that the nonrealization of the direct object with tran-sitive verbs cannot occur grammatically, so in strict terms all the uses of the verb 'hit' here are ungrammatical. The first-person narrator of this passage is the mentally incapacitated Benjy, so the narrative is indeed 'a tale told by an idiot, full of sound and fury', the Shakespearean inspira-tion for Faulkner's title. To capture Benjy's highly idiosyncratic account of men playing golf, Faulkner uses nonrealization as one of a range of stylistic effects that convey Benjy's manner of perceiving and relating to events in his surroundings, that capture, in Leech and Short's term, his 'very unusual mind style' (1981: 202). Fowler suggests that this odd usage with regard to the transitive verb is adopted to imply that 'Benjy has little sense of actions and their effects on objects: a limited notion of causation' (1996: 169). In this way what might be called a syntactic mannerism helps to characterize the style of Benjy's childishly simple world view.

Faulkner's use of nonrealization is unusual enough to create an overt stylistic effect. At the other end of the spectrum there is a type of non-realization that is so commonplace that it more or less goes unnoticed, namely, the lack of subject in imperative constructions. Many treat-ments of English grammar simply note this lack of subject without querying its theoretical status. For example, Gramley and Patzold state: 'The imperative typically appears as the base form of the verb without a subject . . . Imperatives are, despite the lack of a subject, clearly second person, addressed to a hearer-reader . . .' (1992: 174). Huddleston is more aware of the syntactic implications. Comparing the example 'Be good' with 'You be umpire', he notes that the '2nd person subject is omissible' rather than just lacking and that the form 'with *you* absent but "understood" is much more frequent . . .' (1988: 132). The notion of omissibility at least points in the direction of ellipsis, while the appeal to being understood invokes Crystal's caveat. Within one comment, then, Huddleston encapsulates the theoretical debate surrounding subjectless imperatives, but seems to favour the orthodox non-elliptical line of Quirk *et al.*: 'Imperative sentences without a subject . . . cannot be considered comparable to declarative and interrogative sentences with initial ellipsis. The implied subject of the imperative verb is "you", but absence of the subject is the norm with imperatives' (1985: 896).

Quirk *et al.*'s assertion is not as unproblematical as they seem to suggest. An appeal to some implied norm is at least worth examining. It is true that subjectless imperatives are much more common than those where the subject is expressed, as in 'You do the dishes'. On the other hand, as Huddleston also notes, the subject is not always 'you', as in 'Somebody keep the score'. It could be argued that an indiscriminately yelled 'Keep the score' might well imply an unspecified 'somebody' rather than a specific 'you'. Even so, it is clear that the third-person form is highly marked and that the second-person form has a near automatic level of 'understoodness'. An appeal to the norm may be some justification for excluding subjectless imperatives as a type of ellipsis, but it isn't entirely explanatory. Norms have not been established for other types of ellipsis and it would be odd to suggest that once a type of ellipsis has been shown to be more common than its non-elliptical correlate, it should cease to be considered an ellipsis on normative grounds. On the other hand, the consequence of asserting subjectless imperatives as a form of ellipsis might distract from more interesting types. Certain kinds of spoken and written language, such as instructions and recipes, are characterized by the incidence of subjectless imperatives and their patterning is a stylistically significant feature, but this can be taken into account without invoking ellipsis. In any case, given the marked nature of the command with subject rather than without, it is the presence of a subject that is likely to be more noticeably significant to the style of a text.

While the non-elliptical status of subjectless imperatives is not clear cut, it is probably advantageous methodologically to discount them as examples of ellipsis. So as not to abandon them to some theoretical limbo, it is best to place them within the domain of non-realized potential constituents. Above, I argued that expressible predicate arguments and other constituents were variably realized according to both contextual and semantic constraints. Since the category 'subject' is a major predicate argument, it is possible to suggest that in the case of imperatives that grammatical category is expressible, but variably, indeed only exceptionally, realized. This is theoretically explanatory, though not wholly satisfactory, since other cases of nonrealization apply to all the forms of a particular verb rather than just one. Nevertheless, it does allow for a principled categorization of subjectless imperatives which has methodologically sound consequences for stylistic analysis.

Exercise 2.2

Identify the instances of nonrealization in the following examples. How do they contribute to the way the message in each example is conveyed?

(a) Don't drink and drive.
(b) A fee of £15 (variable) will be debited each time a required payment made by cheque or direct debit is returned unpaid.

Inferential gaps

Perhaps an even greater challenge for a theory of ellipsis that wishes to take heed of Crystal's warning against 'a general and uncontrollable notion of being understood' is the way language in use creates inferential gaps to convey meaning. Take the following rejoinder sequences:

A: Are you going to the pictures tonight?
B: I am [ ], if that new Tarantino's on.

A: Are you going to the pictures tonight?
C: That new Tarantino's on at the multiplex.

B's reply in the first sequence has a structural gap, recoverable from the context of A's question, that will need to figure in any account of ellipsis. C's reply in the second sequence is a fully realized sentence that has no obvious structural omissions, yet its quality as a response is less direct, relying on implicit rather than explicit meaning: there is, in other words, an inferential gap in C's answer. The use of the term 'gap' is possibly misleading in this context. Given the structural completeness of C's reply, its inferential gap cannot be accommodated within an elliptical framework. Such a strategy would result in an overgeneralized definition of ellipsis: back to 'being understood' again.

More widely accepted as an explanatorily adequate account of what is understood and how in such rejoinder sequences is the theory of conversational implicature first outlined by Grice (1975). Grice outlines a cooperative principle for language use in conversation which suggests that we at the very least intend to make our communicative acts purposeful. Four operational rules underpin this cooperative principle, which Grice called the maxims of quality, quantity, relevance and manner. Levinson (1983: 101–2) gives a clear outline from which I quote in the following discussion of how Grice's theory may be applied to the inferential gap in the above rejoinder sequence. First, A must assume the cooperative principle is at work, namely that, although C's reply is indirect, it is in some way appropriate to 'the accepted purpose or direction of the talk'. Secondly, if C is obeying the maxim of quality, he is speaking the truth on 'adequate evidence'. Thirdly, is C following the maxim of quantity by making his contribution 'as informative as is required'? C is flouting this maxim by not saying as much as he could. Fourthly, A has to assume that C's reply is relevant to the question. Fifthly, is C obeying the maxim of manner by being 'perspicuous', that is, transparently clear? Although C's rejoinder is brief and orderly, it probably flouts the maxim of manner by not entirely avoiding 'obscurity': at the least it is slightly cryptic. Both the observation and the flouting of Grice's maxims generate conversational implicatures which Levinson defines as: 'inferences based on both the content of what has been said and some specific assumptions about the cooperative nature of ordinary verbal interaction' (1975: 104). We can unpack these inferences, making explicit the relation between a desire to go to the pictures, the attraction of a new Tarantino film and its showing at the local cinema, in order to conclude that C's reply is positive.

In the exchange between A and B above, the process of expanding an elliptical expression, restoring a structural gap, can be seen as an aspect of what Blakemore calls 'explicature'. Following Sperber and Wilson (1986), she defines explicature as 'the result of fleshing out the semantic representation of an utterance' (Blakemore 1992: 59). In this case part of that fleshing out is to make B's reply more explicit by expanding the ellipsis:

> B: I am [going to the pictures tonight], if that new Tarantino's on.

Blakemore goes on to comment that in some cases 'the semantic representation provides only a very skeletal clue as to the explicature the hearer is intended to recover, and the process of developing the semantic representation into an explicature depends heavily on contextual information' (1992: 59).

In the case of B's rejoinder above, where the elliptical aspect of the explicature is straightforwardly supplied by the immediately preceding context, the idea of fleshing out a semantic representation is still a useful one, since even here overall explicature depends on other frames of reference and more general knowledge. For example, speaker B uses the term 'that new Tarantino'. Quite incidentally, I glossed that expression in my subsequent commentary by referring to 'a new Tarantino film'. This applies a quite general metonymic rule, which can be expressed as: call a product by the name of its producer, or more specifically in this context: call a film by the name of its director. Even so, knowing the nature of the product depended on shared cultural knowledge of the kind speakers habitually make assumptions about when encoding meaning. The linguistic and situational contexts of these rejoinders support a particular interpretation of 'that new Tarantino', but it is easy to imagine a situation where a puzzled listener who does not share this specific world knowledge has to ask: 'what's a Tarantino?' Gaps resulting from shared cultural or social knowledge of this kind are a further aspect of explicature: in arriving at the semantic representation of an utterance we flesh out such gaps on the basis of knowing both possible and likely senses within a particular frame of reference. Only when that knowledge is lacking do we resort to overt explicature by asking, for example, 'what's a Tarantino?' The semantic representation of such shared cultural knowledge is part of the explicatory process alongside, but distinct from, the expansion of contextually supported ellipsis.

Exercise 2.3

Compare the following rejoinder sequences. How do the two responses to the same question differ with regard to explicature and inferential gaps?

> A: Is there enough to eat in the Sudan?
> B: Is there ever?
>
> A: Is there enough to eat in the Sudan?
> C: There was a drought last summer.

Discussion of Exercises

Exercise 2.1

Live radio phone-in programmes involve speakers interacting in unscripted and more or less spontaneous conversation, so you would expect the kinds of feature I outlined to figure in their speech: false starts, overlaps, interruptions, fillers, etc. This is indeed the case. One gap, for example, is caused when the chat-show host interrupts his caller who abandons one syntactic structure in order to respond to the host's question:

> A: Erm people who, who eat too much, and I'm overweight myself, people who [ ]
>
> B: How much overweight?
>
> A: I'm probably about a stone and a half overweight.

However, the most interesting contrast here is between the speech styles of speakers A and C. Both use characteristic markers of colloquial speech, such as contracted verb forms like 'it's', 'you're' and 'don't', and affective features like 'I mean'. However, the caller's speech has a number of false starts, pauses and fillers. One of the most interesting is the way speaker A arrives at the word 'studio' in 'I'd like to just address the comment to, to the teacher that you have in the office, er, in the radio sta [tion], the studio today', at one point abandoning a structure half way through a word. The speaker's verbal planning seems to involve a process of elimination that is revealed as he speaks: one could speculate that this process is a commonplace but mostly covert mental operation. By contrast, the language of the studio guest is more or less free of 'normal non-fluency'. Even though speaker C is unscripted, it is likely that he has rehearsed his arguments many times before, so his speech is less spontaneous, less subject to ongoing shifts in verbal planning. That it has a quality sometimes facetiously called 'the broken record effect' is confirmed by the host's interpolation 'Oh yawn yawn'.

Exercise 2.2

(a) The verb 'drink' has both transitive and intransitive senses, like the verb 'read', discussed earlier. In its main transitive sense, defined by *Chambers Dictionary* as 'to swallow as a liquid', its direct object is open-ended, say any one of the set of drinkable things. While this open-endedness isn't invalidated in its intransitive sense, the dictionary notes that alcohol is a frequently implied, but nonrealized, object. This absolute meaning is extended: 'to take intoxicating liquors to excess' (*Chambers English Dictionary* 1992: 433). Compare, for example, 'John drinks coffee in the morning' with 'John drinks in the morning', where the latter strongly implies alcoholic beverage.

The verb 'drive' also has transitive and intransitive meanings. In its transitive sense its direct object is open-ended, say, any one of the set of driveable things. Again, this open-endedness is retained in its intransitive sense. However, in the case of 'drive' there is no frequently implied object, comparable with 'alcohol' for 'drink'. These different implications of nonrealization allow a powerful message 'Don't drink [alcohol] and drive [any vehicle whatsoever]' to be delivered in a snappy style. It is also worth noting that the verbs are subjectless imperatives. Given that nonrealization is the norm in this respect, compare the meaning and stylistic effect of these versions where the subject is realized:

> Don't you drink and drive.
> Don't anybody drink and drive.
> Let no-one drink and drive.

(b) This extract from the terms and conditions of a credit card company contains five passive constructions. In each case the agent is not realized, creating uncertainty about who is responsible for doing what. Possible agents can be realized as follows:

> A fee of £15 (variable) will be debited [by us] each time a required [by us or by some x] payment made [by you] by cheque or direct debit is returned [by some x] unpaid [by you or by some x].

Stylistic insights about the use of nonrealization are helpful when dealing with language of this kind. In particular, the treatment of agentless passives and other forms of nonrealization as stylistically significant features, which was central to seminal work in critical linguistics by Fowler *et al.* (1979) and Kress and Hodge (1979), can tell us a lot about how such language works. Critical linguistics, now more frequently referred to as critical discourse analysis, innovatively demonstrated the power of such nonrealizations to imbue texts, from membership rules and institutional regulations to news reports, with a vague and faceless sense of authority. Such analyses have been both formative and productive in more recent critical discourse analysis of texts, particularly those of a public or bureaucratic nature. For example, Fairclough comments on agentless passives in the reporting of politically sensitive news stories and concludes that their use 'may be to avoid redundancy, if that information is already given in some way. In other cases, it can be obfuscation of agency and causality' (1989: 125).

In the case of these credit card regulations avoiding redundancy doesn't seem to be the motive. This particular regulation is only one of many verbosely worded directives. While obfuscation may not be the aim either, it is the end result. The only message I am clear about after many readings of its wording is that the card holder will pay a fee to the credit card company: perhaps that is the only message that really counts.

Exercise 2.3

In their influential discussion of ellipsis Halliday and Hasan define a rejoinder as 'any cohesive sequel by a different speaker' (1976: 207). Here we have two different sequels to the same question: both are cohesive, but in slightly different ways. The question itself is depressingly familiar and contemporary-sounding, but in fact derives from an early seminal paper on ellipsis by Holzman (1971), who cites 'A: Is there enough to eat in the Sudan? C: There was a drought last summer' as an example of 'elliptical discourse', in that it realizes an implicit relation that needs extralinguistic information for its interpretation. Essentially, there is an inferential gap. Prefiguring Halliday and Hasan, Holzman suggests that a theory of discourse must 'characterize the properties that make a sequence of sentences coherent' (1971: 93–4). In comparing the two rejoinder sequences, we are to some extent doing just that. The question is of the Yes/No type. Any response that fails to provide one of these strains cohesion. B's response to the question, of my own contrivance, is contextually elliptical in a straightforwardly recoverable way. Expanding B's contextual rejoinder is part of the fleshing out process Blakemore (1992) assigns to explicature: 'Is there ever [enough to eat in the Sudan]? But for this question following a question to be cohesive there is still a fair amount of explicature to be done in terms of Sudan's long-standing history of famine related to environmental factors and civil war. The implicature of this is a negative response to the question. In Holzman's example, C's response is not contextually elliptical: there is no recoverable gap to be filled. Explicature here involves glossing the meanings of key terms like 'drought' and 'last year'. The inferential gaps that this reveals can be unpacked, making explicit the relation between lack of rain, crop failure and famine within a particular time scale. Clearly, Holzman's use of the term 'ellipsis' for this kind of inferential gap is at odds with the approach I have outlined in this chapter.

CHAPTER 3

THE LINGUISTIC CONTEXT

One of the earliest attempts to categorize ellipsis systematically, Gunter's seminal paper on ellipsis in American English, established the category of contextual ellipsis where 'the dependency upon context constitutes a grammatical connection between the elliptical sentence in question and its context' (1963: 143). In this chapter I focus on types of ellipsis where this 'grammatical connection' constitutes a cohesive tie between a structural gap and some adjacent text. This cohesive tie allows for the recovery, either full or partial, of elements from the linguistic context: the term 'contextual ellipsis', it is worth reiterating, always implies some linguistic context.

There are two useful distinctions which can be made about the location of this linguistic context with respect to a particular ellipsis site: the first contrasts anaphoric with cataphoric locations, the second intrasentential with intersentential. The first distinction concerns directionality. An ellipsis is anaphoric where the missing linguistic items are recoverable from the preceding context, as in:

Brian won't do the dishes, so you'll have to [ ].

Cataphoric ellipsis relies on the following linguistic context for the recovery of missing elements:

Since Brian won't [ ], I expect I'll have to do the dishes.

The majority of contextual ellipses are, not unexpectedly, anaphoric, reflecting the greater ease of production and reception that is afforded by having the clue to the gap given in advance. The second distinction depends on whether or not the supportive linguistic context is in the same sentence as the ellipsis itself. Some types of ellipsis, like the above examples, are necessarily intrasentential, because they involve an elliptical relationship between a main clause and a dependent subordinate clause. The most prolific source of intrasentential ellipsis is coordination reduction where one or more coordinate structures contain gaps recoverable from another coordinate. I will be discussing various aspects of coordination reduction in more detail in Chapter 6. Other types of ellipsis are necessarily intersentential, the prime example being contextual rejoinders across speakers, as in this exchange from Christopher Hampton's play *The Philanthropist*:

CELIA: You're being cunning.
PHILIP: I'm not [ ]. (1970: 52)

It is worth noting that the boundary between intrasentential and intersentential ellipsis is less clear cut for spoken data. Most written sentences, however idiosyncratically a writer may deploy them, are at least marked by the orthographic conventions of sentence-initial capital letter and sentence-final full stop, so it is usually obvious whether a gap is recoverable within the same sentence or not. Where speech is concerned, the distinction is worth maintaining for rejoinder sequences like the one above where the syntactic relationship between different speakers' utterances is the focus. Longer stretches of speech, particularly single-speaker extended turns, often present us with strings of tone groups that are far from being equivalent to sentences in the orthographic sense. Analysis has to be somewhat *ad hoc*, depending to some extent on whether adjacent clusters of tone groups are syntactically related.

In their influential treatment of cohesive relations within texts Halliday and Hasan view contextual ellipsis as a major component of textual cohesion. In general terms cohesion is 'a semantic relation between an element in the text and some other element that is crucial to the interpretation of it. This other element is also to be found in the text . . .' (Halliday and Hasan 1976: 8). They characterize that semantic relation as one of presupposition, a usage which requires some comment. Trask defines presupposition as follows: 'A proposition whose truth must be taken for granted if some utterance is to be regarded as sensible' (1997: 175). In suggesting that presupposition is the hallmark of cohesion, Halliday and Hasan are indicating, to use Trask's definition as a template, that there is an element whose presence must be taken for granted if some other element is to be regarded as cohesive. In the specific case of ellipsis this cohesion is realized when the absence of an element in one syntactic structure takes for granted its presence in another. Halliday and Hasan go on to characterize ellipsis as a kind of 'substitution by zero' (1976: 145), an essentially textual relation that is mainly anaphoric, but occasionally cataphoric.

In a more recent account of ellipsis in cohesion Toolan takes this notion a step further and eradicates the distinction between ellipsis and substitution altogether by introducing a category of partial ellipsis which he defines as follows: 'Very often the ellipsis is not total; instead, some "abridged" or condensed structure is used, to stand in for the full sequence. This is known as partial ellipsis or substitution, and is very common' (Toolan 1998: 26). He contrasts this category with a 'second subtype of ellipsis, where there is "full" omission of a second mention of items which can be "understood" as implicit, because they are retrievable in the given context' (p. 27).

Part of the data with which Toolan exemplifies partial ellipsis is the following:

KIMBERLEY: Can I look at your watch?
MARTIN: Sorry, I'm not wearing one. (p. 27)

The use of 'one' here is a straightforward example of Halliday and Hasan's substitution category and there seems little point in calling it something else. Indeed, to call this 'partial ellipsis' is misleading, since there is no obvious structural gap. His category of full ellipsis, in which items are properly omitted, is illustrated with, among other things, clausal ellipsis in contextual rejoinders:

ALAN: Don't forget next Monday's a public holiday.
BRIAN: I know [ ].

Toolan adds: 'The distinction between cohesion by partial rather than full ellipsis is sometimes hard to see, which is why they are best treated as variants of a single phenomenon' (p. 28). This seems at odds with his own data, where the differences between the gaps of 'full ellipsis' and the substitutions he calls 'partial ellipsis' are clear to see. Further support for preserving this distinction comes from the analysis of an example from a quite different source, the cookery recipe:

Place the unthawed spinach in a saucepan, cover [ ], and cook [ ] gently for 10 minutes or until softened. Drain [ ] well and transfer [ ] to a food processor. (Tilgals and Gaunt 1996: 70)

Here the structural gap, a direct object, takes for granted the element 'the unthawed spinach' in the preceding sentence. The cohesive relation realized by the ellipsis is really an extension of reference rather than substitution, a kind of 'reference by zero', as Halliday and Hasan might have expressed it. This is confirmed by the way the gap can be filled by pronominal reference:

> Drain it well and transfer it to a food processor.

The gap cannot, however, be filled by substitution:

> *Drain one well and transfer one to a food processor.

The fact that substitution is not an option here gives further point to not treating ellipsis and substitution as variants of a single phenomenon. It even suggests that characterizing ellipsis as 'substitution by zero' is suggestive impressionism rather than an accurate description.

Intrasentential ellipsis: subordination reduction

Where ellipsis occurs within a complex sentence and involves a cohesively semantic relation between main and subordinate clauses, the term 'subordination reduction' signals an appropriate parallel with 'coordination reduction' in compound structures. Strictly, subordination reduction points to an ellipsis in a subordinate clause. However, it is worth including in this category cases where the ellipsis is in the main clause with the subordinate clause providing the recoverable context, as in:

> Because John was going to Silverstone, Jim went [ ] too.

Main clause reduction of this type is anomalous if the order of the clauses is reversed:

> *Jim went [ ] too, because John was going to Silverstone.

This suggests that there is an ordering constraint which is, in effect, a block on cataphoric ellipsis. The sentence is fine, if no ellipsis is assumed:

> Jim went too, because John was going to Silverstone.

Here, however, far from taking for granted that Jim went to Silverstone, we assume that, while Jim also departed, his destination was anywhere but Silverstone. The provision of an anaphorically recoverable context allows the ellipsis to be reinstated, because there is a cohesive tie to support it:

> Louise drove down to Brighton for the day. Jim went [ ] too, because John was going to Silverstone.

Here, we can take for granted that Jim went to Brighton with Louise. With subordination reduction proper, where the ellipsis is sited in the subordinate clause, the cataphoric constraint disappears:

> Because John was going [ ], Jim went to Silverstone too.

Here, we can only assume that John was going to Silverstone.

In the examples discussed so far the missing elements have been uniquely recoverable from the linguistic context. However, that is not the case in all examples of subordination reduction, as the following example from Virginia Woolf's *The Voyage Out* shows:

> Rachel, when [ ] consulted, showed less enthusiasm than Helen could have wished. (1915: 77)

Abbreviated clauses of this kind are readily expanded by a pronominal subject and an appropriate verbal element:

> Rachel, when [she was] consulted, showed less enthusiasm than Helen could have wished.

Neither element meets the criterion of 'verbatim recoverability' from the context. Note also that the gap cannot be filled on the basis of syntactic structure alone, since, for example, pronominal gender is dependent on knowing that Rachel is feminine. The concept of weak contextual ellipsis, derived from Quirk *et al.* (1985), can be applied quite usefully to this kind of example, since there is definitely a gap, but the missing elements are only weakly signalled by the linguistic context on its own.

More problematical is the occurrence of such adverbial clauses without a subordinator:

Left alone, Evelyn walked up and down the path. (Woolf 1915: 346)

The clausal status of the expression 'left alone' is preserved by the presence of a verbal element. We can expand this abbreviated structure in a way that reflects its understood meaning in relation to the linguistic context:

[When she was] Left alone, Evelyn walked up and down the path.

In this case the weak ellipsis is cataphoric, since the gap takes for granted elements that occur later in the text to resolve number and gender. An additional problem is the assignment of a subordinator, whose indeterminacy makes this sentence even weaker as contextual ellipsis than the previous example.

Similar issues arise with abbreviated relative clauses, another common instance of subordination reduction. The way they can be reduced is affected by their restrictive or non-restrictive status. A restrictive relative clause functions as a postmodifier in a noun phrase and uniquely delimits its antecedent head noun, as in the following examples:

Jim said the film which he saw at the multiplex was dire.
The man who was wearing a red cape vanished into the Venetian night.

Ellipsis of the relative pronoun on its own can only occur in restrictive clauses when the pronoun is the object:

Jim said the film [ ] he saw at the multiplex was dire.

The relative pronoun as subject in restrictive clauses can only be omitted together with the auxiliary element of the verbal group:

The man [ ] wearing a red cape vanished into the Venetian night.

In restrictive clauses such as this the ellipsis is again weak in the sense I have adopted for the term: a pronominal subject and an appropriate verbal element can be supplied on the basis of syntactic structure and contextual support, though they are not uniquely recoverable as such.

A non-restrictive relative clause is a separate syntactic structure that relates to its antecedent by providing additional, or even incidental, information. In speech it has a separate intonation pattern that is represented in writing by the use of commas, as this example shows:

The prisoners, who had been left alone, became depressed.

Again, the idea of weak ellipsis is useful in the case of reduced non-restrictive relative clauses:

The prisoners, [ ] left alone, became depressed.

Note that the reduced form is structurally ambiguous. It can be expanded to the relative clause, but can also be interpreted as an adverbial clause without subordinator, as this comparison of examples shows:

[When she was] Left alone, Evelyn walked up and down the path.
The prisoners, [when they were] left alone, became depressed.

In both instances the reduced clause 'left alone' takes on a superficially adjectival quality, but there is a subtle stylistic difference. Coming first in the Woolf sentence, 'left alone' cannot be a reduced relative clause providing incidental information. Since it must be a reduced adverbial clause, it conveys to the reader the sense that Evelyn's pacing is contingent upon, if not caused by, being left alone. In the other sentence, 'The prisoners, [ ] left alone, became depressed', 'left alone', as a reduced relative clause may be providing incidental information, but, as a reduced adverbial clause, it could also be suggesting a reason for the prisoners' depression. The structural indeterminacy of the elliptical expression is a vehicle for ambiguity of meaning and interpretation.

Exercise 3.1

For each of the following sentences, identify any gaps that result from subordination reduction. Suggest possible expansions and note any analytical problems that arise.

If pushed by the other runners, Kathy could well break the record.
Jim broke his ankle, trying to climb Scafell.
The model she had dressed in black swept down the catwalk.
The architects, Glasgow's main players, won the design award.

Intersentential ellipsis: contextual rejoinders

The focus of this section is the fragmented replies and responses that speakers make in dialogue. The term 'fragment' often has negative connotations, as of something broken and incomplete, but its use here is quite positive: fragments are, as my discussion below will illustrate, very often the most effective and efficient type of rejoinder. There are fragments and fragments, of course, and the kind discussed here are not the result of lapses in performance, but a systematic communicative device, a contrast that is worth reinforcing by example. Recall the following sample of spontaneous dialogue from the previous chapter:

> A: I wondered if we, er, aren't, like, taking it a bit slow
> B: Erm
> A: Or is that [ ], would it help [ ]
> B: I think we were taking it a bit slow, but, er, I think I'd find it easier if we did it a bit faster.

A's unsuccessful attempts to say something, 'Or is that [ ], would it help [ ]', are fragments of the first sort. Contextual rejoinders, like Philip's reply in the bit of dramatic dialogue I cited earlier, are of a different order:

> CELIA: You're being cunning.
> PHILIP: I'm not [ ].

The distinction between these different kinds of fragment is usefully made by Matthews (1981: 41) with the terms 'utterance fragment' and 'sentence fragment'. Incomplete utterances or utterance fragments stem from what I have called lapses in performance, false starts, abandoned structures, interruptions and overlaps between speakers and the like. Incomplete sentences or sentence fragments, on the other hand, are elliptical and, despite their incompleteness as sentences, very often constitute a speaker's complete utterance or turn in a conversation. Matthews sums up his position as follows: '[Utterance] Fragments are of no concern to syntax, except as a source of confusion in our data. But ellipsis is constrained by rules' (ibid.). Utterance fragments are an interesting and legitimate object of study for discourse analysts and, as I noted in the previous chapter, Halliday is more positive about accounting for them systematically within a comprehensive grammar of spoken language (1994: 65). However, Matthews is right to suggest that attempting to incorporate them into a theory of ellipsis would be confusing, given the apparent randomness of some types of performance lapse. Sentence fragments, on the other hand, are marked by their 'structural rightness' and functional efficiency in the linguistic contexts where they occur.

The structural rightness of contextual rejoinder fragments is best described in terms of what syntactic element is being ellipted and how the missing element is understood from the surrounding context. Ellipsis operates at sentence, clause and phrase levels as well as on elements within clauses and phrases. My outline is organized around these categories without attempting to provide comprehensive coverage: examples and discussion are indicative of a much wider range of contextual rejoinders. All the examples quoted in this outline are from the rich dialogue of a single play, Christopher Hampton's *The Philanthropist* (1970), to which subsequent page numbers refer.

Maximal ellipsis occurs when a rejoinder omits the whole preceding sentence. Maximal ellipsis entails minimal response:

> DON: Did you find the lemons?
> CELIA: Yes [ ]. (p. 20)

Celia's rejoinder is straightforwardly expanded because the sentence is a simple one with only one clause:

> CELIA: Yes [I did find the lemons].

Note, however, that even in such simple cases of apparently unique recoverability, expansion has to incorporate a change of pronoun, from the question's 'you' to the answer's 'I'. More complex contexts present a greater challenge both for expansion and its analysis:

> CELIA: I suppose you were discussing morphology all night.
>   Or checking her vowel sounds.
> PHILIP: No [ ]. (p. 51)

Philip's minimally direct rejoinder is ambiguous. While it is cohesive with the subordinate clauses of Celia's statement, it is unclear whether it takes account of both clauses or just the second one. The suspicious Celia might assume that, 'No [I wasn't checking her vowel sounds]', means that Philip was indeed discussing morphology all night, denying one metaphor for sexual activity, but conceding another. The embattled Philip, however, is much more likely to be asserting total fidelity: 'No

[I wasn't discussing morphology all night. Or checking her vowel sounds].'

It is this kind of analytical uncertainty, and the communicative ambiguity it affords, that has prompted some theoretical debate as to whether minimal yes/no rejoinders are better seen as clause substitutes. Halliday and Hasan discuss this in relation to their treatment of rejoinders as a cohesive device as follows: 'It is possible to consider yes and no as clause substitutes. But they are not really substitutes; for one thing they can be accompanied by part or even the whole of the clause for which they would be said to be substituting' (1976: 209). Halliday and Hasan are referring here to rejoinders of the following kind:

> ARAMINTA: Are you writing a new novel?
> BRAHAM: Yes, I am [ ]. It's nearly finished. (p. 37)

In this example only the propositional part of the clause is omitted, that is, main verb plus any attached constituents such as object or complement, in this case: 'writing a new novel'. The argument that 'yes' and 'no' cannot be clause substitutes, if they are habitually used alongside partially retained clauses, is a convincing one and there does not seem to be any other justification for discounting minimal yes/no reaction signals from the domain of ellipsis. Their status as ellipsis rather than substitution is not, however, just another aspect of the pedagogical tradition which requires that all answers should be in complete sentences. By classifying minimal yes/no responses as a type of dependent incomplete sentence, we are endorsing the fact that incompleteness is appropriate, at least in spoken exchanges, if not in the written answers to comprehension questions.

There are several other mechanisms whereby the whole of the initiating sentence may be omitted in a contextual rejoinder. Two are particularly common in response to statements. In the first an elliptical superordinate clause is used to comment on a statement:

> ARAMINTA: A lot of people do find me attractive.
> PHILIP: I'm sure [ ]. (p. 49)

A common variant of this is where the superordinate clause is also a question, for example, 'Are you sure [A lot of people do find you attractive]?' as a response in the previous exchange. This has the effect of expressing doubt about, rather than agreeing with, the statement. Secondly, a single question element, either a *wh*-word or an adverbial with rising intonation, may be used to ellipt the whole statement, as in the following examples:

PHILIP: I liked it.
JOHN: Why [ ]? (p. 11)

PHILIP: She left.
CELIA: [ ] Immediately? (p. 54)

This use of the single adverbial, though with a more declarative falling intonation, can also be used to respond elliptically to the whole of a question:

PHILIP: Do you know him?
DON: [ ] Slightly. (p. 16)

The use of single question elements and adverbials closely parallels minimal 'yes' or 'no' responses along with such expressions of indefiniteness as 'perhaps' and 'sometimes'. This parallel further supports the elliptical status of minimal yes/no rejoinders.

Many sentence fragments result from the ellipsis of some part of the initiating sentence, rather than the whole thing. Very often the rejoinder is a word or phrase realizing one of the main functional elements of the sentence: subject, verb, object, complement, adverbial. The following examples of responses to *wh*-questions are typical, in that they only supply the element which contains the information required by the question. In each case I have labelled the functional element realized by the contextual rejoinder:

DON: Who's coming to dinner?
PHILIP: Liz [is coming to dinner]. (p. 16)
Functional element: subject

DON: Who does that leave?
PHILIP: [That leaves] Johnson. (p. 32)
Functional element: object

PHILIP: But . . . who was she?
DON: [She was] A retired lieutenant-colonel. (p. 17)
Functional element: complement

DON: Where's Celia?
PHILIP: [Celia is] In the kitchen. (p. 14)
Functional element: adverbial

The questions here are all simple, one clause, sentences, so the functional element is readily identifiable in each response and what is being omitted is uniquely recoverable from the linguistic context. Where complex *wh*-questions are involved, the rejoinder often consists of a whole clause:

> PHILIP: And why do you think Celia lives by a lie?
> DON: [ ] Because her vanity demands it. (p. 74)

This response can still be described in functional terms: it is a subordinate adverbial clause realizing the functional element 'adverbial' in a fully expanded version of the rejoinder. But, because of the complexity of the initiating question, what is being omitted is ambiguous, as these two possible expansions demonstrate:

> PHILIP: And why do you think Celia lives by a lie?
> DON: [I think Celia lives by a lie] Because her vanity demands it.

> PHILIP: And why do you think Celia lives by a lie?
> DON: [Celia lives by a lie] Because her vanity demands it.

The first expansion simply expresses Don's opinion about Celia, whereas the second makes a more categorical statement. Philip has asked for Don's opinion, but it is clear from his next remark that he assumes Don's response is an assertion of fact:

> PHILIP: I'm not sure about that.

You might ask how Don could have signalled the first expansion without being more definite. This could have been done intonationally: a rising intonation would indicate uncertainty or questioning. If the playwright had wanted Don to sound tentative, he could have indicated this intonation with a question mark in the script. In that case we might have had the following exchange:

> PHILIP: And why do you think Celia lives by a lie?
> DON: Because her vanity demands it?
> PHILIP: You may be right.

In this version Philip clearly assumes that Don's remark is an expression of opinion and responds accordingly. In the context of Hampton's play and the characters involved, though, the assertiveness of Don's reply is appropriate to his more forthright personality. My discussion merely serves to show how ellipsis has a built-in potential for ambiguity because an apparently unique recoverability may turn out to be less unique than it at first seems.

In the examples discussed so far, ellipsis has been seen to operate on whole categories: sentences, clauses, functional elements. However, in many cases rejoinders consist of partial elements that do not have constituent status, as in the following example:

> ARAMINTA: Is that nice?
> PHILIP: Very. (p. 40)

Philip's reply may be expanded to: 'That is very nice' which makes explicit the fact that there is more than one ellipsis site: '[That is] Very [nice].' It is worth considering whether these two ellipses operate independently. The first one could have applied on its own. Philip could have replied: '[That is] Very nice'. This may be analysed as a complement, one of the functional elements noted earlier. In this case, the complement is realized as an adjective phrase: 'Very nice.' The second ellipsis reduces this adjective phrase by omitting the adjective and leaving only its modifier: 'Very.' This second ellipsis could not have applied on its own. Philip could not have replied: ★'That is very [nice].' This suggests that where there is more than one ellipsis in a single syntactic structure there can be ordering constraints on the operation of these ellipses that block ungrammatical strings.

Another rejoinder with more than one ellipsis site shows that this ordering constraint is structure-specific rather than universal:

> DON: And did it raise much money?
> BRAHAM: [ ] Enough [ ] to cover my fee. (p. 27)

The first ellipsis, of pronominal subject and main verb, like the previous example, creates a functional sentence element, in this case an object, '[It raised] Enough money to cover my fee', realized as a noun phrase. The second reduces this noun phrase by omitting the head noun: '[It raised] Enough [money] to cover my fee'. Unlike the previous example, however, the ellipses in Braham's reply can be applied independently of each other. Applying the second ellipsis on its own produces an acceptable structure. Braham could have replied: 'It raised enough to cover my fee.' These different options in the deployment of ellipsis constitute a stylistic choice for the playwright putting words into a character's mouth. And, at a less conscious level for the most part, such choices are also being made by speakers in natural conversation.

Exercise 3.2

Suggest possible expansions for the ellipses in the following rejoinder sequences from T. S. Eliot's *The Waste Land*. Comment on any problems that arise with respect to contextual recoverability and suggest how any perceived anomalies contribute to the atmosphere of the exchange as a whole.

> 'What is that noise?'
>   [ ] The wind under the door.
> 'What is that noise now? What is the wind doing?'
>   [ ] Nothing again nothing . . .
>
>   . . . 'What shall we do tomorrow?
> What shall we ever do?'
>   [ ] The hot water at ten.
> And if it rains, [ ] a closed car at four.
>
>   (1963: 67–8)

Discussion of Exercises

Exercise 3.1

Subordination reduction is a general term for ellipsis in subordinate clauses, such as abbreviated adverbial clauses and reduced relative clauses. Adverbial clauses comment on such things as how, why or when the event of the main clause occurs. In the first example the adverbial clause is conditional, telling us under what conditions the event of the main clause is likely to occur:

> If [she is] pushed by the other runners, Kathy could well break the record.

Note that the subject in the restored gap is a co-referential pronoun marked for person, number and gender, not the uniquely recoverable

'Kathy'. The omission of the auxiliary verb also means that the subordinate clause is non-finite or tenseless. The tense of the missing element is cued by the verb in the main clause. This verbal element isn't strictly recoverable from the context. Although an appropriate part of BE is the most obvious expansion, a range of less determinate elements is possible, such as 'gets', 'happens to be', etc. Even so, a general rule for this kind of weak ellipsis emerges as: 'fill the gap with a co-referential pronoun subject plus a finite verbal element'. We can see this in operation on a parallel sentence:

> Although [he was] pushed by the other runners, Trevor didn't break the record.

This kind of 'subordination reduction rule' applies straightforwardly to the next example, but in addition the subordinating word or subordinator is also omitted. This subordinator is to some extent indeterminate. For example, more than one temporal subordinator is appropriate:

> Jim broke his ankle, [while he was] trying to climb Scafell.
> Jim broke his ankle, [when he was] trying to climb Scafell.

Despite this indeterminacy, the subordinator is also constrained by the context. For example, a conditional marker would be wholly anomalous:

> *Jim broke his ankle, [if he was] trying to climb Scafell.

On the basis of these examples it is possible to suggest an extension of the general rule to cover this pattern of subordination reduction: 'fill the gap with a contextually appropriate subordinator plus a co-referential pronoun subject plus a finite verbal element'.

The other two examples may be seen to contain reduced relative clauses. The first is restrictive, identifying a particular model among implied others:

> The model [whom] she had dressed in black swept down the catwalk.

Note that the omitted pronoun is the object of the relative clause. I have accordingly chosen the relative pronoun's objective form 'whom'. However, this is also a stylistic choice, since it is increasingly restricted to formal usage, mostly in writing. Colloquial speech and less formal written language is marked by the use of 'who', even where the relative pronoun is the object.

The relative clause in the second example is non-restrictive:

> The architects, [who are] Glasgow's main players, won the design award.

All the architects within the frame of reference are included in the additional information provided by the relative clause. Note that the verb in my expansion is in the present tense: incidental non-restrictive clauses do not need to adopt the tense marker of the main clause. It is also worth noting that some descriptive grammars avoid an elliptical analysis of such examples by using the notion of apposition. Since 'the architects' and 'Glasgow's main players' are co-referential, they are said to be appositive noun phrases: the second is simply juxtaposed to the first, rather than derived from some underlying relative clause. This has some merit in descriptive terms and doesn't prevent the stylistic effect of such structures from being recognized.

Exercise 3.2

Most of the examples of rejoinders I discussed exhibited uniquely recoverable ellipsis, but not all rejoinders are susceptible to a uniquely recoverable expansion. The extracts from T. S. Eliot's *The Waste Land* have instances of both types. They are from the section of the poem entitled 'A Game of Chess' whose general theme is marital relations. The exchanges here represent a rather odd communicative situation between wife and husband. The first gap expands unproblematically:

> 'What is that noise?'
> [That noise is] The wind under the door.

The second rejoinder is best seen as a reiterative response to the second of the wife's questions:

> 'What is that noise now? What is the wind doing?'
> [The wind is doing] Nothing again nothing.

The ellipses in the second sequence are not uniquely recoverable, since a strict contextually derived expansion results in semantically odd expressions:

> . . . 'What shall we do tomorrow?
> What shall we ever do?'
> *[Tomorrow we shall do] The hot water at ten.
> *And if it rains, [we shall do] a closed car at four.

An acceptable expansion based on the given linguistic context needs to be more specific than this. Since 'do' is a highly generic action verb, one way of achieving a sensible expansion is to supply appropriate hyponyms, action verbs that relate more specifically to the object elements left by the elliptical process. My own expansion is along the following lines:

> [Tomorrow we shall order] The hot water at ten.
> And if it rains, [we shall take] a closed car at four.

Other hyponyms of the verb 'do', appropriate to the sense, would do just as well. This strategy does, of course, stretch the notion of contextual recoverability rather a lot, but seems warranted by the oddity of the exchange.

The anomaly of the final sequence reinforces the strangeness of the passage as a whole: even the other sequences, if not problematical in terms of recoverability, are, as I noted, discursively odd. The fact that the questions are in quotation marks, whereas the responses are not, is a key to this oddity. This is Eliot's way of representing an anxious and fretful woman talking aloud to an indifferent husband who maintains his silence, but answers in his head. The husband's final unvoiced enumeration of routine events underlines the atmosphere of marital unease. Here we have a failing relationship in 'The Game of Chess', Eliot's suggestive metaphor for the marital relationships he depicts.

CHAPTER 4

THE SITUATIONAL CONTEXT

With reference to language in use, the term 'context' has two general meanings. First, as we saw in the previous chapter, the term refers to the actual language surrounding an utterance or sentence: the linguistic context or co-text, as it is called in some treatments. My use of the term 'contextual ellipsis' refers exclusively to the linguistic context. The second major use of 'context' implies the variety of extralinguistic factors that may contribute to our understanding of a language event, such as setting, participants, objects and actions. The more explicit 'context of situation' captures this meaning. This distinction between linguistic and situational contexts is frequently labelled by the referential terms 'endophoric' and 'exophoric', respectively pointing to those elements 'within the text' and 'outside the text'. Even though some definitions of ellipsis build in a requirement that missing elements are recoverable from the linguistic context, ruling out situational factors altogether, the distinction between linguistic and situational contexts is fundamental to my own treatment of ellipsis. The working definition I arrived at in Chapter 1 incorporates this distinction: structural gaps that can be related to: (a) omitted elements recoverable from the linguistic context, (b) other potential syntactic forms, (c) the situational context. In this chapter and the next I explore some of the ways in which we can recover gaps and understand elliptical sentences on the basis of knowing the likely structures they relate to in the situational context where they occur. This chapter deals specifically with two major categories of ellipsis: sentence-initial and situational.

Sentence-initial ellipsis

The type of linguistic gap that is the main topic of this section is both very common in everyday speech and widely recognized in the literature on ellipsis. However, its discussion by linguists raises a number of issues as to the most explanatory way of describing its elliptical status. This brief extract from a meal-time conversation I recorded provides a good example:

A: Well, strawberries or
B: Oh strawberries
A: you'll not like the look of those.
B: Um, syrup, oh no
A: I got two tins just in case.
B: Ugh, oh well, in syrup.
A: [ ] Any good?

The question here is readily expanded to:

A: [Are they] Any good?

The basis for this expansion is not some contextually recoverable element, so this kind of ellipsis clearly needs to be resolved in relation to its likely syntactic form in this particular situational context. In isolation, an expansion is achievable on syntactic potential alone. As the initiator of a conversation, for example, 'Any good?' is readily expanded to a number of forms, such as 'Is it any good?', 'Was he any good?'. The context of situation supports an appropriate meaning, as it does in the above conversation. The role of situational context in such examples suggests that these kinds of omission are a type of situational ellipsis. That view is supported by Carter and McCarthy in their corpus-based study of spoken English grammar. They note a significant number of ellipses where subject pronouns and copular or auxiliary verbs 'are retrievable from the contextual environment', citing such examples as '[there's a] Foreign body in there' (Carter and McCarthy 1995: 146). The fact that such truncated expressions can initiate a conversational turn gives rise to their categorization as sentence-initial ellipsis, though utterance-initial may be more appropriate, since they are commonly, though not exclusively, features of colloquial speech. Three related issues regarding sentence-initial ellipsis need to be addressed: (a) the kinds of elements that are omitted, (b) its context-independence or conventionality, (c) its status as a prosodic rather than a syntactic feature. These issues are discussed in turn in the rest of this section.

The most commonly omitted items in sentence-initial ellipsis are of two kinds: verbal operators, that is, auxiliary elements such as 'be', 'do' or 'have', and pronominal subjects or existential markers. Both kinds appeared in the examples previously cited:

[Are they] Any good?
[There's a] Foreign body in there.

If these combinations are the norm for omitted items, then it is worth testing how much less or more than this norm can be subject to sentence-initial ellipsis. Statements allow for the omission of pronominal subject alone, as in such formulaic fragments as the emphatic:

[I] Told you!

Questions allow for the omission of the verbal operator alone:

[Have] You got any money?

These are the minimal elements for this kind of ellipsis. An interesting variation on the norm of subject and operator occurs where the verb is copular BE. As one of the few lexical verbs in modern English that can act as an operator, BE allows for such expressions as:

[Are you] Hungry?

Here copula and subject are omitted before the subject complement. Literary examples occur where writers wish to capture the speech quality of their personae, as in T. S. Eliot's poem 'Portrait of a Lady':

[He is] So intimate, this Chopin, that I think his soul
Should be resurrected only among friends. (1963: 18)

By applying sentence-initial ellipsis Eliot not only indicates colloquial speech but also allows the complement to be foregrounded at the start of the line.

The fact that a lexical verb is subject to sentence-initial ellipsis raises the possibility that other verbs and their attachments might figure too. With respect to their example '[ ] Foreign body in there', Carter and McCarthy go on to suggest that '[I can see a] is an equally possible candidate for the understood part of the message' (1995: 146). This degree of indeterminacy is similarly exemplified by a much simpler utterance like '[ ] Coffee?'. This has a wide range of possible expansions, depending on the context in which it is uttered: 'Would you like some coffee?', 'Is that coffee?', 'Have you got any coffee?' are just a few that spring to mind. Although the range of possible structures is not open-ended, it is clear that the apparent omission of these elements cannot be described in terms of a few simple categories like pronominal subject and operator. Examples like '[ ] Coffee?' and those cited by Carter and McCarthy are much more obviously dependent on the situational context for any particular expansion of the understood element of the message.

While some sentence-initial ellipses, then, are open to a wider range of expansions, the majority, like '[Are they] Any good?' and '[Are you] Hungry?', are restricted to a few possibilities which are predicted by syntactic rule. Although the situational context plays a part in determining the exact nature of the gap, the linguistic context is not involved in the recovery. This context-independent expansion based on one or two syntactic categories that characterizes much sentence-initial ellipsis has prompted the term 'conventional' in, for example, Thomas's typological treatment of ellipsis (1979: 46). This contrasts nicely with the term 'contextual' and underlines the fact that sentence-initial ellipses do not rely on linguistic contexts other than their own syntactic structure for their resolution.

By way of reinforcing that contrast, compare the following examples of a sentence-initial ellipsis and a contextual rejoinder:

[ ] Got any money?
[ ] $8\frac{1}{2}$.

The first of these readily expands to 'Have you got any money?' without any support from the linguistic context whatsoever. In isolation, this is the default expansion. It also reflects the most likely meaning in most situational contexts, though we have to allow for a situation where, say, '[Has she] Got any money?' is the understood message. The second, apart from its numerical value, is more or less meaningless without its context. It could be the answer to a sum, a hat size, an interest rate and so on. It is, however, the response in the following snippet of conversation:

A: What's your favourite Fellini?
B: [ ] $8\frac{1}{2}$.

On the basis of this particular context we can expand B's rejoinder to: 'My favourite Fellini is "$8\frac{1}{2}$"', resolving any uncertainty about its meaning out of context. The metonymic gap, discussed in Chapter 2 with regard to 'that new Tarantino', is again in evidence. Speaker A's use of 'Fellini' to mean 'film directed by Fellini', was clearly part of B's shared knowledge and not a problem.

This contrastive exercise suggests that to the extent missing items in sentence-initial ellipsis can be automatically supplied, they are conventional in a way that those of conversational rejoinders are not. However, the term is slightly misleading when used in this exclusive way, since most types of ellipsis are conventional to some extent, that is, subject to syntactic rules and constraints. Furthermore, no sentence-initial utterance is likely to be independent of a situational context which gives it meaning beyond its conventional derivation.

The third issue concerns the possible prosodic nature of sentence-initial ellipsis, that it is an extension of the type of spoken elision I noted in Chapter 1 with regard to the example: 'They doctored the apes, and made 'em think'. Prosodic features of language, such as intonation, accent, volume and the elision of sounds in running speech, have been proposed as an alternative or possibly supplementary explanation for the most conventional types of sentence-initial ellipsis, for example, in Quirk *et al.*:

> It is difficult to say whether the missing syllables are lost because their utterance is subaudible, or because of more abstract phonological principles . . . Whatever the correct explanation of such initial ellipsis may be, it seems unquestionable that the omissions are at least partly phonologically determined. (1985: 896)

It is worth looking in some detail at what a phonologically determined omission generally means, to see if it really can be applied to sentence-initial ellipsis. Let's take the following example:

Did you get the tickets?

Those elements likely to disappear are, according to a syntactic analysis, the verbal operator and the pronominal subject: 'did you'. Phonologically, the citational form /dɪd ju/ is likely to be reduced, especially in informal speech, because these elements are weakly stressed syllables. Possible reductions are /dɪdʒu, dɪdʒə, dʒu, dʒə/. These variants can be properly called phonological reductions, since they involve either a reduction in the number of phonemes or recourse to a weaker vowel or both. It is possible, of course, that this process of reduction can be taken to the point where nothing is pronounced at all. This explanation could go hand in hand with a syntactic analysis, since the abstract phonological principles invoked could be related to grammatical categories. However, such covert psycholinguistic processes are outside the scope of my own analysis of sentence-initial ellipsis. In general, a syntactic explanation of such reduced sentences is descriptively adequate for the stylistic aims of this book, which is not to deny the theoretical interest of prosodic explanations.

An alternative way of describing the syntactic basis of sentence-initial ellipsis may be derived from the systemic approach of Halliday and Hasan. They outline a basic structure for clauses or simple sentences that consists of a modal element plus a propositional element (1976: 197). The modal element consists of the subject and the operator or finite part of the verbal group, while the propositional element is the rest of the verbal group together with any objects, complements or adjuncts, as the following simple example shows:

Modal Element	Propositional Element
Liam is	singing in the band

Either element may be ellipted in different contexts. In the following rejoinder sequence the modal element is omitted:

A: What is Liam doing?
B: [ ] Singing in the band.

In the next one it is the propositional element that is missing:

A: Who is singing in the band?
B: Liam is [ ].

If we look at some of the examples of sentence-initial ellipsis discussed above, it is clear that the category 'modal element' captures the nature of the missing items:

Modal Element	Propositional Element
[Are they]	Any good?
[There's a]	Foreign body in there.
[Are you]	Hungry?
[He is]	So intimate, this Chopin.

The advantage of this analysis is that sentence-initial ellipsis can be seen in terms of what appears to be a general syntactic rule that applies to other types of sentence. Even where only one item within the modal element is ellipted, as in '[I] Told you!' and '[Have] You got any money?', it is at least possible, though less neatly satisfactory, to account for the gap in terms of 'weak' modal ellipsis.

Exercise 4.1

Although sentence-initial ellipsis is characteristic of colloquial speech, there is one written genre which regularly exploits it: the diary. The following examples are extracts from two fictional diaries: Sue Townsend's *The Secret Diary of Adrian Mole* (1982) and G. and W. Grossmith's *The Diary of a Nobody* (1892). Make a list of the omitted sentence-initial items and comment on any patterns of ellipsis that emerge from your analysis.

The Secret Diary of Adrian Mole

Came home. Fed dog. Read a bit of *Female Eunuch*. Felt a bit funny. Went to sleep. (p. 29)

Got *Waiting for Godot* out of the library. Disappointed to find that it was a play. (p. 63)

Not had a postcard from my love yet. (p. 102)

Just got back from London. (p. 121)

Took Bert's Woodbines round to the home. (p. 158)

The Diary of a Nobody

Painted the bath red, and was delighted with the result. (p. 42)

Still a little shaky, with black specks. (p. 59)

Nearly late for church, Mrs James having talked considerably about what to wear all the morning. (p. 83)

Went to Smirksons', the drapers, in the Strand. (p. 129)

Quite looking forward to the seance this evening. (p. 219)

Situational ellipsis

We have seen that most sentence-initial ellipsis operates on a fairly narrow set of conventionally prescribed items, mainly in speech, where the situational context supports or resolves meaning. Sentence-initial gaps do not rely on the recovery of material from the surrounding linguistic context, making them very distinct from the types of ellipsis I discussed in Chapter 3: there is always an exophoric dimension to sentence-initial ellipsis. There are also gaps where the missing elements are only recoverable from the situational context: the basis for their resolution is always extralinguistic. Within Halliday and Hasan's schema for cohesion such gaps are not strictly cohesive, because the understood part of their message is entirely within the context of situation. For these exclusively exophoric gaps I use the term 'situational ellipsis'.

The difference between contextual and situational ellipsis can be demonstrated by using the same expression to illustrate both types. First, here is a typical contextual rejoinder sequence:

> A: I think I'll go and see The Spice Girls.
> B: I wouldn't [ ], if I were you.

Here, B's response is uniquely recoverable from the linguistic context, an example of contextual ellipsis. Imagine now a scenario that must have been acted out in dozens of B movies, both westerns and films noirs: gunman A is being held up by gunman B; A has dropped his weapon conveniently close to where he stands; being a foolhardy fellow, he decides to have a go at reaching for his gun at which point gunman B says: 'I wouldn't [ ], if I were you'. In isolation this expression can be understood as a warning or recommendation not to do something or other. As a contextual rejoinder the precise nature of this action is recoverable from the linguistic context. In the movie scenario the action can only be understood from the situation. The example does suggest that there will always be some degree of indeterminacy in the recovery of situational ellipsis, but gunman A will get the message whether he understands some general expression like 'move' or 'do that' or a more specific 'reach for your gun'.

Situationally resolved gaps in spoken language can be compared with gaps related to lapses in performance and false starts. In general, Matthews' (1981) concepts of sentence fragment and utterance fragment, outlined in Chapter 3, are useful here. In the above example situational ellipsis results in a sentence fragment like 'I wouldn't [ ], if I were you', whereas lapses in performance create utterance fragments, such as 'because the, erm [ ]', 'or is that [ ]', and 'I don't mind, it's [ ]' discussed in Chapter 2. Although the contrast seems to follow Matthews' distinction between syntactically ordered sentence fragments and randomly structured utterance fragments, it is also worth looking at possible prosodic differences. A genuine situational ellipsis is likely to be contained within a complete intonation pattern, whereas utterance fragments typically break off in the middle of an intonation pattern and leave it unresolved. There will, of course, always be cases in the give and take of spoken language that seem to fall somewhere in between. Take the following exchange between two friends I recorded, as one prepared to go shopping:

A: (putting on coat): Anything you want up the er [ ]?
B: Would you mind taking [ ] (stops speaking as A picks up video)

Note that A's turn begins with a sentence-initial ellipsis typical of the structures discussed in the first part of this chapter: '[Is there] Anything you want up the er [ ]?'. The second gap is much less determinate. Even though the situation can suggest likely things speaker A might have said, such as 'street' or 'shops', these are not recoverable in the way that the gunman's action was in my earlier example: there is no exophoric ellipsis. Although A was not interrupted, the hesitation marker and the break in intonation contour suggest that this was a lapse in performance which, by Matthews' criteria, results in an utterance fragment. Speaker B's turn is harder to judge in this respect. It can be seen to omit the object of 'taking', because that object is recoverable from the situational context and A's action in picking up the video allows for a meaningful gap. In that respect it is closer to: 'I wouldn't [ ], if I were you', a situationally supported sentence fragment. On the other hand, the intonation pattern breaks off rather than completes its contour, creating uncertainty about its status as a situational ellipsis. This example is a useful reminder of the challenges posed by the analysis of raw conversational data, which often refuses to fall neatly into the categories we have devised for it.

The incidence of situational ellipsis in writing is very common, occurring in a variety of signs, notices, manufacturers' labels on goods and the instructions on containers of household products.

Instructions are usually framed as subjectless imperatives. The most frequently omitted constituent is the direct object of the imperative verb, as in the ubiquitous 'Push [ ]'. Though we hardly need to stop and think about it, this only makes sense if we understand that the object of the verb is whatever the instruction is written on, a door, a button in a lift, or whatever. The physical object to which the sign is attached resolves the situational gap. The situational ellipsis of direct objects of this kind is straightforward as long as the sign or notice refers unambiguously to the thing it is written on, as with, for example, 'Do not remove [ ] from this notice board' printed in bold on a list of exam results. Where containers are concerned, the potential for ambiguity becomes interesting. On a spray can of air freshener, for example, I found two consecutive instructions as follows:

> Do not pierce or burn [ ] even after use.
> Do not spray [ ] on a naked flame.

The omitted object of the verbs in the first instruction must be 'the can', but the object of 'spray' in the second has to be whatever is in the can, however that is specified, 'the air freshener', 'the contents'. Since we mostly manage to avoid blowing ourselves up with such items, it is clear that these ambiguities are communicatively unproblematic. Even so, the implicit understanding assumed by this kind of situational ellipsis is worth noting, as the wording illustrated here appears to be fairly standard across a wide range of products.

Situationally resolved gaps are also to be found in the information that accompanies a product, usually on the packaging. The most commonly deleted constituent is the subject, as in '[ ] Contains natural herbal extracts', found on a bottle of skin cream. Here, the subject must be the contents of the bottle, the cream itself, and not merely the container. In a survey of my own household products, I found far fewer ellipses of the subject in informational sentences than of the object in instructions, perhaps because retaining the subject allows the manufacturer to repeat the brand name or emphasize the product. Where subject ellipsis did occur on a container, it always seemed to imply the contents rather than the container itself. Some informational sentences omit more than just the subject, though the ones I found were restricted to food products, as in '[ ] Suitable for home freezing'. Here, the subject, presumably the whole package rather than just the contents, as it was a carton of orange juice, is omitted with copular BE. As with spoken situational ellipsis a degree of indeterminacy is inherent, but a reasonable expansion can be suggested, such as '[This product is] Suitable for home freezing'.

Situational ellipsis, both in speech and writing, has been defined and illustrated here to indicate a very specific way in which language interacts with its environment. This is a considerable narrowing of its definition compared with other, more comprehensive treatments, where situational ellipsis tends to be a superordinate category including all forms of ellipsis that are not strictly recoverable from the linguistic context. While acknowledging the importance of situational context to all forms of ellipsis, including those which are strictly linguistic, I have reserved the term 'situational ellipsis' for an exclusively exophoric relation. As defined, situational ellipsis is unlikely to prove a central feature of wider samples of either spoken or written English, though its sustained occurrence in a text would undoubtedly constitute a marker of some stylistic significance.

Exercise 4.2

The following are all examples of written communication taken from real situations. Each has a brief indication of that context in brackets. Identify any situational ellipses and suggest reasonable expansions based on the contexts provided. Comment on any patterns you discern and any problems that arise.

> Dry clean only (on a silk jacket)
> Does not contain CFC which damages ozone (on a can of hair spray)
> Please do not bend (on an empty cardboard envelope)
> Avoid contact with eyes (on a tube of foot balm)
> Kills germs even after the flush (on a bottle of lavatory cleaner)
> Keep out of the reach of children (on a packet of pain relief tablets)
> Keep clear (on a garage door)
> Shake well before use (on a carton of pineapple juice)
> Best served chilled (on a can of lager)

Discussion of Exercises

Exercise 4.1

These two fictional diaries were written nearly one hundred years apart. The Grossmiths mock the pompous respectability of late Victorian suburban life, while Townsend wittily exposes teenage angst in the late twentieth century. Despite the very different content, both Townsend and the Grossmiths seek to recreate a diaristic style appropriate to 'nobodies' rather than polished writers with an eye on publication. This diaristic style has some features in common, as these samples of sentence-initial ellipsis bear out. The most obvious omission is, of course, the first-person pronoun: all fifteen instances of initial ellipsis lack 'I'. Diarists know they are the subjects of their entries and can safely omit the first-person pronoun: accordingly, these writers apply this stylistic trait to their fictional diarists. In neither diary could I find a sentence-initial gap where the subject was a third person. Third persons have to be made explicit at the outset, though once their identity is established, further references to them can be subject to other forms of contextual ellipsis. Nine of the sentence-initial ellipses omit the first-person pronoun alone, immediately before a simple past tense verb, stating an action, as in these examples: '[I] Came home. [I] Fed dog. [I] Read a bit of *Female Eunuch*. [I] Felt a bit funny. [I] Went to sleep'; '[I] Went to Smirksons', the drapers, in the Strand'. The other instances omit both subject and operator. Unlike conversation, the main reason for this pattern is not to ask abbreviated questions: diaries are not interactive in that way. In four cases the operator is an auxiliary verb: '[I was] Disappointed to find that it was a play'; '[I have] Not had a postcard from my love yet'; '[I have] Just got back from London'; '[I am] Quite looking forward to the seance this evening'. In the other two examples ellipsis involves 'I' together with part of BE as a main verb: '[I am] Still a little shaky, with black specks'; '[I was] Nearly late for church, Mrs James having talked considerably about what to wear all the morning'. Note that the tense of the verbal element is cued by the syntax of the elliptical diary entry. It is also worth noting that five of these more complex ellipses begin with a negative particle or an adverb, such as 'Still' or 'Nearly'. I found this to be a common pattern in both diaries for entries that omitted more than the first-person pronoun on its own.

Exercise 4.2

The examples can first of all be divided into those which are informational and those which are instructional. The informational sentences all conform to the pattern I noticed in my earlier discussion by omitting the subject:

[ ] Does not contain CFC which damages ozone (on a can of hair spray)
[ ] Kills germs even after the flush (on a bottle of lavatory cleaner)
[ ] Best served chilled (on a can of lager)

In all three cases the situationally supplied subject has to be understood as the contents of each container rather than the container itself. Note also that the last example is a passive construction which also omits the auxiliary BE:

[This lager is] Best served chilled.

The instructional sentences show more variation and raise some analytical problems. Most of them conform to the pattern I noticed in my earlier discussion by omitting the direct object:

Dry clean [ ] only (on a silk jacket)
Please do not bend [ ] (on an empty cardboard envelope)
Shake [ ] well before use (on a carton of pineapple juice)
Keep [ ] out of the reach of children (on a packet of pain relief tablets)
Keep [ ] clear (on a garage door)

The first four of these may be seen to omit reference to the physical object they are written on, in the first case the jacket, in the others the relevant container. Although the point of not bending the cardboard envelope is to protect its contents, because this item is reusable, the printed directive remains valid even when the envelope is empty. Most directives on containers lose their point when the container is empty, as, for example, the instruction regarding pain relief tablets. It is the tablets themselves that need to be beyond children's reach: an empty packet would be harmless. This elliptical directive contrasts nicely with one on the packet of a different brand of pain relief tablets: 'Keep all medicines out of the reach of children'. Here the general instruction spells out a direct object of 'keep' which includes this particular packet of pain relief tablets by implication. In an interesting paper that informs some of my ideas here, Sadock explores the syntactic and semantic properties of labels on medical products. He notes that a deleted object cannot be combined with one that is not omitted, as in: *'Keep [ ] and other medication out of the reach of children' (Sadock 1974: 600). This may account for the occurrence of either the specific directive with situational ellipsis, 'Keep [this packet of pain relief tablets] out of the reach of children' or the more general directive without ellipsis: 'Keep all medicines out of the reach of children.'

The instruction on the garage door is essentially about not parking in the road outside the garage door. 'Keep clear' is a highly abbreviated way of saying this. The situationally ellipted object of 'keep' is not so much ambiguous as in need of a fairly elaborate interpretation, along the lines of 'Keep [the road onto which this garage door opens] clear'.

The final example, 'Avoid contact with eyes' is exceptional, in that it does not omit the direct object of its imperative verb, and problematical, because there is no obvious ellipsis site and an expansion is difficult to make. The directive tells the user to avoid letting the substance in the tube come into contact with eyes. However, that is a paraphrase of the message rather than a principled suggestion for what is omitted. Clearly, 'Avoid [letting the substance in the tube come into] contact with eyes', does not identify the ellipsis of a valid constituent. My conclusion is that this sentence is not a genuine example of situational ellipsis as I have defined it, but spills over into a more general category of abbreviated language, telegraphic ellipsis, that is the subject of my next chapter.

CHAPTER 5

TELEGRAPHIC ELLIPSIS

Two examples of language in use which I discussed in the previous chapter could not quite be accommodated within the categories of ellipsis they seemed at first to fall into:

Coffee?
Avoid contact with eyes.

The first, I suggested, is superficially like sentence-initial ellipsis: the gap precedes the expression and the expression itself is similar to other question fragments which can initiate conversational exchanges. On the other hand, if we wish to define sentence-initial ellipsis in fairly precise terms, restricting it to a closed set of syntactically determined elements like pronominal subject and operator, then expressions like 'Coffee?' have to be categorized in some other way. Although the range of possible structures is not open-ended, it has a much wider set of possible expansions that are closely linked to the situational context:

A: [Would you like some] Coffee?
B: Not for me, thanks.

A: [Did you get any] Coffee?
B: Oh sorry, I forgot to buy some.

In each case the expansion spells out the situationally determined interpretation of the respondent rather than supplying syntactically predictable items.

The second example arose from my trawl of expressions on product labels. It seemed to have the superficial characteristics of other situational ellipses, but closer analysis showed that the imperative verb 'Avoid' cannot be understood by simply assuming its direct object is the container it is written on or, indeed, the contents of that container. As with

'Coffee?', this expression has a range of possible and plausible expansions, such as:

> Avoid [the substance in this tube coming into] contact with eyes.
> Avoid [allowing] contact [of the substance in this tube] with eyes.

Furthermore, situational ellipsis was seen to omit a situationally identifiable single syntactic constituent, signifying the product or its container, whereas the gaps indicated by these expansions cut across constituency boundaries.

These two examples, then, have a number of things in common: uncertainty of expansion, syntactic indeterminacy, omission of elements that are not properly defined as constituents and a high dependence on situational context for their resolution. These are characteristics which are generally associated with a form of abbreviated verbal communication that is widely known as telegraphic language. The term itself is rather dated, since it was meant to imply those linguistic structures which are abbreviated, truncated or otherwise incomplete in ways that are suggestive of telegrams. The language of this somewhat outmoded form of communication, motivated primarily by reducing costs in a form of communication where the sender was charged per word, reflects a very basic categorization of word classes in language, as the following example shows:

> Arriving Gatwick Tuesday 1440. Flight SN663. Peter.

This constitutes a fairly coherent message for someone expecting Peter to be coming home from Brussels in the near future, even though it omits at the very minimum the following words in order: I, am, at, on, at, on, from.

Words can mostly, though not absolutely, be divided into two broad categories called content and structure words or, meaning roughly the same thing, lexical and grammatical words. Content words include the traditional major word classes like noun, main verb, adjective and adverb, while structure words belong to classes like pronoun, auxiliary verb, preposition and conjunction. In broad terms, content words bear the main weight of meaning in a sentence or utterance, while structure words make explicit the grammatical relations between content words. To some extent, it is possible to omit most or even all structure words without damaging a message beyond comprehension: telegrams take advantage of this to cut costs and in so doing create the characteristic telegraphic mode. As is clear from the first examples discussed above, the transfer of the term 'telegraphic' to the kind of language I am discussing in this chapter is no more than suggestive: telegraphic ellipsis covers a much wider range of linguistic elements than so-called structure words. Nevertheless, the analogy between the pared-down messages of telegrams and the abbreviated structures of everyday spoken and written texts is a useful one.

Headlinese

A form of written language which typically uses telegraphic ellipsis is the newspaper headline. Headlines are smiled at and groaned over for their punning word play and have become the stylistic hallmark of rival newspapers, both tabloid and broadsheet. However, the grammar of 'headlinese', and in particular the lack of completeness of many head-lines, has been seen as problematical in more traditionally prescriptive treatments. For example, Jespersen set the tone as follows in his influential comprehensive treatment of English: 'Headlinese combinations are not in themselves sentences and often cannot be directly supplemented so as to form articulate sentences: they move, as it were, on the fringe of ordinary grammar' (1949: 125). Jespersen's view depends on a particular conception of the sentence as a syntactically complete and fully realized structure. While most contemporary linguists have moved away from a rigid distinction between sentences and non-sentences, the ideal of completeness still informs many definitions. For example, Carter and Nash have a supplementary category 'fragmentary sentence . . . from which some element has been deleted' (1990: 260). My approach to ellipsis is also informed by the notion of sentence completeness, but wishes to challenge its definitional exclusivity. Even if telegraphic sentences are on the fringe of ordinary grammar, whatever that might imply, they are part of English in use and warrant explanation rather than perfunctory dismissal. I would prefer an alternative account of headlinese that refor-mulates the first part of Jespersen's statement as follows: 'headlinese combinations are in themselves incomplete sentences and usually can be directly supplemented so as to relate to fully realized sentences'.

As with most telegraphic texts, the grammatical clues in headlinese suggest likely, though not wholly determinate, expansions. The following headline above an article about the introduction of citizenship lessons in schools is a useful example of this:

Citizenship heads for secondary schools. (*TES*, 14.5.99)

There are at least two structural possibilities here, depending on the syntactic constituency of the phrases involved and where gaps are discerned:

| Citizenship heads | for secondary schools |
| *Subject* *Verb* | *Adverbial* |

Citizenship heads   for secondary schools
Subject   *Verb*   *Adverbial*

Citizenship   heads for   secondary schools
Subject   *Verb*   *Object*

The first structure omits the verb, a major sentence element, so an expansion would need to indicate that: 'Citizenship heads [are to be appointed] for secondary schools'. The second structure, with 'heads for' as a phrasal verb, does not omit a major sentence element. The first structure's subject noun phrase condenses something like 'heads of department responsible for citizenship' in typical headlinese fashion. The second likens 'citizenship' to an impending visitor or perhaps an approaching hurricane. The meanings made possible by these different structural analyses are both relevant to the topic, since the newspaper article to which this headline is attached, concerns proposed government policy on the teaching of citizenship. The ensuing text dis-ambiguates the headline to some extent, as there is no mention of a new teaching post called 'head of citizenship'. This does not rule out that such posts will be created to implement government policy, but it makes the second structural analysis more likely. Grammatical clues present in the headlines themselves thus interact with contextual information from the setting to encode retrievable meaning. This process is essentially cataphoric in that headlines refer forward to the main body of the text, a fact exploited by editors and sub-editors on a daily basis to encourage headline-spotters to read on. Gunter probably still has the most succinct statement to this effect: 'Telegraphic ellipses depend, for their expansion to underlying form, only upon the grammatical clues present in the elliptical forms themselves, with hints supplied from the setting in which each occurs' (1963: 142). My own formulation, 'structural gaps that can be related to other potential syntactic forms or to the situational con-text', includes, though much less elegantly, telegraphic ellipsis and attempts to situate it within a wider range of phenomena where situation and syntax interact to facilitate meaning.

Exercise 5.1

The following headline was attached to an article about the prosecution and conviction of a drug dealer. Suggest its potential structure in terms of major sentence elements and fill in any gaps you think pertain to this structural analysis.

> Cannabis man jailed for year
> > (*Waltham Abbey Gazette*, 1.10.98)

Lists, headings and things

In the case of headlines a telegraphic structure often constitutes an entire orthographic sentence. However, telegraphic structures also occur as parts of longer, more complex orthographic entities, for example, in mundane settings such as shopping lists, the ingredients of recipes and lists of things to do. This listing potential of telegraphic structures can also be put to literary use, particularly in the compressed language of poetry or poetic prose. The following passage from Lawrence Durrell's novel *Balthazar*, is an interesting example of this:

> Landscape tones: brown to bronze, steep skyline, low cloud,
> pearl ground with shadowed oyster and violet reflection.
> > (1968: 11)

This consists of a chain of paratactic telegraphic structures, that is, juxtaposed with or without overt markers of coordination. Here, the first structure, 'Landscape tones', acts as a kind of heading: the other structures exemplify such tones in terms of colour, shape and shade. An expansion which reflects this heading function would be something like: '[Here is a list of] Landscape tones'. Four of the five structural elements of the text are single noun phrases: 'landscape tones', 'steep skyline', 'low cloud', 'pearl ground with shadowed oyster and violet reflection'. The last of these incorporates quite complex postmodification, 'with shadowed oyster and violet reflection', of the head noun 'ground'. However, the fifth structure, 'brown to bronze', is more difficult to describe. It is probably best seen as a complex adjective phrase, by analogy with phrases like 'fair to middling', and therefore a truncated version of something like '[in the colour range from] brown to bronze'.

Although there is no strictly contextual recoverability for such an expansion, the structure of the phrase, together with its adjacent structures, weakly determine this underlying form. Telegraphic ellipsis is most readily understood by assuming the most obvious structure compatible with surrounding language and/or the situational context. In this case, syntactic uncertainty does not cause semantic ambiguity, as would be the case if 'to bronze' were also potentially an infinitive, as in 'Sheep to fold'. Here, structural uncertainty is a source of semantic ambiguity and its interpretation can only be resolved by the context of situation. The meaning of 'Sheep to fold' depends on whether, let's say, it is the headline of a story on rescued lambs ('Sheep [are safely returned] to [the] fold') or the title of a chapter in a book of origami ('[Model] Sheep [for you] to fold'). It is usually possible to contrive a context for a telegraphic sentence that would prompt a different expansion, such as '[Mr] Brown [is off] to bronze [in Benidorm]' as the headline for a report on some famous person's holiday plans. However, 'brown to bronze' is not ambiguous here because it is embedded within a text whose linguistic structures and denotational range reinforce a particular interpretation.

Other linguistic phenomena which are best included in the category of telegraphic ellipsis are headings, titles and notices. Quirk *et al.* distinguish a separate category called 'Block Language' which they characterize as follows: 'Block language appears in such functions as labels, titles, newspaper headlines, headings, notices and advertisements. Simple block language messages are most often nonsentences' (1985: 845). The use of the term 'nonsentence' recalls Jespersen's notion that such structures are 'not in themselves sentences' but are 'on the fringe or ordinary grammar'. It is therefore unsurprising that Quirk *et al.* include headlines within their category of block language. As with Jespersen's statement, I would reformulate Quirk *et al.* as follows: 'simple block language messages are most often incomplete or minor sentences'. With this shift in descriptive stance most of what Quirk *et al.* call 'block language' may be included in the broader category of telegraphic ellipsis. Certain kinds of spoken sentence fragments, labels, headlines and some literary usage have features in common that are characteristic of this category, such as verblessness, single noun phrase constituency, uncertainty of ellipsis site, non-recoverable omissions, indeterminate expansions, close reference to situational context. Notices, headings and titles also often have these features and it is preferable to include them in a single category of language in use whose syntactic structures can be related to definable situational contexts.

In functional terms, titles and headings stand in a similar relationship to text as the headlines of newspaper articles do. Their grammatical structure encodes one or more meanings which the ensuing text elaborates upon or, where necessary, disambiguates. Titles and headings refer cataphorically to the text they relate to. This relation between heading and text can be seen operating as a kind of cohesive signalling device which can be extended into the text at the level of subheadings in newspapers and magazines. For example, an article in the magazine *Sibyl*, on the relationship between feminism and the superficial trappings of femininity, has the following heading and array of subheadings:

> Heading of article: Strappy ideals
> Subheadings in sequence: The closer shave, Now you see me . . . , Eyeshadow feminists, Making up is never easy, Identity parade, Frock-me shoes (*Sibyl*, September/October 1998)

The first heading relates to the article as a whole, as the highlighted introduction indicates:

> Why does being a feminist, particularly a lesbian feminist, have to entail a rejection of femininity? Louise Carolin recounts what happened when she stopped shaving her head and embraced hair dye and high heels. (p. 29)

The heading sets a tone of light-hearted polemicism with its pun on high-heel shoe straps and stroppy attitudes. Each subsequent subheading introduces a short section of text, 'telegraphing' its main point, such as head-shaving, make-up as a feminist issue or lesbian representation and identity, and maintaining the tone set by the title with ironic phrases and double-entendres. The final subheading signals a conclusion which asserts feminist assertiveness:

> Why succumb to cheap frills when you could be working a stroppy little frock? Who'd wear 'come-and-get-me' shoes, when there are shoes which shout, 'I'm coming to get you'? (p. 31)

Five of these heading/subheading structures are single noun phrases characteristic of other free-standing telegraphic strings, such as notices and signs. Just as notices and signs introduce, direct our attention to, or otherwise give us information about, objects in our situational context, so these headings and subheadings similarly relate to their textual environments.

Exercise 5.2

The following brief stretch of text from J. P. Donleavy's novel, *The Ginger Man*, consists of three separate orthographic sentences, that is, strings demarcated by an initial capital letter and a final full stop. How does the sentencehood of each structure relate to its textual function?

> Christmas. Lying here on my back listening to carol singers in the street.
> Two weeks ago I woke up in this room and Mary was gone.
> (1965: 320)

Telegraphic speech, telegraphic thought

Perhaps the most common context in which telegraphic ellipsis is illustrated and discussed, even though the term ellipsis itself is not often used, is that of children's telegraphic speech. Most commentators on child language development see telegraphic speech as an intermediate stage between the single word expressions, or holophrases, that very young children use, and the more fully realized syntax of four to five year olds, who have acquired most of the syntactic patterns of adult speech. For example, Steinberg cites such utterances as, 'More milk', 'Red car' and 'No sleep'. He notes the lack of function words and suggests that, 'The child uses combinations of content words with the expectation that the listener will understand the relations between items . . .' (Steinberg 1993: 8). Clearly, the child's meaning and our understanding of it are both highly context dependent, but we can, as Steinberg does, assume a 'mature speaker's equivalent' of each utterance along the lines of: 'I want some more milk', 'This is a red car', 'I don't want to go to sleep'. In practical terms, these equivalents fill the structural gaps in the child's utterances in the same way that we can expand on telegraphic ellipses in other contexts. Even more so in this case, however, such expansions do not pretend to capture the psycholinguistic processes which facilitate very young children's use of language.

The majority of children fairly quickly leave wholesale telegraphic speech behind in the normal course of language acquisition and development.

As we have seen, the patterns of adult speech contain telegraphic elements, such as 'Coffee?' and the like, but speech that consisted almost entirely of such elements strung together would seem odd. In Chapter 10 I look in some detail at sports commentary, a speech style that has a comparatively high incidence of telegraphic ellipsis, but even here telegraphic speech occurs in the context of other syntactic structures. The oddity of an exclusively telegraphic adult speech style is, however, brilliantly captured by Charles Dickens for his character Mr Jingle, a loquacious and feckless strolling player who pervades the early chapters of Dickens's first major novel, *The Pickwick Papers*. Here is a sample of Jingle's jargon from his reaction to the town of Rochester in Kent, where members of the Pickwick Club have just arrived:

> Ah! fine place . . . glorious pile – frowning walls – tottering arches – dark nooks – crumbling staircases – Old cathedral too – earthy smell – pilgrims' feet worn away the old steps – little Saxon doors – confessionals like money-takers' boxes at theatres – queer customers those monks . . . (1837: 82)

Jingle's entire mode of speaking is, according to Dickens's own description, 'a lengthened string of similar broken sentences' (p. 77). There are twelve such 'broken sentences' here. The majority of these expressions, eight in all, are single noun phrases: 'fine place', 'glorious pile', 'frowning walls', 'tottering arches', 'dark nooks', 'crumbling staircases', 'earthy smell', 'little Saxon doors'. Structurally as well as functionally, they are very similar to the child's utterance 'Red car'. They point to or identify an object in the environment and assign it an attribute or, in the case of 'little Saxon doors', two attributes. The other four expressions in this brief sample of Jingle's speech are more obviously truncated sentences. There is a sentence-initial ellipsis in '[There's an] Old cathedral too'. Dickens signals a new turn in Jingle's speech with the capital letter. This and the other truncated sentences typically omit function words: '[The] pilgrims' feet [have] worn away the old steps', '[The] confessionals [are] like money-takers' boxes at theatres'. The final expression uses an inversion characteristic of colloquial speech which allows emphasis to be put on an aspect by bringing it to the front of the utterance: '*queer customers* those monks [were]'. This kind of preposing can also be analysed as a sentence initial ellipsis: '[They were] *queer customers* those monks'. By means of this highly telegraphic syntax Dickens creates a sense of structureless rush to Jingle's eccentric speech style. It is debatable whether someone who spoke like Mr Jingle would always be intelligible in real conversational circumstances. In terms of text processing, de Beaugrande suggests that highly telegraphic spoken language will tax the problem-solving of most listeners: '. . . ellipsis as extensive as Mr Jingle's is not convenient to hearers who have to perform inferencing in many directions at once in limited time. Having the text preserved in print makes matters easier' (1980: 158). Strangely, then, the intelligibility of Jingle's speech does not seem to be a problem for the other characters, who respond with instant understanding, though the narrator does remark on one occasion that the only reason Mr Pickwick can comprehend Jingle's 'rapid and disjointed communication' is because he is 'sufficiently versed' in his 'system of stenography' (p. 163).

Exercise 5.3

The brief extract from James Joyce's *Ulysses* below is typical of the way the author represents his main protagonist's 'stream of consciousness'. Here, as Leopold Bloom wanders the streets of Dublin, he contemplates the nature of civilizations and their cities. Classify the syntactic structures Joyce uses to capture Bloom's thoughts in the same way I did for Jingle's speech above. Then, attempt to summarize his meaning in your own words. Suggest, in particular, why telegraphic structures may be the syntax of choice for representing thought in this way.

> Houses, lines of houses, streets, miles of pavements, piled-up bricks, stones. Changing hands. This owner, that. Landlord never dies they say. Other steps into his shoes when he gets his notice to quit. They buy the place up with gold and still they have all the gold. Swindle in it somewhere. Piled up in cities, worn away age after age. Pyramids in sand. Built on bread and onions. Slaves. Chinese wall. Babylon. Big stones left. Round towers. (1922: 156–7)

Notices and signs

In this final section I want to look briefly at the notices and signs that give us information about objects in our environment or give us directions or warnings so that we can negotiate that environment sensibly. Such signs are often telegraphic according to the criteria I outlined earlier. Take, for instance, the ubiquitous 'NO CYCLING'. This is readily paraphrased according to its conventional meaning: 'you must not cycle here'. However, an expansion that incorporates the noun phrase itself is rather awkward, for example, 'you must do NO CYCLING' or 'NO CYCLING is allowed', confirming the typical syntactic indeterminacy of telegraphic ellipsis. The formulaic nature of these telegraphic structures means that they are generally unambiguous, their interpretation conventionalized even in isolation. Since their normal occurrence is within a specific context of situation, however, one would expect the situation to support and, if necessary, disambiguate intended meaning. A good example of this is the sign 'NO BIKES'. In the window of my local town library the notice 'NO BIKES' expands to something like 'There are NO BIKES allowed in here', a sensible prohibition. The same sign could mean something rather different and much more gloomy on the door of the local cycle shop: 'There are NO BIKES for sale in here'.

The way abbreviated notices interact with their situational contexts was brought home to me by two signs found many miles apart that are identical in layout and phraseology: only one word is different.

WARNING
NO RUBBISH BEYOND THIS POINT

WARNING
NO LIFEBUOYS BEYOND THIS POINT

The first of these is to be found on the exit gates of a civic waste disposal tip: it forbids us to dump rubbish beyond a certain point. The second is on a stretch of sea wall. Far from forbidding us to take lifebuoys beyond a certain point, it warns us that no lifebuoys are provided and therefore even greater care is needed when walking along the sea wall. There is nothing in the syntactic structure of the signs or even in the minimal difference in vocabulary that can account for the differences in meaning. It is perfectly feasible to hypothesize situations where the meanings are reversed, where rubbish is not available and lifebuoys are forbidden. What we can say is that in the situational contexts in which they are found these telegraphic strings allow for the 'most sensible' interpretation to be made. If we extend Grice's theory of conversational implicature, discussed in Chapter 2, from conversation to written communication, then it is possible to explain our understanding in terms of the cooperative principle and its associated maxims. For example, the first sign obeys the maxim of quality by referring to rubbish we want to get rid of and not, the kind we might want, in another context, to acquire. The second sign can be seen to obey the maxim of quantity by being only as informative as is necessary. Both signs are assumed to be situationally relevant and perspicuous in manner.

Despite structural uncertainties and other analytical problems, in this chapter I have made a strong case for granting telegraphic structures the status of sentences, rather than treating them as beyond the grammatical pale. Clearly, these structures do pose challenges for syntactic description, yet their structure is motivated in a way that random word strings, nonsense strings and even reasonable intelligible false starts and lapses are not. We have seen, even on the evidence of brief extracts, that the clustering of telegraphic structures in spoken or written texts acts as a marker of stylistic significance whose recognition can contribute to a wider analysis of both non-literary and literary language.

Discussion of Exercises

Exercise 5.1

There is really only one likely structure for this particular headline in terms of major sentence elements:

Cannabis man	jailed	for year
Subject	*Verb*	*Adverbial*

Once this basic syntactic structure is discerned, then certain gaps become apparent. The noun phrase subject requires an article: '[A] Cannabis man'. The verb phrase is a truncated passive form: '[has been] jailed'. The prepositional phrase that realizes the adverbial slot also lacks an article: 'for [a] year'. Note that these omitted items are all structure words by my previous definition, so the headline is truly telegraphic. Although not elliptical as such, since there is no structural gap, it is also worth noting that 'cannabis man' is a cleverly compressed way of indicating someone convicted of taking cannabis.

Exercise 5.2

The three orthographic sentences that comprise this extract from Donleavy's novel are of very different status with regard to sentencehood.

The first is an isolated noun. The second has two non-finite clauses in parataxis. The third compounds two fully realized past tense clauses. These very different sentence structures closely reflect textual function. The word 'Christmas' here may be seen as a subheading for the rest of the text. Although it is not marked as such by having a line to itself or being underlined, the relationship between 'Christmas' and what follows bears comparison with the subheadings from *Sibyl* magazine that I illustrated and discussed above: its function is to provide a setting for the text that follows as well as a point of orientation for the reader. This introductory function moves into the narrative *via* a sentence with sentence-initial ellipsis situating the narrator in a present from which the past tense narrative can unfold: '[I'm] Lying here on my back listening to carol singers in the street'. Narrative proper ensues with the tensed verbs of the final sentence: 'Two weeks ago I woke up in this room and Mary was gone'.

Exercise 5.3

The early years of the twentieth century saw a radical development in the representation of thought in fictional texts, particularly among those writers, like Joyce, associated with the modernist movement in literature. The most obvious way of representing the thoughts of fictional characters is to quote them with a verb of thinking:

> 'A landlord never dies they say', thought Bloom, as he wandered the streets of Dublin.

This technique is usually called 'direct thought' because it closely parallels 'direct speech', where the exact words a character says are quoted directly. The only difference is the verb of thinking instead of a verb of saying. In a passage of dialogue where the identities of the characters have been established, it is possible to omit the names of the speakers and the verbs of saying, as long as this doesn't cause the reader to lose track. This way of representing dialogue can be called 'free direct speech'. The parallel for thought representation is 'free direct thought': the name of the thinker and the verb of thinking are omitted. The extensive use of free direct thought was one of the radical techniques used by writers like Joyce to 'get inside the heads' of their characters. But allowing thoughts to float free on the page was not enough for Joyce. He sought also to devise a literary technique which would radically differentiate narrative from the so-called 'interior monologue' of his characters. In her discussion of the stylistic qualities of interior monologue in *Ulysses*, Wales notes that it is distinguished by its:

> 'imitative' or 'symbolic' style, which attempts to suggest the inchoate thought-processes, the flow of thoughts, abrupt topic shifts, random associations etc. Since thought is not only verbal but non-verbal, such a style must inevitably be 'symbolic' in its attempt to suggest the chains of visual images and memories, as well as other mental stimuli such as sensations, feelings etc. (Wales 1992: 72)

This is a useful reminder that the relationship between language and thought is far from perfectly understood and that any literary device for the representation of thought is necessarily impressionistic.

There are fifteen orthographic sentences in this particular passage of interior monologue. The first of these is a chain of noun phrases: 'Houses, lines of houses, streets, miles of pavements, piled-up bricks, stones'. With these Bloom points to or denotes the things he sees. There are a further five free-standing noun phrases in the passage: 'Pyramids in sand', 'Slaves', 'Chinese wall', 'Babylon', 'Round towers'. These clearly cannot be references to directly observed items. They map points in the associative train of Bloom's thought. Structurally more coherent, though still fragmented, sentences serve to connect these points. Some of these truncated sentences omit function words and are readily expanded: '[A] Landlord never dies they say', '[There's a] Swindle in it somewhere', '[They are] Piled up in cities, worn away age after age', '[They are] Built on bread and onions', 'Big stones [are] left'. One or two sentences are more indeterminate in structure or opaque in meaning. They require content words to flesh out their meaning, as in, for example, '[These houses are always] Changing hands'. This is elaboration rather than expansion. The elliptical aphorism, 'This owner, that [owner]', still requires further elaboration along the lines of 'This owner [has it], that [owner has it]'. Particularly interesting is: '[Some] Other [landlord] steps into his shoes when he gets his notice to quit'. This involves a contextual ellipsis referring back to 'landlord' in the previous sentence, but also involves the telegraphic omission of a function word 'some'. There is one coordinate sentence without any ellipsis: 'They buy the place up with gold and still they have all the gold'. The lack of abbreviation and in particular the repetition of 'gold' seem designed to capture Bloom's puzzled exasperation at the successful greed of landlords. On the basis of these analyses, my own interpretative summary is as follows:

> Bloom reflects on the urban sprawl he's walking through, thinking that no matter how often properties change hands, there's never a shortage of landlords, whose continuing exploitation must be corrupt in some way. Bloom shifts to the houses themselves, their gradual decay, and this triggers thoughts of past buildings, the pyramids built using ill-fed slave labour, the great wall of China, the ruined towers of Babylon.

In comparison with this rather dull summary Joyce gives us a vivid impression of the fragmentary nature of interior monologue. This is not only a remarkable literary achievement, but also coincidentally parallels hypotheses about the nature of thought and its relation to language that were emerging at the time he was writing *Ulysses*. In the years between the two World Wars the most innovative work was being done by the Soviet psychologist, Vygotsky, whose treatise, *Thought and Language*, was first published in 1934, though it was not translated into English till the 1960s. Vygotsky introduces the concept of 'inner speech' with the following characterization: 'Our experiments convinced us that inner speech must be regarded, not as speech minus sound, but as an entirely separate speech function. Its main characteristic trait is its peculiar syntax. Compared with external speech, inner speech appears disconnected and incomplete' (1986: 235). Vygotsky goes on to argue that one of the main syntactic features of inner speech is its omission of the subject and its attachments, so that the syntax becomes a series of predicates. He likens this to two types of 'external speech': abbreviated contextual rejoinders and telegraphic expressions where 'the subject is plain from the situation' (p. 236). He concludes that, since we always know the subject and situation when we are thinking, inner speech is similarly abbreviated. If we broadly assume predicates to include main verbs, objects and complements, then we can see that many of Joyce's orthographic sentences are predicative, as my expansions indicate. Even the single noun phrases can be seen as predicative in the sense that Vygotsky intends. For example, the noun phrases in a paratactic chain are objects of Bloom's attention, as an expansion along the following lines captures: '[I can see] Houses, lines of houses, streets, miles of pavements, piled-up bricks, stones'. Vygotsky reached his conclusions about the nature of inner speech after much empirical investigation, including the careful study of children's egocentric speech to which it is closely related. However, it is worth reiterating that such characterizations of inner speech are essentially impressionistic. That remains as true in today's much more sophisticated climate of psycholinguistic study as it was when Vygotsky developed his pioneering theories. It is also true of Joyce and others in the modernist enterprise of representing thought on the page. However ingenious Joyce's very distinctive brand of interior monologue is, it remains very much a literary device.

CHAPTER 6

COORDINATION REDUCTION

In Chapter 3 I made an initial contrast between subordination reduction, where ellipsis occurs within main and subordinate clauses in complex sentences, and coordination reduction, which is a general term for a range of elliptical features that occur in coordinate structures. Coordination is potentially the most abundant source of ellipsis in English, since it is both convenient and communicatively efficient to omit elements that are readily understood from adjacent conjuncts. Most coordination reduction has a high level of unique recoverability from the surrounding linguistic context, so it is very much within the domain of contextual ellipsis, as I have previously defined that term.

Most coordination reduction is by definition intrasentential, since most coordination creates compound structures within an orthographic sentence or within the utterance turn of a single speaker. However, there are exceptions to this that render the coordination intersentential. For example, coordinate constituents do occur across speakers. This feature of everyday conversation is frequently captured by writers of fictional dialogue, as in this extract from Jean Rhys's novel *The Wide Sargasso Sea*:

> I said gently, 'I know that after your father died, she was
> very lonely and unhappy'.
> 'And very poor', she said. (1968: 107)

Here, two speakers share what is essentially a single coordinate structure in which the second speaker supplies a final coordinate constituent or conjunct as a kind of afterthought to the first speaker. Even outside the representation of dialogue, authors frequently represent coordinate constituents as separate orthographic sentences, as the following line by Dylan Thomas shows: 'See my sad, Grecian stare. And the longing to be born in my dark eyes' (1963: 54). While the orthographic separation does not alter the grammatical fact of coordination, it is possible to suggest that it indicates an additional emphasis in the meaning of the second conjunct. The pause after 'stare' and the capitalization of 'and' give it a weight that is lacking in: 'See my sad, Grecian stare and the longing to be born in my dark eyes'. If this is the case, it involves a fairly subtle stylistic choice on the part of the writer.

In this chapter, however, the nuanced effects of intersentential coordination, interesting though they are, are not a major focus. My main concerns are twofold. First, I want to explore the levels at which coordination is seen to operate, since this is an important factor in deciding whether an ellipsis needs to be recognized. Secondly, having established principled strategies for identifying coordination reduction, I will outline several distinctive categories and their characteristic features.

Levels of coordination

Even a cursory review of the way linguists have treated coordination reduction reveals a shift from an exclusive assumption of clause coordination to arguments for coordination at other levels. One common type of clause coordination is exemplified where two or more main clauses are joined by a conjunction, resulting in a compound sentence, such as the Donleavy sentence discussed in the last chapter:

Two weeks ago I woke up in this room and Mary was gone.

Either of the clauses could stand on its own as a simple sentence:

Two weeks ago I woke up in this room.
Mary was gone.

The conjunction can be omitted so that there is no overt marker of coordination and the clauses are merely juxtaposed, another instance of parataxis:

Two weeks ago I woke up in this room, Mary was gone.

Where, as here, both clauses are fully realized without any apparent gaps, a theory that only recognizes clause coordination presents no problem. However, this approach to coordination presents some difficulties for a wide range of common structures, like this extract from Rhys's dialogue quoted above:

She was very lonely and unhappy.

If coordination is at clause level, then this has to be seen as a reduction of:

She was very lonely and [she was very] unhappy.

An analysis of this kind has the advantage of rule economy, since all coordination reduction can be treated in a uniform way. On the other hand, it proliferates the amount of ellipsis that needs to be recognized. One way of obviating this is to site coordination at the next level down, as it were, that of the phrase:

She was very lonely and [very] unhappy.

Here, coordination is between two adjective phrases which constitute the complement of the verb. This still doesn't eliminate the need to recognize an ellipsis altogether. If, however, the coordination of phrasal elements is recognized, then a non-elliptical reading is possible. In this case, it is the adjectives themselves, 'lonely and unhappy' which are coordinated. The intensifier 'very' simply applies to, or has scope over, both of them.

This approach approximates quite closely to what Wilder (1994: 291) calls the 'small conjunct hypothesis' supported by an 'Across-The-Board (ATB) rule application' that allows elements to have scope, as I have called it, across a variety of coordinate constituents. As Wilder's detailed critique shows, such an approach is not without its detractors. Indeed, his expressed aim is to demonstrate that the small conjunct hypothesis is false and that ATB-rule application is theoretically pro-fligate (p. 304). It is fair to say that recognizing coordination reduction at three levels, between clauses, between phrases and between phrasal elements, does not have the theoretical constraint argued for in Wilder's paper. Nevertheless, this strategy avoids an approach based exclusively on clause coordination and only acknowledges ellipsis where coordinate structures do not yield proper constituents. My approach is also broadly in line with that of other commentators, such as Huddleston:

no one would want to push ellipsis analysis to the extreme of deriving all coordination from clause coordination . . . we shall

> make minimum use of ellipsis, resorting to it only when the actually present terms in the coordination are not independently identifiable as constituents. (1984: 387)

This approach requires some discussion of what constituents are acceptable as 'present terms' or conjuncts in coordinate structures. Linguists of different persuasions, using terminology appropriate to their theoretical stance, seem to evoke two criteria: syntactic category and functional role. Conjuncts should be parallel in these respects. That parallelism usually implies identical structures, as anomalous sentences tend to prove:

> *Chewing gum and to walk are hard to do at the same time.

Here, 'chewing gum' and 'to walk' both function as subjects, but the first is participial and the second is infinitival and this blocks the coordination. There seem to be exceptions to this, though:

> He spoke quietly but with menace.

Both 'quietly' and 'with menace' function as adverbial elements. Even though one is an adverb and the other a prepositional phrase, the coordination is acceptable because functional role mitigates structural difference. Oostdijk, advocating a strategy that takes structure and function into account, goes on to suggest:

> Since the coordination of identical categories (on the condition that they are dominated by one and the same function node) is always possible and the coordination of different categories only in some cases, the description of coordination should basically be category-based and supplemented by information concerning the function of the node immediately dominating the coordinated (categorial) constituents. (1986: 185)

This position makes it possible to look at the range of constituents at each level in terms of structure and function in order to ascertain when an elliptical analysis might or might not apply.

Main clauses in coordination, as I noted above, are conjoined simple sentences: for that reason, clause coordination is quite often referred to as sentential coordination. As simple sentences, clauses can be assigned familiar syntactic structures and corresponding functional roles, such as statement, question, command and exclamation. We might expect that clauses of the same type will coordinate easily and that there will be some constraint on cross–coordination. This seems to be borne out by the ubiquity of sentences like:

Two weeks ago I woke up in this room and Mary was gone.

This happily conjoins simple statements in marked contrast with the awkwardness of the following example:

*Why did you have a hit in August and don't have a flop at Christmas.

Even though each clause is syntactically well-formed, this coordination of question and command is unacceptable. One thing we can't do, then, in expanding an ellipsis in coordination, is to assume a different syntactic category and functional role from the full conjunct, as this example shows:

Why did you have a hit in August and [ ] a flop at Christmas?

This cannot be interpreted as an elliptical version of the above sentence:

*Why did you have a hit in August and [don't] have a flop at Christmas.

However, it readily expands to a coordination of parallel questions:

Why did you have a hit in August and [why did you have] a flop at Christmas?

Another issue that needs to be addressed is why structures of this kind cannot, on grounds of analytical economy, be seen as non–elliptical coordinations of conjuncts at a lower level. In this case 'a hit in August' and 'a flop at Christmas' appear to be phrases. However, in the context of this sentence, each of these strings has two constituents, a direct object noun phrase, 'a hit', 'a flop', and an adverbial element in the form of a prepositional phrase, 'in August', 'at Christmas'. In Huddleston's formulation, 'the actually present terms in the coordination are not independently identifiable as constituents'. My analysis, in fact, follows Oostdijk's strategy quite closely in making category-based judgements supplemented by information concerning the function role of the constituents.

The status of phrasal constituents is clearly important in deciding to recognize an ellipsis and locating its site within a coordinate structure. It is appropriate in this context to review the major syntactic categories that operate at phrase level. There are five major phrasal categories: noun phrase, verb phrase, adverbial phrase, adjectival phrase, prepositional phrase. Besides the usual phrasal configurations, many of which we have seen in examples quoted so far, it is worth remembering that the first four of these phrasal categories can be realized by single words: our expectation that a phrase will have two or more words is misleading in that respect. For example, a noun phrase may consist of a proper noun or a personal pronoun, a verb phrase may be just a lexical verb, and so on. As far as functional role is concerned, phrases can usually be seen to realize the major functional sentence elements: subject, verb, object, complement and adverbial.

We have seen that where a conjunct consists of more than one phrasal element, fulfils more than one functional role or has some other constituency problem, it is more or less inevitable that coordination reduction will need to be recognized. A further example confirms this:

> Sharon ordered a rice dish, Sandeep went for the fish and Amina the lamb.

If we take 'Amina the lamb' to be a single phrasal constituent, then we would have to recognize phrasal coordination here between 'the fish' and 'Amina the lamb'. Both would be the objects of 'went for'. This would give Sandeep a rather odd culinary taste and makes us wonder what kind of restaurant gives personal names to its meat sources on the menu. Clearly, 'Amina the lamb' is not a single constituent. Its present terms are 'Amina' as subject and 'the lamb' as object, in which case an ellipsis has to be recovered from the immediately preceding context:

> Sharon ordered a rice dish, Sandeep went for the fish and Amina [went for] the lamb.

Compare that with the following example:

> Sharon ordered a rice dish, some fish and a nan bread.

Here, three coordinate noun phrases are all legitimate constituents, in the same syntactic category and serving the same functional role as objects of 'ordered': there is no need to recognize an ellipsis at clause level.

Recognizing constituents at the third level of coordination, between phrasal elements, is a less certain process. However, each major phrase type has a set of structural components and these may be seen as the subphrasal constituents that can enter into coordination. For example, noun phrases are generally ascribed the following structure: (premodification) head noun (postmodification). A range of elements can occur as premodification, such as numerals, genitives, adjectives and other nouns, as the following noun phrases respectively exemplify: 'three sisters', 'Abigail's party', 'hard times', 'city slickers'. Coordination across these different elements is awkward or unacceptable, as in '*three and Abigail's sisters', '*hard and city times', whereas elements in the same category coordinate happily: 'three or four sisters', 'hard and fast times'. This suggests that these elements are distinctive constituents of phrases according to syntactic and functional criteria and do not need to be seen as ellipting the head noun in the way that the following expansions would imply: 'three [sisters] or four sisters', 'hard [times] and fast times'.

A set of guidelines of the kind explored here, for the recognition of constituents at each level of coordination, allows us to look at types of coordination reduction in a principled way. A strategy for acknowledging an ellipsis in coordination should be based on the smallest constituent principle. Wherever possible, all conjuncts should be recognized at the sub-phrasal level, eliminating the need to allocate an ellipsis site at a higher level. Text can then be scanned for the recognition of phrasal coordination. This process will rule out some ellipsis that would have been included in an approach based exclusively on clause coordination. Finally, some examples will be unequivocally recognized as instances of coordination reduction within conjoined clauses. Although this strategy is an apparently negative one of rejecting and ruling out, its net effect is to identify the structurally most interesting kinds of ellipsis in coordination. These are also likely to be more significant as markers of style and stylistic variation.

Exercise 6.1

Apply the strategies outlined in the above section to the following data. Identify the constituent status of conjuncts at whatever level of coordination is appropriate and comment, where useful, on functional role. Decide if and where an ellipsis site needs to be recognized and note any problems associated with your analysis.

There is a time for living and for generation.
That old man and woman seem to be lost.
Their terms of engagement ruled out old men, women and children.
The red and yellow flags were flapping in the wind.
Albert knew he was between a rock and a hard place.
Give peace a chance and war a rest.
Hingis lost to Novotna but Davenport didn't.
Swann fell in love with Odette and Marcel with Albertine.

Categories of coordination reduction

My discussion at the end of this chapter of the data in Exercise 6.1 concludes with the idea that the site of the ellipsis in coordinate structures can form the basis for categorizing the main types of coordination reduction. Gaps can be seen to occur to the left, right and centre of conjuncts and the following outline is organized accordingly. The terminology of coordination reduction is associated with, and often derived from, generative syntactic theory. For the most part, I will attempt a theoretically neutral description, while acknowledging theoretical terms that have gained some wider currency. In general, my outline will be concerned with the types of element omitted, the constituency of the reduced conjunct and any constraints or problems associated with particular categories of ellipsis within coordinate structures.

Leftmost coordination reduction

In the second, third or subsequent conjuncts of a coordinate structure it is possible, though not compulsory, to omit elements that are uniquely recoverable from the first conjunct. This element may be on the left of the conjunct:

'Give peace a chance and [give] war a rest'.

Ellipsis of leftmost elements is frequently called 'conjunction reduction', especially in generative grammar. This term is easily confused with coordination reduction and I will try to avoid it, though it is worth knowing if you are delving further into the syntax of coordination, particularly from a generative standpoint. For example, in an early, but influential formulation Hudson notes: 'The first property of conjunction reduction, then, is that it removes items from the left of the conjuncts. More properly, of course, we can say that it removes them *from the left hand edge of the conjuncts*, since no non-shared items may be to their left . . .' (1976: 552, my italics).

The leftmost siting of omitted elements is worth stressing in this way. The introduction of a non-shared item to the left of the conjunct effectively shifts the site of the ellipsis to a central position, as an addition to the previous examples shows:

> Today give peace a chance and tomorrow [ ] war a rest.

Not even shared items are allowed to interfere with the leftmost siting of the gap, as a slightly different version of the sentence demonstrates:

> Why give peace a chance and why give war a rest?

Leftmost ellipsis is fine here, as long as all items are omitted:

> Why give peace a chance and [ ] war a rest?

But if we try to retain a shared leftmost item, the site of the ellipsis not only becomes central but results in an ungrammatical string:

> ★Why give peace a chance and why [ ] war a rest?

Given the characteristic word order of English sentences, leftmost coordination reduction typically involves the subject plus a verbal element. The verbal element may be a single lexical verb or a more complex verbal group, as in the following examples:

> Mars gave peace a chance and [ ] war a rest.
> Mars ought to be giving peace a chance and [ ] war a rest.

In yes/no questions the auxiliary element, preceding the subject as operator, may be omitted on its own from the second conjunct:

> Is Venus prevailing and [ ] Mars complying?

Given that ellipsis is leftmost, the omission of sentence elements that normally follow the verb is less prevalent. Many sentences involving apparent gaps of this kind can be seen as instances of phrasal or subphrasal coordination, without the need for an elliptical interpretation, as in:

> They made Jeannette director and chief executive.

Here, the noun phrases, 'director' and 'chief executive' coordinate as object complements. The presence of a further constituent to the right in each clause, however, will create a structure that requires an elliptical analysis:

> They made Jeannette director last year and [ ] chief executive in the spring.

In this case, the addition of an adverbial element means that 'director last year' and 'chief executive in the spring' are not single recognizable constituents. The elements remaining in the reduced second conjunct here are typical for leftmost coordination reduction, since they occur later in the characteristic order of English sentences. In general, these conjuncts combine objects, complements and adverbials, as in the examples discussed: 'war a rest' (indirect object + direct object), 'chief executive in the spring' (object complement + adverbial). The conjunct in the reduced question, 'Is Venus prevailing and [ ] Mars complying?' is of a rather different constituency. Owing to the inversion of subject and operator, the leftmost omitted item is the auxiliary part of the verb phrase, leaving 'Mars complying' (subject + lexical verb).

Rightmost coordination reduction

The ellipsis of elements on the left of conjuncts stands in most direct and obvious contrast with rightmost coordination reduction, not just in relation to the site of the gap, but also with regard to the elements omitted and the constituency of the reduced conjunct. Let's take another look at an example quoted in Exercise 6.1:

> Hingis lost to Novotna but Davenport didn't [lose to Novotna].

Here, the constituency of the reduced conjunct is 'Davenport' as subject and 'didn't' as verbal auxiliary, in this case the operator marked for negation. The omitted elements, 'lose to Novotna' consist of the lexical verb and an adverbial. While the ellipsis is truly contextual with regard to recoverability in the first conjunct, note that the recoverability is not unique, but weak in the sense in which I used that term in Chapter 3, since the form of the verb has to be adjusted to accommodate the negative particle.

What is interesting about the relation of reduced conjunct to ellipted elements here is the way it coincides with Halliday and Hasan's structural division for clauses, modal element plus propositional element, which I outlined in Chapter 4. Recall that the modal element consists of the subject plus a verbal auxiliary, while the propositional element is the rest of the verbal group together with any objects, complements or adverbials. The ellipsis here could be plotted as follows:

Modal Element   *Propositional Element*
Davenport didn't   [lose to Novotna]

Rightmost coordination reduction can be seen, then, as a kind of propositional ellipsis within coordinate structures. This is close to its treatment within generative grammar as a category of verb phrase deletion. Within generative grammar the term 'verb phrase' signifies not just the verbal group, but any objects, complements or adverbials attached to it, in fact, the predicate in more traditional terms. Accordingly, the verb phrase in the second conjunct of the above sentence is 'didn't lose to Novotna'. Verb phrase deletion is, by this token, a fairly accurate term for an ellipsis that results in 'didn't [ ]'. Again, it is a useful term to be familiar with for anyone wishing to extend their study of coordination reduction into generative grammar accounts.

It is also worth noting that rightmost ellipsis of the kind illustrated here, whether it is called verb phrase deletion, propositional ellipsis or some other term, is not exclusive to coordination reduction. It occurs, for example, in the context of subordination: 'Hingis lost to Novotna, even though Davenport didn't [ ]'. In such structures, there is no block on the ellipsis being cataphoric, as this version shows:

Even though Davenport didn't [ ], Hingis lost to Novotna.

Compare this with the ordering constraint on coordination reduction which results in the following anomalous sentence:

*Davenport didn't [ ] and Hingis lost to Novotna.

Rightmost ellipsis is also common in contextual rejoinders of the following type:

A: I thought Davenport might lose to Novotna.
B: Well, she didn't [ ].

Clearly, then, rightmost coordination reduction has to be seen as a sub-category of a wider phenomenon with features and constraints specific to its occurrence in coordinate structures.

There is another form of ellipsis which requires specific attention within this section, since it involves the omission of rightmost elements, but its analysis is complicated because one of the conjuncts interrupts the other, as the following example demonstrates:

Jerry Lewis was, and De Niro wanted to be, the king of comedy.

This particular form of ellipsis is characterized by two discontinuities, marked in speech by intonational breaks and shifts in stress and signalled in writing by appropriately sited commas. This structure is very distinct-ive and has genuine rhetorical potential in that a key piece of informa-tion normally provided in the first conjunct is held back and, with well-orchestrated pausing at the break points, can be held in suspense. This stylistically interesting structure does, however, present some prob-lems for analysis, not least in deciding where the ellipsis is sited. There are two possibilities. First, the gap could be sited cataphorically in the first conjunct:

Jerry Lewis was [the king of comedy], and De Niro wanted to be, the king of comedy.

In this case, though, there is no motivation for the second discontinuity, but if we remove it, the sentence becomes anomalous:

*Jerry Lewis was [?], and De Niro wanted to be the king of comedy.

As my question mark suggests, the gap is no longer recoverable from the context: what Jerry Lewis was becomes unknown. The second option is to site the gap in the second conjunct:

Jerry Lewis was, and De Niro wanted to be [the king of comedy], the king of comedy.

This can be related to the more commonplace rightmost coordination reduction:

Jerry Lewis was the king of comedy and De Niro wanted to be [the king of comedy].

According to this analysis, the second ellipted conjunct has been displaced and inserted into the structure of the first conjunct. This accounts for both intonational breaks. In commentaries with a generative orientation this displacement is called 'right node raising', indicating that a structure at one syntactic level has been moved to a higher level in the grammatical hierarchy. Blevins, for example, discusses theoretical issues arising from the discontinuities in right node raising with regard to the sentence:

Max likes and Ida hates anchovies. (1994: 353)

This displaced form of rightmost coordination reduction can also be seen to be a subcategory of wider patterns of rightmost ellipsis in, for example, sentences involving subordination:

Even though Jerry Lewis was, De Niro wanted to be [ ], the king of comedy.

Central coordination reduction

Elements central to a second or subsequent conjunct may be uniquely recoverable from the first conjunct, as in the sentence I quoted in Exercise 6.1:

Swann fell in love with Odette and Marcel [fell in love] with Albertine.

Ellipsis of such central elements is usually called 'gapping'. This term, although it has its origins in generative linguistics, is now more or less standard and I use it throughout this section. As with other forms of coordination reduction, gapping is essentially anaphoric. Attempts to violate this directionality constraint are usually ungrammatical:

*Marcel [ ] with Albertine and Swann fell in love with Odette.

However, this constraint in ordinary spoken and written English may have literary exceptions, especially in the context of highly wrought parallelism. With reference to such exceptions in gapping, Fabb notes:

This typical pattern is violated in poetry, for example in the poetry of Alexander Pope, where the first of two elements may be gapped:
Now leaves [ ] the trees, and flowers adorn the ground.
(1997: 147)

Here, the gap 'adorn' in the first conjunct is cataphoric, anticipating contextual resolution in the second, but this is clearly far from the norm in modern English.

Given the centrality of the gap, we might expect that the most frequent element to be omitted in gapping would be the verb, which is central to the characteristic order of elements in English: subject, verb, object/complement. This is indeed the case and early formulations of gapping suggested that the verb alone was subject to gapping. However, as my own example shows, phrasal attachments or other contiguous elements can be omitted along with the verb, as with 'fell in love', on the condition that the gap remains central. The minimal gapping is probably an auxiliary whose centrality is preserved by the surrounding subject and lexical verb:

Bottom will weave and Starveling [ ] sew.

Gapping of the entire verbal group is always possible where a preceding subject and a following object or complement preserve its centrality:

Bottom will play Pyramus and Snug [ ] the lion.

A range of other clause elements can be gapped along with the verb: in these cases the centrality of the gapping is usually preserved by a rightmost adverbial. In the following examples the constituency of the gapped elements is given in brackets:

Bottom played his part plaintively and Snug [ ] roaringly.
(verb + direct object)
Pyramus died lovingly for Thisbe and Thisbe [ ] for Pyramus.
(verb + adverbial)

Besides the centrality of the gap, it is also clear that a verbal element figures in all my examples. We can test whether this verbal element is essential to gapping by attempting to omit other elements without omitting the verb:

> *Swann fell in love with Odette and Marcel fell [ ] with Albertine.
> ?Bottom played his part plaintively and Snug played roaringly.
> Pyramus died lovingly for Thisbe and Thisbe died for Pyramus.

The first sentence is anomalous, though this is partly because 'fall in love' is more or less a phrasal verb whose parts cannot be split, so a non-elliptical reading is ruled out. The other sentences can only be interpreted as having no ellipsis at all. This makes the second somewhat odd as 'played' has to be read as intransitive. The third sentence is well-formed but it doesn't tell us how Thisbe died. On the basis of even these few examples, it is fairly safe to conclude that gapping must include a centrally sited verb with or without other sentence elements uniquely recoverable in an adjacent conjunct.

Exercise 6.2

The following extracts all contain examples of gapping. Identify the sites of the gaps and suggest suitable expansions. How do these instances of gapping contribute to linguistic parallelism in each text?

> *The Daytrippers* may well be the most archetypal American indie film ever made. Its backdrop is the mean streets and loft apartments of New York; its cast list a roll call of indie regulars (Parker Posey, Campbell Scott, Stanley Tucci, Liev Schreiber). Its budget is minuscule ($30,000); its shooting schedule hectic (16 days). (X. Brooks in *The Big Issue*, 20–26.7.98: 34)

> Christie at the office again, next day. Yesterday there was a Skaterless silence, today a letter from Skater's solicitors, not from Skater. Christie passed it straight to Wagner: not without thought. (B. S. Johnson 1973: *Christie Malry's Own Double-Entry*, p. 61)

> Nay, rather would not my daunger have beene her death, my mishap her miserie, my torture her torments, and my fatall destinie her finall destruction? (R. Greene 1587: *The Carde of Fancie*, p. 247)

Discussion of Exercises

Exercise 6.1

The examples presented for this exercise cover a fair range of coordination types, some of which require an elliptical analysis, while others can be seen to involve gapless conjuncts at the phrasal or subphrasal level.

According to the smallest constituent principle outlined above, the first example involves conjoined prepositional phrases, 'for living' and 'for generation'. These function as postmodifiers and are valid subphrasal constituents, so an elliptical reading, 'a time for living and [a time] for generation', is unnecessary.

The next two sentences might easily be said to exemplify 'the old man and woman syndrome', so frequently do examples involving these stock characters appear in the literature. Discussion centres around whether a coordination like 'That old man and woman' relates to some underlying form: 'That old man and [that old] woman'. Our strategy avoids this problem: head nouns like 'man' and 'woman' are valid constituents within noun phrases and the premodification 'That old' has scope over both nouns. This is confirmed by the fact that, to avoid implying the woman is also old, coordination would need to take place at phrase level and involve additional material, such as 'That old man and the woman he's with' or at the least 'That old man and that woman'. Where the scope of the premodifier cannot, on semantic grounds, apply to all conjuncts, then it is clear that coordination must be at the level of phrases, as in 'old men, women and children'. Here, plural nouns like 'women' and 'children' act as noun phrases in their own right and coordinate as such with 'old men'. An elliptical reading of these conjuncts, ★'Old men, [old] women and [old] children', is anomalous.

The next example exposes the potential for ambiguity inherent in much coordination. If the adjectival premodifiers 'red' and 'yellow' are in subphrasal coordination, then there is no ellipsis and all the flags are parti-coloured. On the other hand, the conjuncts can also be analysed as noun phrases with an ellipsis of the head noun: 'The red [flags] and yellow flags'. In this reading, some of the flags are exclusively red and some are exclusively yellow. While this meaning is less favoured, it is both plausible and easily reinforced, as in: 'Both the red and yellow flags were flapping in the wind'.

Prepositional phrases, such as 'to the lighthouse', are generally described as consisting of a preposition 'to' plus a complement 'the lighthouse'.

'The smallest constituent principle would allow for the coordination of such complements, as in, for example, 'to the lighthouse and the gatehouse', without the need to recognize an ellipsis of the preposition. This analysis is supported by the formulaic expression in the next sentence: 'between a rock and a hard place'. Here, the prepositional complements have to be conjuncts, since phrasal coordination with ellipsis of the preposition is nonsensical: *'between a rock and [between] a hard place'.

The last three examples all involve major clause coordination with some form of ellipsis. Tests for constituency at levels below the clause fail to recognize valid conjuncts according to the criteria set out in this chapter. In the first sentence, 'peace a chance' and 'war a rest' each consist of two elements, the indirect and direct objects of the verb, so an elliptical clause coordination applies: 'Give peace a chance and [give] war a rest'. The next sentence has no possible conjuncts except the clauses themselves, the second of which omits elements contextually recoverable from the first: 'Hingis lost to Novotna but Davenport didn't [lose to Novotna]'. Again, in the final sentence coordination is at clause level. The conjunct, 'Marcel with Albertine', is not an identifiable constituent and an ellipsis has to be recognized: 'Swann fell in love with Odette and Marcel [fell in love] with Albertine'. Note that the site of the ellipsis in these three sentences is, respectively, to the left, right and centre of the conjuncts concerned. This positioning underpins the categorization of the major forms of coordination reduction discussed in the second half of this chapter.

Exercise 6.2

Parallelism is the general term for a range of rhetorical effects based on structural repetition. This repetition may be achieved in a number of ways, but here the focus is on syntactic structures, which are the most obvious source of parallelism. While the syntactic structure is repeated, some of the content is changed or omitted, allowing for parallels to be drawn between the different realizations of the same structure. This device is nicely used in the first example, where the film review repeats the same basic structure four times in all, but in two parallel pairs. This structure has the form, 'its x is y', where 'its x' is the subject and 'y' the complement. If we strip away other detail, this form is realized by the first pair as follows:

Subject	Verb	Complement
Its backdrop	is	the mean streets and loft apartments of New York;
its cast list	[ ]	a roll call of indie regulars.

Note that the complements here take the form of noun phrases, whereas in the second pair the complements are adjectives:

Subject	Verb	Complement
Its budget	is	minuscule;
its shooting schedule	[ ]	hectic.

The verb is gapped in the second conjunct of each pair, its omission giving structural variation and reinforcing the parallelism involved. Note that the conjuncts are paratactically juxtaposed, rather than overtly co-ordinated by 'and'. A final rhetorical point: if we take the bracketed detail into account, the second pair exhibit perfect parallelism:

Its budget is minuscule ($30,000); its shooting schedule [ ] hectic (16 days).

The first pair, on the other hand, lacks a parallel bracketed term in its first conjunct:

Its backdrop is the mean streets and loft apartments of New York (?); its cast list [ ] a roll call of indie regulars (Parker Posey, Campbell Scott, Stanley Tucci, Liev Schreiber).

As this extract shows, gapping, and the parallelism it contributes to, is to be found in non-literary writing as well as the highly wrought verses of Augustan poetry. The next two extracts further exemplify that diversity, although they are both taken from literary prose works.

The second piece of text brings together a number of elliptical features of which gapping is only one. It begins with a scene-setting telegraphic sentence that locates the time and situational context of the subsequent narrative: 'Christie at the office again, next day'. There then follows a pair of juxtaposed sentences that exhibit both parallelism and gapping in the second conjunct. Their structure may be logged as follows:

Adverbial	Existential + Verb	Complement
Yesterday	there was	a Skaterless silence,
today	[ ]	a letter from Skater's solicitors.

Note the presence of a leftmost adverbial element to preserve the centrality of the existential marker and verb, without which gapping could not take place. The telegraphic afterthought to this sentence, 'not from Skater', is then paralleled by a structurally identical addition, 'not without thought', to the next sentence: 'Christie passed it straight to Wagner'. The cumulative effect of ellipsis and parallelism is to give the text a compact symmetry.

The final extract gives evidence that gapping has been around a long time in the history of English. In fact, it is characteristic, along with other features of parallelism, in the euphuistic prose of the Elizabethan era. This particular passage strings together four conjuncts which are parallel in structure. The second and subsequent conjuncts gap elements recoverable from the first. An analysis of this is complicated by the archaic syntax of the overall sentence. The ellipted verb phrase, 'would not have beene', is discontinuous and an analysis based on reduced clause coordination requires the recognition of two ellipsis sites, as in:

> Nay, rather would not my daunger have beene her death,
> [would not] my mishap [have beene] her miserie,
> [would not] my torture [have beene] her torments,
> and [would not] my fatall destinie [have beene] her finall destruction?

These parallel clauses are questions and, as the first clause makes clear, the first verbal auxiliary, together with its negative particle, has been inverted with the subject to act as operator in question formation. In the subsequent clauses the omission of this operator has to be seen as a leftmost coordination reduction. This displacement of the operator allows the second site in this discontinuous ellipsis to figure as a partial gapping of the rest of the verb phrase, central to parallel structures:

Subject	Verb	Complement
my daunger	have beene	her death,
my mishap	[ ]	her miserie,
my torture	[ ]	her torments,
my fatall destinie	[ ]	her finall destruction?

The omission of these verbal elements allows parallel subject and complement noun phrases to be juxtaposed for maximum stylistic effect. These noun phrases are structurally identical. Contrastive possessive determiners, 'my' and 'her', reinforce a series of alliterative nouns, culminating in the double alliteration of 'fatall destinie' and 'finall destruction'.

CHAPTER 7

THE ROUGH GUIDE TO GAPS

The first six chapters of this book have looked at and analysed the most common types of elliptical gap as they occur in quite a wide variety of spoken and written English. The main focus has been linguistic and, for much of the time, predominantly syntactic. In other words, I have been mainly concerned to identify, describe and analyse the structural possibilities for, and constraints upon, ellipsis. In identifying grammatical patterns and investigating the rules that seem to govern and constrain them, I have sometimes adopted the techniques of a particular approach to linguistic enquiry, such as manipulating and test-casing contrived examples. For the most part, though, I have described and analysed real data, using a fairly eclectic range of ideas and techniques. The study of the structural patterns and syntactic rules of a specific linguistic feature is a valid enterprise and ellipsis can, like any other syntactic feature, be studied in its own right. However, even while focusing on the syntactic scheme of things, I have given a fair amount of space to matters that might be broadly called 'stylistic'. There are two main reasons for this. First, my own commitment to an integrative approach: I noted in Chapter 1 that questions of style can go hand in hand with linguistic analysis, making a holistic approach to ellipsis possible. Secondly, this approach is invited by the nature of ellipsis itself. As we have seen, it is a fairly messy, fuzzy-edged phenomenon in the way it relates to the situational as well as the linguistic context, becoming more of a property of discourse than a syntactic feature at times. The fact that ellipsis is common to literary artistry and the most mundane of everyday language uses also allows for comparative and contrastive analysis within a very broad conception of 'style'.

The main purpose of this chapter is to provide a succinct summary of the material explored in previous chapters and, in addition, to give you the framework for a more open-ended exercise in data gathering and classification. An overview at this stage will help to establish and clarify the range of categories and subcategories of ellipsis that were discussed in the preceding chapters with respect to fairly diverse data. In addition, it will provide a kind of checklist of elliptical categories that will be useful in subsequent stylistic analyses. With that end in mind, this overview is presented in tabular form with an accompanying commentary that summarizes key points relating to each category.

The types of elliptical phenomenon that I have identified are summarized in Table 7.1. Its title, 'The rough guide to gaps', is meant to be

Table 7.1   The rough guide to gaps

ELLIPTICAL GAPS

RELEVANT CONTEXT: LINGUISTIC (CONTEXTUAL ELLIPSIS)
INTRASENTENTIAL (within sentences)
Subordination reduction:

Brian won't do the dishes, so you'll have to [ ]. (p. 38)
Because John was going to Silverstone, Jim went [ ] too. (p. 41)
The model [ ] she had dressed in black swept down the catwalk. (p. 52)

Coordination reduction:
Leftmost:

Mars gave peace a chance and [ ] war a rest. (p. 93)

Rightmost:

Hingis lost to Novotna but Davenport didn't [ ]. (p. 94)

Central (Gapping):

Pyramus died lovingly for Thisbe and Thisbe [ ] for Pyramus. (p. 98)

INTERSENTENTIAL (between sentences or utterance turns)
Conversational rejoinders:

DON: Where's Celia?
PHILIP: [ ] In the kitchen. (p. 48)

RELEVANT CONTEXT: SITUATION + LINGUISTIC FORM
Sentence initial ellipsis:

[ ] Got any money? (p. 58)
[ ] Quite looking forward to the seance this evening. (p. 61)

Telegraphic ellipsis:

[ ] Cannabis man [ ] jailed for [ ] year. (p. 73)
[The] pilgrims' feet [have] worn away the old steps. (p. 77)
NO BIKES (p. 79)

Situational ellipsis:

B says: 'I wouldn't [ ], if I were you' (as A reaches for his gun). (p. 62)
Keep [ ] out of the reach of children (on a packet of pain relief tablets). (p. 65)

Table 7.1 (cont'd)

NON-ELLIPTICAL GAPS

Lapses in conversation:

A: Or is that [ ], would it help [ ]
B: I think we were taking it a bit slow . . . (p. 23)

Nonrealization:

Then they put the flag back and they went to the table, and he hit [ ] and the other hit [ ]. (p. 29)

Inferential gaps:

A: Are you going to the pictures tonight?
C: That new Tarantino's on at the multiplex. (p. 31)

---

appropriate in a number of ways. The summary is rough in the sense that some of its detail is approximate: as we have seen, some aspects of ellipsis resist a wholly precise description. There is also the implication that a guide to ellipsis cannot be fully comprehensive: the table presents a credible set of categories without claiming to be an exhaustive typology. Lastly, in the spirit of rough guides, this summary aims to provide an accessible tool for mapping a route through the territory of ellipsis.

The table is arranged to show the relationship between form and linguistic context and/or context of situation. To emphasize this relationship as the basis for categorizing and subcategorizing types of ellipsis, the rough guide to gaps reorders, where necessary, the material of the preceding chapters. However, each category is illustrated by page-numbered examples from those chapters, so that relevant discussion can be readily located.

Given that there appears to be a wide variety of contexts and motivations for gaps to occur in language, the twin questions, 'what is ellipsis?' and 'what isn't ellipsis?', prompt the initial categorization of elliptical and non-elliptical gaps. Elliptical gaps are structural omissions that can be described, however imprecisely, in terms of syntactic rules and constituents and whose recovery is supported, usually in quite specific ways, by contextual and/or situational information. Non-elliptical gaps do not, for various reasons, fulfil these criteria. For example, where there is a structural gap, it may not be subject to general syntactic rule or, where situational information supports recoverable meaning, there may be no actual structural gap. Non-elliptical gaps are nevertheless included in the rough guide, for contrastive purposes, because they are significant discourse features that are often discussed in the literature in terms of ellipsis and because some examples are ambivalent as to their status, suggesting some overlap or gap continuum.

Elliptical gaps characterize structurally incomplete sentences. Our sense of that incompleteness derives from the potential forms such sentences might take. In many cases that potential form can be related to elements recoverable from the linguistic context. This gives us the basis for the major category of contextual ellipsis, which, with its many subcategories, is the most widespread elliptical type. The rough guide to gaps itemizes the factors that inform the subcategorization of contextual ellipsis.

A useful, though not entirely unproblematical, distinction is made between intrasentential and intersentential contexts. The linguistic source of a gap is frequently to be found within the confines of a multi-clausal compound or complex sentence or the intonationally signalled equivalent in a speaker's utterance. In other words the gap is intrasentential. Subordination and coordination are the syntactic relations which organize such sentences and ellipses which occur in these contexts are called subordination reduction and coordination reduction. With regard to subordination reduction, it is worth noting that the gap can occur in either a main clause or a subordinate clause, as along as it is retrievable from the linguistic context. A general point about coordination reduction is that coordinate clauses or other conjuncts do not necessarily have an overt marker of coordination, but can be simply juxtaposed by means of parataxis. Subcategories of coordination reduction are based on whether the site of the ellipsis is to the left, right or centre of the conjunct. Note that rightmost ellipsis, widely known as verb phrase deletion, is not confined to coordination, but patterns similarly in subordinate clauses, conversational fragments and other linguistic contexts. This flexibility allows for the phenomenon called 'multiple VP ellipsis' by Klein and Stainton-Ellis (1989: 1119). They discuss examples which involve two or more ellipsis sites, such as the following exchange:

A: You never go swimming.
B: That's because I don't look good in a swimming costume.
     I might [ ] if I did [ ]. (p. 1123)

Normally verb phrase ellipsis is contextually resolved by the nearest verb phrase antecedent. In the case of 'I might [ ]', this would be 'look good in a swimming costume', which is clearly not the meaning intended by speaker B. The anaphoric link that supports this gap has to cross over the nearest verb phrase antecedent and pick up the earlier 'go swimming' for the gaps to be filled appropriately: 'I might [go swimming] if I did [look good in a swimming costume]'. Klein and Stainton-Ellis call this kind of anaphoric resolution 'crossing-dependency' and suggest such aspects of multiple verb phrase ellipsis are particularly interesting for the demands they make on clause comprehension and what that can tell us about the wider issue of human sentence-processing.

Central ellipsis is commonly known as gapping and figures significantly in literary parallelism. Similar processing and comprehension constraints on the relative distance between a potential ellipsis site and its antecedent also pertain to gapping and other types of coordination reduction. In a corpus-based study of ellipsis in coordination, for example, Meyer points out: 'As the distance between the ellipsis and antecedent sites becomes greater, however, the likelihood of ellipsis decreases because the processing load becomes heavier for both the addresser and addressee . . .' (1995: 253). This psycholinguistic constraint is a major factor in the linguistic balancing act between avoiding redundant repetition and creating potentially unintelligible gaps.

Where the recoverable material that supports a gap is to be found outside the sentence in which it occurs, in some adjacent or contiguous sentence, the notion of intersentential ellipsis applies. The most widespread category of intersentential ellipsis occurs in contextual rejoinders across speakers in dialogue or conversation. Strictly, conversational rejoinders are utterance turns. However, intersentential ellipsis also occurs between written sentences other than those representing dialogue, as in this brief example from Deborah Levy's novel *Billy and Girl*:

I've hardened up. Scholars have to [ ]. (1996: 107)

Here the verb phrase deletion of the second sentence is understood in the context of the first: 'Scholars have to [harden up]'. Psycholinguistic constraints on the processing of gaps are less severe in the case of writing. Even so, the linguistic context relevant to an intersentential ellipsis is normally an immediately adjacent sentence. In an empirical study, Garnham compared informants' reactions to the following types of contrastive data:

Margie wanted the recipes.
The main dish was mouthwatering.
The dessert was delicious.
Tom did too.

The main dish was mouthwatering.
The dessert was delicious.
Margie wanted the recipes.
Tom did too. (1987: 65)

There were significant differences in judgements about acceptability and the time taken to make these judgements in favour of elliptical sentences which immediately followed their antecedent, as in the second example: 'Margie wanted the recipes. Tom did [want the recipes] too'. Where the ellipsis did not have an immediately preceding antecedent, the data was significantly harder to process. Garnham concludes: 'This result suggests that rapid loss of memory for surface form is a general property of the language understanding system, and that it imposes severe constraints on the way the language processing system operates.' (p. 67). This consolidates the points made by Klein and Stainton-Ellis and Meyer and further underlines the insights elliptical phenomena can provide in relation to cognitive theories of language.

The other major category of ellipsis is based on the fact that the potential form of a truncated expression can be deduced from its syntactic structure supported by clues from the situational context. The notion of recoverability is inappropriate in the sense that there is no linguistic material to be traced in the surrounding context. On the other hand, the gaps are variously reconstitutable. The degree to which their form is determinate is a factor in subcategorizing ellipses within this overall type. At one end of the spectrum of determinacy is sentence-initial ellipsis. Here syntactic structure more or less dictates the missing elements from the onset of the sentence. In this respect such ellipsis is conventional. In those cases where the gap allows for only one possibility, Thomas underlines this conventionality with the term 'self-defining elision' (1979: 46). Although his use of the term 'elision' here is not meant to imply a phonological dimension to conventionality, another view, explored by Quirk et al. (1985: 896), is that sentence-initial ellipsis is closer to phonological elision. Syntactic and phonological explanations are not incompatible and abstract phonological principles may be at work with regard to sentence-initial ellipsis. However, an analysis based solely on syntactic categories is favoured in this book.

Some instances of telegraphic ellipsis where the likely gap is at the beginning of a sentence are superficially like sentence-initial ellipsis. Closer analysis shows that the telegraphic gap is not confined to the narrow set of functional elements that fill most sentence-initial gaps, but is much less determinately reconstituted. The balance between structure and situation shifts away from the conventions of syntax towards the role of exophoric reference in resolving meaning and ambiguity. Telegraphic strings with multiple ellipsis sites take on a highly abbreviated and possibly cryptic message quality in, for example, the quasi-literary contexts of newspaper headlines and advertisements.

The term 'situational ellipsis' is reserved for those gaps that can only be reconstituted with reference to an extralinguistic act or object. In writing, these are not as rare as one might imagine, since they occur formulaically on a wide range of commercial and domestic packaging. In spoken contexts, outside certain contrived routines, situational ellipses are likely to be heard as possible lapses in performance, such as false starts and other normally non-fluent failures to complete sentences, rather than genuine exophoric gaps.

It is appropriate that the rough guide to elliptical gaps concludes with a category that shades into a type of non-elliptical gap, the conversational lapse. For the most part, lapses in performance result in structural gaps, but, despite the desire of some linguists to incorporate these spoken features into a whole speech grammar, it remains doubtful that any general syntactic rules could be devised to account for them systematically.

The nonrealization of predicate arguments and other potential constituents does result in gaps of a kind compared with some maximally full realization of all possible elements. However, there is no sense of structural incompleteness, unless, of course, the nonrealized constituent is compulsory for the grammaticality of the sentence, as in the case of the direct object of a transitive verb. The treatment of nonrealization as 'indefinite ellipsis' creates more problems than it explains. The term itself is appropriately ambiguous, since it suggests not only that the ellipsis is of uncertain specification but also that there is no end to the attribution of potential gaps.

The final category of non-elliptical gap seems a contradiction in terms, since no actual structural gap is discernible. However, inferential gaps, as I have called them, are the most interesting and significant of the non-elliptical gaps, since accounting for the difference between what is said and what is meant is probably the most challenging aspect of discourse analysis as a whole.

Exercise 7.1

The following examples cover the range of categories outlined in the rough guide to gaps. Identify the ellipsis, if any, in each example and categorize each sentence according to the rough guide.

A: Yeah, well, I, yeah, we can put some work in on it if you
      like, because . . .
B: Yeah let's do that.

Wayne likes Muti for Mahler and Solti for Bruckner.

Like another prawn ball?

Dave's going swimming, if Denzel is.

A: Do you know Rajvinder?
B: Slightly.

SHOP TO LET

Charles fell about laughing, but the director didn't.

Enjoy!

Contains paracetamol (written on a packet of pain relief tablets).

Boxer loved work and Napoleon power.

GEOFF: Dave's a pretty good swimmer.
ROBERT: And I'm Johnny Weissmuller.

Exercise 7.2

A more open-ended empirical exercise. In the light of your performance of Exercise 7.1 and my discussion of its outcomes, find examples
for each of the categories of ellipsis to compile your own rough guide
to gaps. Try to use real data wherever possible, but remember that
appropriately made-up examples are also valid.

Discussion of Exercises

Exercise 7.1

I have placed the examples in the order of the rough guide to gaps.
Ellipses, if any, are indicated together with a brief comment on examples,
where appropriate.

ELLIPTICAL GAPS

Subordination reduction:

> Dave's going swimming, if Denzel is [going swimming].

The gap is in the subordinate clause and is typical of so-called verb phrase deletion as in rightmost coordination reduction.

Coordination reduction:
Leftmost:

> Wayne likes Muti for Mahler and [Wayne likes] Solti for Bruckner.

Rightmost:

> Charles fell about laughing, but the director didn't [fall about laughing].

Compare so-called verb phrase deletion here with the example for subordination reduction. Note in this case the adjustment of the lexical verb to accommodate the negative particle: 'fell' relates to 'didn't fall'. In this respect the ellipsis is weakly rather than uniquely recoverable.

Central (Gapping):

> Boxer loved work and Napoleon [loved] power.

A straightforward gapping of the lexical verb only: even so, it creates a strong sense of parallelism.

Conversational rejoinders:

> A: Do you know Rajvinder?
> B: [I know Rajvinder] Slightly.

The whole sentence is ellipted in this reply. An interesting theoretical issue is raised by the fact that an actual full reply would almost certainly have pronominalized Rajvinder: 'I know him slightly.' Should an expansion reflect this? Since expansions are an analytical tool for making syntactic relations explicit, they should probably reflect uniquely recoverable antecedents as closely as possible.

Sentence initial ellipsis:

> [Would you] Like another prawn ball?

It is possible that specific situational contexts will support other expansions, such as: '[Would she] Like another prawn ball?' In the absence of a specified situation, the given expansion is most likely, assuming the question is a direct address.

Telegraphic ellipsis:

[This] SHOP [is] TO LET

This minimal expansion identifies the omission of function words appropriate to a specific situation: an estate agent's sign on a shop in the high street. The structural indeterminacy of telegraphic strings and their situational dependence is demonstrated by the fact that a different situation would prompt a different expansion. For example, as the title to a box advertisement in a newspaper, valid expansions might be:

[There is a] SHOP TO LET
[X is announcing a] SHOP TO LET.

Situational ellipsis:

[The product in this packet] Contains paracetamol (written on a packet of pain relief tablets).

The label clearly refers to the contents and not the packet itself, but the verb 'contains' is singular, so some generalized subject has to be inferred: 'product' rather than 'tablets'.

NON-ELLIPTICAL GAPS

Lapses in conversation:

A: Yeah, well, I [ ], yeah, we can put some work in on it if you like, because [ ] . . .
B: Yeah let's do that.

The first gap results from a false start, the second from an interruption. Neither can be accommodated within a set of rules for ellipsis.

Nonrealization:

Enjoy [ ]!

This formulaic incitement by service providers is an interesting development in usage. The verb 'enjoy' is strictly transitive and requires a direct object. That object is not realized in this formula. To the extent that the verb refers to an item in the context of situation, 'your food', 'the movie', the gap can be seen as situational ellipsis. However, there is a sense of nonrealization in this usage which suggests that the verb 'enjoy' is in the process of becoming intransitive as well, like 'read'. If that is the case, we may soon hear people saying 'are you enjoying?' without wondering 'enjoying what?'.

Inferential gaps:

> GEOFF: Dave's a pretty good swimmer.
> ROBERT: And I'm Johnny Weissmuller.

The meaning of Robert's droll rejoinder depends on conversational implicature. Robert is clearly not Johnny Weissmuller, so his assertion severely violates the maxim of quality. Weissmuller was a great Olympic swimming champion before becoming the star of the Tarzan films of his era, so Robert's false claim to be Weissmuller implies that he is as far away from being an Olympic champion at swimming as Dave is from being a pretty good swimmer. He thus calls into question Geoff's opinion of Dave's prowess and suggests it is not only false but exaggerated. In effect, Robert implies that Dave is hopeless at swimming. The exchange crucially relies on Geoff knowing who Weissmuller was, of course.

Exercise 7.2

You may have used the data in Exercise 7.1 as a comparative checklist when finding your own examples. If not, comparing your own examples with those provided for Exercise 7.1 should help you to judge your performance. One thing you are almost certain to have found is that some categories of gap are much more widespread than others in actual language use. For example, gaps resulting from false starts and other conversational lapses are so common as to appear natural, while most spoken exchanges have examples of elliptical rejoinders. On the other hand, you may have had to search quite hard for an example of gapping and may well have decided to contrive one instead. The exercise should have sharpened your awareness of categories of ellipsis in the course of listening and reading. This alertness is essential for analysing and commenting upon ellipsis as an exponent of style.

PART TWO

THE STYLISTIC EFFECTS OF ELLIPSIS

CHAPTER 8

STYLE AND STYLISTICS

This chapter explores various ideas about, and theories of, style in an attempt to establish a framework for describing how ellipsis can be seen to contribute to the style of particular examples of spoken and written discourse. Different definitions and theories of style prompt, of course, different takes on the occasionally maligned notion of stylistics. My approach here is to make explicit connections between the two. Style is notoriously difficult to define, as Wales notes at the beginning of her set of definitions of the term, the first of which might be deemed 'the bottom line':

> At its simplest, **style** refers to the manner of EXPRESSION in writing or speaking, just as there is a manner of doing things, like playing squash or painting. We might talk of someone writing in an 'ornate style', or speaking in a 'comic style'.
> (Wales 1989: 435)

This definition suggests that style is concerned with two things: (a) the formal properties of a text rather than what it is about, (b) the choices that creators of texts make. This bottom-line definition embodies the commonly debated split between form and content, the idea that 'the same thing' can be expressed in more than one way. Leech and Short (1981: 14–26) call this view of style 'dualism' and contrast it with 'monism'. A fundamental tenet of monism is that language is not just a formal representation of prior content. Rather, there is no meaning without form. In that case even variations which are apparently formal will imply a different meaning. In effect, this theory claims that the dualistic split between form and content is anomalous. Furthermore, formal differences take on even greater significance when they are not just expressive variants. From this perspective, stylistics, the study and explication of style, need only be concerned with the formal properties

Table 8.1   Style and stylistics

Style may be to do with one or more of the following:	To the extent that it is, Stylistics may be seen to be:
FORM	FORMAL
FUNCTION	FUNCTIONAL
INDIVIDUATION	AUTHORIAL
ACT OF LISTENING OR READING	AFFECTIVE

of text. This broadly coincides with Bradford's concept of 'textualism' which is a preoccupation with text, particularly literary text, 'as a cohesive unity of patterns, structures and effects' (1997: 73).

A purely textualist stylistics is probably neither possible nor desirable. Contextual and discursive factors lead us away from a preoccupation with the formal and expressive properties of language alone: content, in a very broad sense, begins to matter after all. As Wales goes on to say in her definitions of stylistics: 'The goal of most stylistic studies is not simply to describe the FORMAL features of texts for their own sake, but in order to show their FUNCTIONAL significance for the IN-TERPRETATION of the text . . .' (1989: 437–8). While it cannot be equated with 'content', functional significance implies closer attention to what a text is about. Once an interpretative goal is cited, further-more, it is difficult to avoid the idea that content is involved. By this token, stylistics is now concerned with a much wider range of prop-erties and their consequences. This wider concern is captured by Brad-ford's concept of 'contextualism', whose 'unifying characteristic is its concentration on the relation between text and context' (1997: 14). Context here, as Bradford's subsequent discussion shows, entails not only the immediate situation of text, but also wider social, psychological and political considerations.

The rest of this chapter elaborates on the four categories of style and stylistics set out in Table 8.1. This is far from being a comprehensive survey, since it is biased towards the textual aspects of style, in Brad-ford's terms, though some contextual issues are inevitably touched upon where appropriate. Table 8.1 maps a number of key factors in the consideration of style on to corresponding categories of stylistics. The following discussion presents general points about these selected categor-ies but attempts to show how ellipsis can be seen to operate within each one.

Form —— Formal

Style, as I noted above, is in a very basic sense always a matter of form, since whatever factors are involved in stylistic variation, they are realized by differences at one or more levels of linguistic organization. It was an emphasis on formal differences that gave the formalists both their focus and their name. The formalists were scholarly theorists of language and literature, based in Moscow and St Petersburg during and after the Russian revolution. They influenced, and in the person of Roman Jakobson, helped to found the Prague School of Linguistics, the other most prominent formalist group. Formalists are, in Bradford's terms, the archetypal textualists. However, the formalist exploration of textual patterns and structures is very rarely neutral or unmotivated: a formalist approach always wants to consider the 'effects' of structural difference. My discussion centres on two related concepts that formalists found significant: deviation and defamiliarization.

The concept of deviation depends on some idea of linguistic ordinariness, a norm from which other varieties of language can be seen to be deviating. The nature of the deviation is usually explained with regard to one or more of the levels of linguistic organization, so we might point to lexical deviation, if a text contains unusual or inappropriate vocabulary, or cohesive deviation, if a text disrupts the normal requirements of logical discourse. One problem with the concept is that it can easily be associated with deviance, evoking notions of oddity and weirdness. Clearly, it is possible that linguistic deviation may result in texts that are structurally and semantically odd or even perverse and this possibility can be exploited, especially in literature. However, the concept of deviation is applicable to a much wider range of language in use. Compare, for example, the following two sentences:

> If you haven't got a *Financial Times*, you'll be so ill-informed you won't be able to make a comment.
> No *FT*, no comment.

The snappy telegraphic sentence is the ideal advertising slogan, because it crams all the implications of the first sentence into a few words as well as accommodating a further connotation of distaste for anyone who doesn't have a *Financial Times*. It is not that the slogan is a 'version' of the longer sentence. A minimal expansion on the basis of identified ellipsis sites would be something like:

[If you've] No *FT*, [you've] no comment.

Nevertheless, the telegraphic string, in so far as it lacks elements in relation to fully realized grammatical sentences, can be seen as a deviation from a background norm.

Although the concept of deviation has been applied to other uses of language in the way I have demonstrated here, it has been particularly prominent in relation to literary texts. In one of the best-known treatments of the topic, Mukařovský, a member of the famous Prague School of Linguistics, calls the background norm, in the context of which poetic language can be seen to deviate, 'standard language' (1964: 17). Mukařovský doesn't define this term explicitly, but his discussion suggests he does not mean some hierarchically superior variety, but rather something like 'normal everyday usage'. This exposes the second problem with the concept of deviation: in asserting a norm, however innocuously, the issue of whose norm is always open to question. Take this extract from Alice Walker's epistolary novel *The Color Purple*:

Nobody cook like Shug when she cook.
She get up early in the morning and go to market.
Buy only stuff that's fresh. (1983: 178)

Against a background norm of 'standard language', presumably standard American English, this passage consistently deviates by omitting the third person singular marker from its verbs. This represents in written form a morphemic variation that is typical of a large number of speakers of African American Vernacular English, a distinct variety. As a perceived deviation from 'standard American English' this distracts from any other formal properties that might be stylistically significant. If, however, the African American Vernacular English variety is taken as the norm integral to this text, then attention can move from the morphemic variation to a genuine ellipsis:

[She] Buy only stuff that's fresh.

As we saw in Chapter 4, this kind of sentence-initial ellipsis in writing is characteristic of diary entries. In *The Color Purple* this particular ellipsis reinforces our sense that Celie's highly personal letters have a diaristic quality: they are a narrative for, as well as of, the self.

For Mukařovský, literary language takes the resources of everyday language, encompassed in his notion of 'standard', and consciously and pleasurably introduces deviations that 'de-automatize' text. In a much earlier paper the Russian formalist Shklovsky rehearses similar arguments, using a slightly different terminology. In what amounts to a formalist manifesto Shklovsky argues that perception becomes automatic as it becomes habitual. Applied to language, this process of habituation means that our ordinary, everyday speech becomes unthinkingly automatic. The purpose of art, in this case poetic language, is to counteract that state of habituation by means of linguistic forms which create a sense of 'defamiliarization'. Shklovsky elaborates on his enduring concept as follows: 'The technique of art is to make objects "unfamiliar", to make forms difficult, to increase the difficulty and length of perception because the process of perception is an aesthetic end in itself and must be prolonged' (1917: 20). Shklovsky seems to tie his concept of defamiliarization into a particular aesthetic viewpoint that is less obviously applicable to present-day popular cultural theory and artistic accessibility. Even so, the idea that literary discourse must make strange the normally habituated use of everyday language is a compelling one. True to its formalist origins, treatments of defamiliarization tend to focus on how the shape and structure of the literary message, its specifically linguistic properties, manifest deviations that challenge the habituated reader. As a syntactic feature of language that creates structural gaps, ellipsis has the potential to contribute to the defamiliarizing qualities of poetic texts.

Exercise 8.1

Identify any elliptical gaps in the following passage from Ezra Pound's *The Cantos*. To what extent do such gaps create structures that deviate from 'standard language' in Mukařovský's sense of the term? Do you think the text makes objects unfamiliar? If so, what part, if any, does ellipsis play in this sense of defamiliarization?

> Autumn moon; hills rise about lakes
> against sunset
> Evening is like a curtain of cloud,
> a blurr above ripples; and through it
> sharp long spikes of the cinnamon,
> a cold tune amid reeds. (1987: 244)

Function ——— Functional

In some very basic way virtually all speech events are functional in the sense that they fulfil some strategic use, but specifying the particular function of a speech event or the range of functions that can be recognized have both proved quite elusive. Particularly problematic is the multifunctional nature of language. Any speech event is likely to be fulfilling more than one strategic use at a time, depending on various factors in the situational context. For example, a television weather forecast has informative and predictive functions, but to the extent that it projects the personality of the forecaster it also fulfils personal or expressive functions. Most functional approaches to style get round this by what can be called the 'dominant function principle', which asserts, in the words of its most influential proponent, that: 'The verbal structure of a message depends primarily on the dominant function' (Jakobson 1960: 353). A treatment of television weather forecast style would, at least initially, focus on those verbal structures associated with its dominant informative function. If a comparison of individual weather forecaster styles were being made, then linguistic exponents of personal or expressive functions would also need to be taken into account in relation to the dominant function.

There are two main strategic problems with a functional approach to style. The first is to establish the dominant function of a text or speech event. A range of criteria is usually invoked for this purpose, such as: the importance of the addresser or encoder, a focus on the addressee or decoder, the relation of text to situational context, the nature of that situational context. These and a host of other factors contribute to establishing the dominant function of some piece of language in use. At their most general functions are given such names as referential, persuasive, expressive, instructive. These general categories tend to be illustrated with reference to more specific uses of language, for which I have used the term 'functional style'. For example, the persuasive function is associated with the functional style of advertising, the instructive with recipes or car manuals. Such functional styles are also called registers. Montgomery *et al.* suggest that register signifies 'the fact that the kind of language we use is affected by the context in which we use it, to such an extent that certain kinds of language usage become conventionally associated with particular situations' (1992: 55). They go on (pp. 56–7) to itemize three factors in the situational context that particularly influence register: the medium, the participants and the purpose or field. The first of these is essentially about speech versus writing, though this apparently straightforward division has complexities that I touch upon in Chapters 9 and 11. The social roles of, and relationships between, participants affect the 'tone' of a register, particularly with regard to the degree of formality realized by means of, for example, terms of address. Montgomery *et al.* link the purpose or function of language in use to its field or, in a very general sense, its subject matter, so that, for example, football commentary will have structures appropriate to its purpose and 'field-specific' vocabulary, something I explore in more detail in Chapter 10.

The second major problem with a functional approach to style is contingent upon the dominant function principle: in what way does the verbal structure of a message, its form, depend on, or even relate to, its apparent function? The following exercise in 'dualism' serves to illustrate the nature of the problem. The first example below is a constructed version in the manner of a diary entry of the second example which is the opening of Gerard Manley Hopkins's poem 'The Windhover'.

Went up the Blue Heaps this morning to catch the sunrise: dappled clouds etc. Saw a falcon hovering just as dawn broke.

> I caught this morning morning's minion, king-
> dom of daylight's dauphin, dapple-dawn-drawn Falcon, in
> his riding
> Of the rolling level underneath him steady air . . .
>
> (Gardner (ed.) 1963: 30)

One of the propositions of a functional stylistics is that, even where certain factors like subject matter are held constant, differences in dominant function will correlate with formal variation. To some extent these examples confirm that proposition. The diary entry functions within the so-called emotive or expressive functional range. The focus is the writer's own experience and reactions to it. The writing self is so taken for granted that it need not be verbally coded, resulting in the typical sentence-initial ellipses of diary entries: '[I] Went up the Blue Heaps . . . [I] Saw a falcon hovering . . .'. So there is at least some justification in saying that the verbal structure of the message depends on its dominant function. The Hopkins poem also focuses on the writer's own experience, his reactions to it, his interpretation of its significance. Yet it has none of the features that mark the style of the diary entry. From a functional perspective it is possible to argue that, while the expressive function is clearly fulfilled, it is not the dominant function here. The main focus is the message as verbal construct: its visible shape, its verbal and rhythmic texture depend on its being a poem rather than a self-referential mnemonic device. It is a focus on such characteristics as these that Jakobson (1960: 356) associates with the poetic function and which dominates this text's functional range.

The comparison of a non-literary functional style or register with a highly marked poetic style may seem contrived to support a functional stylistics. It does show that specific texts have features associated with their function, sentence-initial ellipses in the case of diary entries, alliteration, rhyme, repetition and other forms of verbal play in the case of poems. What a functional stylistics cannot claim, of course, is that all diary entries, let alone all poems, manifest the same verbal structures. Any generalization will need to be severely hedged. This is the line taken by Carter and Nash with regard to their notion of 'text convention':

> There are conventional regularities in the use of language in many contexts and situations; if stylistic differences in texts are to be accounted for perhaps one of the main constituent factors will be the function of these codes and conventions and the use of language either in association with them or in breaking them. (1990: 11)

There is in the notion of text convention a degree of circularity. Do we recognize a functional style by its text conventions or do we discover its text conventions on the basis of knowing its functional style? Nevertheless, the recognition of text conventions allows us, for example, not only to judge whether a particular diary entry is 'diaristic' but even to construct texts in the manner of a diary entry. The notion of text convention might even help us to decide whether a poem is 'poetic' or not. Since text conventions pertain to particular functional styles, the concept is likely to be most useful in comparing different examples within the same genre.

Exercise 8.2

Compare the following samples of weather forecasts, one from teletext, the other from a newspaper. To what extent is the notion of a set of text conventions valid across the two samples? What part does ellipsis play in the conventions you discern?

FORECAST   UK TUE 6pm to WED 6am
(Green) Windy. Gales. Frequent squally showers. Clear spells.
3–6C
(Yellow) Windy. Odd showers. Clear spells. 2–6C
(Blue) Overcast. Windy. Gales. Locally heavy rain then
showers. 5–9C
(White) Locally heavy rain, easing later. 8–11C
(The entries refer to a colour-coded map)
                              (ITV Teletext, 27.10.98: 104)

Weather
Windy. Cold in the north. Mild in the south.
Cent S & SE England, London, E Anglia, Midlands: Windy
and cloudy with some rain and drizzle at times. A fresh to
strong south-westerly wind. Max temp 15–17C (59–63F).
Tonight, mild and windy. Min temp 12–14C (54–57F)

(This is followed by similarly formatted entries for six further
regions)
Outlook: Periods of rain interspersed with sunshine and showers.
                              (*The Guardian*, 27.10.98: 19)

Individuation —— Authorial

The previous two sections of this chapter, with their concern for the
formal properties of texts and their relation to effects or functions, have
been, in the sense promoted by Taylor and Toolan (1984), 'objectivist'.
In their schematic guide to the various branches of stylistics they note:
'Objectivist stylisticians believe style to be an inherent property of the
text itself, taken as an utterance of the language' (1984: 88). As my
discussion of the weather forecasts sampled in Exercise 8.2 indicates,
texts fulfilling the same function can be seen to have some properties in
common, so we are justified in recognizing, say, the text style of weather
forecasts. But I also note that other contextual factors, such as media
provenance, seem to correlate with textual differences, so there is clearly
a need to discriminate the text style of newspaper weather forecasts from
the text style of teletext weather forecasts. We could, of course, compare different newspapers or teletext channels to differentiate further
text styles. Although these texts are anonymous, they do not write themselves: ultimately someone is responsible for compiling them. However,

we can assume that no single individual is always the author of a particular weather forecast and that others can compile stylistically identical forecasts, as the need arises, by adhering to their text conventions.

The idea that style is inherent in the text itself, especially with regard to functional styles, suggests a rather impersonal quality, that to some extent runs counter to what might be seen as the 'common sense' definition of style. That view is encapsulated by Short as follows: 'Style can be perceived in any consistent writing, literary or otherwise, or indeed in *any consistent behaviour*, linguistic or otherwise. Individual novelists can be said to have styles, but so can weather forecasters, singers or runners' (1996: 329 (original italics)). While it is still the outcome of consistent behaviour that manifests style, whether this is running, singing, weather forecasting or making literary texts, this view asserts that style is bound up with individual behavers. This shifts the focus somewhat. Style can be seen as an individuating feature which, as Short exemplifies, is not confined to language and, within language, not restricted to the literary domain. While television forecasters will adhere to the text conventions of broadcast weather reports, they will also be individuated by the manner they express themselves within that functional style. In this respect style is almost a synonym for idiolect, that set of individual linguistic traits which make us all unique language users.

To the extent that a focus on the individual addresser or encoder of language correlates with the expressive function, a stylistics that pays attention to style as an individuating feature is distinguished by Wales as 'expressive'. She notes: 'expressive stylistics may be seen to survive in notions of style as idiolect: in the idea that Dickens has a style that is different from Trollope's or Thackeray's. Certainly this view of style is central to STYLOMETRY, involved in historical questions of authorship' (1989: 166). Style as individuation is, then, particularly interesting in literary studies. Despite theories of textual autonomy and critical reappraisals of the status of authorship, we are interested in understanding the stylistic markers that characterize and trace the development of individual writers. This interest asserts the integrity of text in human terms. Given that our individual way of using language is the basis for this literary individuation, I have chosen the term 'authorial' for this type of stylistics. Authorial stylistics can, of course, be applied to speakers, from stand-up comedians to members of the cabinet, and to non-literary writers. It is also the basis for certain kinds of computational or statistical studies of texts. These can be used to characterize a writer's style in terms of frequency of certain features, such as vocabulary items, syntactic structures or figures of speech. Such methods can be used, as Wales mentions, to establish authorship in old or disputed texts, as well as for non-literary purposes, such as the gathering of forensic evidence in criminal proceedings. Nevertheless, the main concern of authorial stylistics is to analyse and interpret the characteristic textual features of individual authors.

Exercise 8.3

Analyse the most significant stylistic features of these extracts from two of Charles Dickens's novels, *The Pickwick Papers* and *Bleak House*, identifying any ellipses that contribute to your analysis. How do these elliptical features contribute to Dickens's authorial style?

The Pickwick Papers
Everything was so beautiful! The lawn in front, the garden behind, the miniature conservatory, the dining-room, the drawing-room, the bed-rooms, the smoking-room, and above all the study with its pictures and easy chairs, and odd cabinets, and queer tables, and books out of number, with a large cheerful window opening upon a pleasant lawn and commanding a pretty landscape, dotted here and there with little houses almost hidden by the trees; and then the curtains, and the carpets, and the chairs, and the sofas! (1837: 895)

Bleak House
Fog everywhere. Fog up the river, where it flows among green aits and meadows; fog down the river, where it rolls defiled among the tiers of shipping, and the waterside pollutions of a great (and dirty) city. Fog on the Essex marshes, fog on the Kent heights. Fog creeping into the cabooses of collier-brigs; fog lying out on the yards, and hovering in the rigging of great ships; fog drooping on the gunwales of barges and small boats. (1853: 5)

Act of listening or reading —— Affective

As a reaction to treatments of style that are objectivist, theoretical positions have been developed which suggest that style is, at least in part, a perceptual category influenced by the interaction between listener and speech event or reader and text. These receptive theories of style are almost exclusively concerned with the reader and, even more narrowly, with the reader's response to literature. Before discussing this main focus of affective stylistics, as these theories are collectively referred to, it is worth asking if they can be applied to everyday oral communication.

One area of investigation that seems to involve a valid listener-response theory is Tannen's treatment of female—male conversation. Her thesis is that mismatches and breakdowns in communication between women and men, particularly in intimate relationships, can be explained by gender-based differences in speech style or 'genderlects'. Much of Tannen's treatment is objectivist in the sense that it shows how the style of women's speech has subtly different text conventions from that of men. However, her approach to these differences is essentially 'contextualist', in Bradford's sense, which I outlined in the first section of this chapter. Tannen claims, for example, that 'boys and girls grow up in what are essentially different cultures, so talk between women and men is cross-cultural communication' (1992: 18). Although the concept of genderlect implies that differences in style stem from the encoder of the message, it is clear from many of Tannen's examples and comments that the role of the decoder is also vitally important. In other words, men and women hear the style they want to hear, to which they are socially and culturally primed. Indeed, she concludes that intimate communication between the sexes is best improved not by changing speech styles but by raising listener awareness of genderlect differences. She makes a plea for a more effective affective stylistics, though not in these terms.

The idea that the predisposition of the decoder is a major factor in the stylistic interpretation of texts is chiefly associated with reader-response theory as a form of literary criticism. At its most extreme this view asserts that we more or less impose style on text according to our expectations. The most famous and controversial exposition of this view is Fish's account of how groups of students impose all kinds of interpretations on the following list of linguists' names, simply because they have been told it is an example of seventeenth-century religious iconographic poetry:

Jacobs-Rosenbaum
    Levin
      Thorne
      Hayes
        Ohman(?) [Fish 1980: 323]

In a witty commentary Fish himself admits that the names are fortuitously helpful in promoting the students' interpretation, since most of them have biblical connotations. Nevertheless, he uses this experiment, which he claims to have replicated many times, to justify the theory that: 'Interpretation is not the art of construing but the art of constructing. Interpreters do not decode poems: they make them' (p. 327).

In a cogent critique of Fish's position regarding this 'poem', Bradford (1997: 198–200) queries why readers made nothing of the poem's apparent lack of formal structure, while acknowledging that some might have found such formlessness stimulating. One idea which he overlooks is that this list of names is highly elliptical: minding the gaps in this 'poem' invites the affective readings Fish reports. The distinction Barthes makes between 'readerly' and 'writerly' texts is useful here. In simple terms, texts which make fewer interpretative demands on the reader are *lisible*: they can, in Fish's words, be construed. Texts which require the interactive effort of the reader are *scriptible*: they must, in Fish's words, be constructed (Barthes 1990: 4–6). As a poem, Fish's list of names is highly *scriptible*, not, in this case, because of its rich plurality, but because of its indeterminate code. That indeterminacy is structurally realized by its highly elliptical form. So much is missing that readers have literally to write the poem themselves.

To suggest that affective stylistics works best on highly elliptical texts would be a clear overgeneralization. There are many other textual and contextual factors that can render a text *scriptible*. We can, however, fairly safely say that highly elliptical texts make interpretative demands on readers. This is a matter of both quality and quantity. Contextually unsupported gaps or telegraphic strings of indeterminate structure are qualitatively more challenging to readers in quite specific ways. In quantitative terms, the more gaps there are in a text, especially of these types, the more its meanings will require active construction by the reader. Grant-Davie has a very positive view of these demands and a fresh angle on their implications:

> . . . ellipsis can have the effect of creating a bond of respect and shared assumptions between the author and the reader. They become collaborators in the discourse. Consequently, the elliptical text is exclusive in the sense that it is not designed for all readers, just for those who can bridge the gaps within the text. (1995: 461)

The highly elliptical *scriptible* text, then, not only challenges readers, but when they have met that challenge, gives them membership of an exclusive group: the constructors of the text. Perhaps the real attraction of Fish's list of names for those who have poured over its meaning is the promise of entry it gives to such a group or at least the knowledge that such an act of reading is a very exclusive one.

Exercise 8.4

The following text is a 'found poem' compiled in the same manner as Fish's list. With the information that it is an early modernist love lyric, construct a plausible meaning by bridging the gaps within this *scriptible* text.

> Paris
> (The Inextinguishable)
> The Year 1905
> Clouds
> The Girl from Arles:
> A Song of Summer.

Discussion of Exercises

Exercise 8.1

Canto 49 of Pound's vast poetic discourse *The Cantos* is commonly known as 'The Seven Lakes Canto' because of its first line: 'For the seven lakes, and by no man these verses' (1987: 244). The canto consists, for the most part, of translations and reworkings of Chinese poems accompanying paintings of river scenes. This provenance is a clue to the elliptical lyricism of the extract. Pound's concept of the poetic image as a presentational rather than an explanatory device is closely linked to the notion that the Chinese ideogram is a perfect medium for such images, an idea he derived from the sinologist Ernest Fenollosa whose paper, 'The Chinese Written Character as a Medium for Poetry', he discovered in 1915 (Wilson 1997: 99–103).

In translating and reworking Chinese ideograms into English, Pound tries to find structural equivalences in an attempt to create an ideogrammatic feel to the very different verbal textures of the English language. In earlier poems derived from the Chinese, especially those collected in *Cathay* (1915), Pound tended to 'fill out' the English syntax. Commenting on this process, Qian suggests a likely reason: 'In translating Chinese poetry, especially in the early decades of the twentieth century when Western audiences were still unfamiliar with the "elliptical method", I think it was well-advised to insert missing pronouns, connectives, noun forms, and verb forms where necessary' (1995: 162). However, as Qian goes on to note, when translating passages from the Chinese in *The Cantos*, Pound 'adopts the elliptical technique without reserve'. This extract from 'The Seven Lakes Canto' exemplifies that technique. The opening telegraphic phrase, 'Autumn moon', sets the scene, acting as a subheading for what follows. It presents, without obvious sentence structure, its image, upon which subsequent images hang. A less drastic deviation from 'standard language' in Mukařovský's sense of the term is the omission of definite articles in such phrases as: 'against [the] sunset', '[the] Evening', '[the] sharp long spikes of the cinnamon', 'amid [the] reeds'. Definite articles, as their name suggests, act to identify specific referents within particular contextual frames. Their omission creates indefiniteness: this is not a specific sunset on a particular evening, but an image of timeless recurrence like the ancient painting it originally relates to. This is reinforced by the lack of verbally realized action in 'and through it [the] sharp long spikes of the cinnamon [ ]'. Here the gap can be filled with appropriate verbs, such as 'emerge', 'protrude', 'stick out' or even the more static 'are visible'. The lack of a main verb emphasizes the presentational quality of the image for the reader. And so it is with the final line, 'a cold tune amid reeds', whose structural ambiguity renders its relation to the preceding text uncertain. As a noun phrase, it seems to provide an aural equation for the protrusion of long spikes of cinnamon: '[they are like] a cold tune amid [the] reeds'. As a new reduced clause, it apprehends some unidentified sound in the scene, as this possible expansion suggests: 'a cold tune [can be heard] amid [the] reeds'. The first of these readings makes objects startlingly unfamiliar. The second, by presenting new, unexplained detail, contributes to defamiliarization in a less drastic but no less effective way. Telegraphic ellipsis and paratactic juxtaposition have made such ambiguities possible, adding to the timelessly fresh depiction of a recurrently familiar event.

Exercise 8.2

Since weather forecasts are about an extralinguistic phenomenon in the real world, they are functionally referential. Within that general function, their purpose is twofold: to report current conditions and to predict a usually quite short-term future outlook. Both samples here are of written forecasts, despite the very different media from which they are taken, so we might expect them to have certain text conventions in common, even though superficially they are rather different. The newspaper provides a brief national summary, 'Windy. Cold in the north. Mild in the south', before going through the regions, and a general outlook at the end, 'Periods of rain interspersed with sunshine and showers'. The teletext provides neither of these, though further forecast periods are given on subsequent pages. Both reports are organized according to regions, a text convention that also applies to broadcast weather forecasts. The newspaper has to label each regional entry, while the teletext uses a colour code relating to a map, thereby saving on text and creating a more interesting and visually distinguishable presentation. Both forecasts are very modestly predictive as well as reportive, using vague temporal markers, such as 'then', 'later' and 'at times', though the newspaper risks the more precise 'tonight'. This temporal/predictive vocabulary can be seen as a lexical text convention along with more specific weather terms: 'squally showers', 'gales', and the more precise 'fresh to strong south-westerly wind'. Both reports are conspicuously devoid of technical meteorological terminology, though the newspaper has some of this on an accompanying map. Both texts give a temperature range for each region: the teletext only provides Celsius, whereas the newspaper gives both Celius and Fahrenheit.

While each entry in the newspaper forecast is slightly longer than those on teletext, it is the deployment of ellipsis that is the most notable text convention of both examples. The entries are highly elliptical, being made up of telegraphically juxtaposed words and phrases: 'Windy. Gales. Frequent squally showers. Clear spells', 'Tonight, mild and windy. Min temp 12–14C (54–57F)'. There are no finite verbs in either sample, though the teletext uses a participial clause, 'easing later'. As a reduced relative clause, this has the expansion: '[which will be] easing later', the verb form reflecting its predictive function. This syntactically stripped down style allows the casual reader or viewer to scan for regionally relevant information in as concise a form as possible. Incidentally, or perhaps not so incidentally as all that, it facilitates a generality that, to some extent at any rate, makes the forecast very flexible: 'Windy. Odd showers. Clear spells', 'Windy and cloudy with some rain and drizzle at times'.

Exercise 8.3

Dickens wrote *The Pickwick Papers* as a young man. The comedy of its picaresque episodes stands in sharp contrast to the much later social criticism of *Bleak House*. Yet these brief extracts have structural devices in common that allow Dickens to sustain very different themes and tones. The first extract presents with unconcealed approval Pickwick's final home in the last chapter of the novel, while the second paints a sombre picture of fog-bound London at the very outset of *Bleak House*. Both extracts are notable for their accumulation of detail achieved by list-like enumeration. Like most lists, the language is essentially paratactic, juxtaposing and coordinating phrases and attendant clauses. The passage from *The Pickwick Papers* begins with a complete sentence: 'Everything was so beautiful!' By means of contextual ellipsis the rest of the passage enumerates every item that 'was so beautiful'. The number of gaps depends on the level at which juxtaposition and coordination are recognized. Taking into account phrasal coordination and constraints on constituents, I would gap the passage for this ellipsis as follows:

> The lawn in front [was so beautiful], the garden behind, the miniature conservatory, the dining-room, the drawing-room, the bedrooms, the smoking-room [were so beautiful], and above all the study [was so beautiful] with its pictures and easy chairs, and odd cabinets, and queer tables, and books out of number, with a large cheerful window opening upon a pleasant lawn and commanding a pretty landscape, dotted here and there with little houses almost hidden by the trees; and then the curtains [were so beautiful], and the carpets, and the chairs, and the sofas!

Note that some expansions have to be adjusted for plural items, a case of weak ellipsis of the type I discussed with respect to subordination reduction in Chapter 3. As the ellipsis consists of main verb plus complement, the whole of this long sentence lacks any fully realized main clause. In addition, there are two reduced relative clauses which further concentrate the wealth of detail: 'a pretty landscape, [which was] dotted here and there with little houses [which were] almost hidden by the trees'.

The passage from *Bleak House* is similarly verbless in its main clauses. Here, however, the opening sentence also lacks a fully realized structure: an ellipsis is apparent at the outset and the sentence doesn't provide a recoverable context for what follows. There are two potential sites for the series of ellipses that characterize the passage. One is central: 'Fog [is] everywhere.' etc. The other is sentence-initial: '[There is] Fog everywhere.' etc. An expansion involving existential sentences and clauses along these lines captures the presentational nature of the passage,

[There is] Fog everywhere. [There is] Fog up the river, where it flows among green aits and meadows; [there is] fog down the river, where it rolls defiled among the tiers of shipping, and the waterside pollutions of a great (and dirty) city. [There is] Fog on the Essex marshes, [there is] fog on the Kent heights. [There is] Fog creeping into the cabooses of collier-brigs; [there is] fog lying out on the yards, and hovering in the rigging of great ships; [there is] fog drooping on the gunwales of barges and small boats.

This reading has one practical flaw in that some of the sentence-initial ellipses are not at the beginnings of orthographic sentences. Since there is no contextually recoverable expansion, these gaps cannot be seen as reductions of paratactic clauses. These structures may be alternatively categorized as telegraphic. This is reasonable, given the affinity between some sentence-initial and telegraphic ellipses. This problem is obviated by recognizing the central elliptical site, since all the ellipses may then be seen to be telegraphic: 'Fog [is] everywhere. Fog [is] up the river . . . fog [is] down the river . . .' etc. Both readings are equally attractive in also providing a syntactic account of the elliptical parallelism that marks the passage.

How do these elliptical features contribute to Dickens's authorial style? Clearly, a writer as prolific and multifaceted as Dickens shows a considerable amount of stylistic variation. Yet, as Leech and Short note, 'this variation takes place within the encompassing medium of a pervasive Dickensian style' (1981: 63). They go on to illustrate and discuss some of the traits that contribute to this pervasive style, including 'the formal rhetoric of parallelism . . . characteristic of Dickens in many of his moods' (p. 64). As we have seen, ellipsis helps to realize that parallelism in the passages of very different mood discussed in this exercise. The authorial style we know as 'Dickensian' is the product of a wide range of linguistic features as well as social and historical detail, of which elliptical parallelism is only a small, but nevertheless significant, device.

Exercise 8.4

Any interpretation of this 'found poem' depends on an interaction between what the reader brings to the act of reading it and the meanings made possible by the text itself. Given the information that it is an early modernist love lyric, the reader can, for instance, assume a series of elliptically encoded images of place, time and person. My own minimal

expansion of this series of telegraphic ellipses results in the following
version:

[In] Paris
(The Inextinguishable [city])
[In] The Year 1905
[Through] Clouds
[Came] The Girl from Arles:
A Song of Summer [ensued].

This construction of the poem suggests it records the onset of a significant love affair, a construction the text allows, but does not dictate.
Semantic relations that the reader can elaborate upon are hinted at by
juxtaposition, for example, in the way that the bracketed '(The Inextinguishable)' comments on 'Paris' or 'The Girl from Arles' prefigures 'A
Song of Summer'. The poem was found by listing the titles of six pieces
of music read at random from CD covers on a shelf. As a final exercise
in affective stylistics, you could make a 'found poem' for yourself and
elicit 'constructions' from several different people, comparing the results
of these various acts of reading.

CHAPTER 9

SPEECH STYLES AND ELLIPSIS

In previous chapters I have used specific examples of spoken language, such as casual conversation and radio phone-in debate, to illustrate different aspects of ellipsis. In this chapter I want to outline one or two of the more general factors by which speech styles may be classified. Representative or indicative examples of some speech styles will be discussed in relation to these factors, noting, where relevant, stylistic characteristics with particular reference to elliptical features.

Most types of spoken language are best described within a framework of functional styles or registers of the kind I outlined in Chapter 8. There I noted that a range of factors were involved in the variation of functional styles. These include: the field of discourse, such matters as subject and theme as well as overall purpose; the tenor of discourse, as manifest in levels of formality according to participant roles and relationships; the setting, in the way it influences not just levels of formality but also formulaic or ritual patterns of language. The other major factor is, of course, the fact of speech itself, as compared to writing: the medium is, to some extent, the fundamental basis of stylistic variation. This is sometimes referred to as the modality factor. In this context the term has nothing to do with verbal mood or the use of modal auxiliaries. The modality factor is specifically concerned with the deployment of speech as a mode or medium of language. In this respect the main distinction is between speech used in a natural or straightforward way and more complex or oblique ways, some of which may be a consequence of modern technology.

We can probably agree that, all other factors considered, speech is at its most natural and uncomplicated as a medium, when there is one addresser and one addressee who is present and can hear the speaker and respond, if appropriate. In this sense, speech is most itself when it is dialogic, interactive and face-to-face. Speech is more complex as a medium when one or more of these facets does not apply. By this token, monologic speech is less natural because, for instance, feedback and response is restricted to non-verbal cues, laughter, sighs, yawns and facial expressions. At least some element of interactivity is possible, if an audience is present, but if there is no addressee, the use of speech is further complicated. One of the most interesting examples of audienceless monologue is young children's egocentric speech, which is used, among other things as a kind of self-monitoring device to accompany action during, for example, play.

Egocentric speech is less widespread, but hardly unknown, among adults. It surfaces at moments of elation or distress, during prolonged isolation and in many other contexts. We probably all 'talk to ourselves' at times, though doing so in public has long been associated with mental disturbance, as countless literary characters, not least Hamlet, attest. More recent technology allows us to speak in monologue to an absent addressee, by means of the telephone answering machine. This technology allows for a very different kind of speech event in which a monologue addressed to someone who isn't there takes on many characteristics of interpersonal communication, such as the minimal ingredients of 'phatic' language: greetings, introductions, farewells and the like. For example, I transcribed a dozen voice mail messages and all but one addressed the receiver by name with varying levels of formality and familiarity. All used a phatic signing off formula, ranging from the plain 'Thank you' to the more casual 'Speak to you soon' and 'Cheers, bye'. There was a reasonable amount of normal non-fluency, including false starts and ongoing adjustments, such as 'I've got my [ ] I've got your fax number', as well as the usual range of fillers and hesitation phenomena. Given the uninterrupted nature and specific focus of these messages, however, they were clear in content and structure. The messages I transcribed may not be typical, of course, but they do suggest that an orientation towards the virtual addressee, manifested by some features of face-to-face conversation, helps to lessen the potential for impersonality in 'remote' forms of communication made possible by new technology.

Another complicating aspect of speech as a medium is introduced when one of its primary purposes is to be written down by others. As so-called dictation, this has a marked effect on speech style in terms of speed, pausing, repetition and overtly expressed indicators of punctuation. This kind of dictation is increasingly rare nowadays, but even in less rigid conditions, speech being written down affects delivery. For example, in educational settings, when teachers are in 'transmission mode', even though they are not strictly dictating, the fact that their students are writing down or taking notes on almost everything they say, gives their monologic speech style a markedly different quality from their interactive speech in seminar or small group settings.

Table 9.1   Speech styles: typological factors

SPONTANEITY	
Spontaneous	Non-spontaneous
Low degree of rehearsal	High degree of rehearsal
No written basis	Based on writing
NUMBER OF PARTICIPANT SPEAKERS	
One	More than one
Monologic	Dialogic
Passive audience	Interactive audience

Issues of modality cut across the discussion is this chapter, which is organized around two primary factors of spoken language: levels of spontaneity and number of participant speakers. Aspects of each of these factors are presented in Table 9.1. These aspects are listed in contrastive, more or less polarized columns, providing references points in the following discussion. However, as that discussion shows, language in use operates in more complex ways than such simple contrasts would suggest.

Levels of spontaneity

As a factor in the stylistic variation of speech, spontaneity can only be taken into account in respect of overt performance. An apparently spontaneous utterance may have been mulled over and mentally prepared for anything from a matter of minutes to days, weeks or even years. No doubt we have all experienced thinking about what we are going to say in a particular situation. But we also know that our actual speech often fails to match our carefully thought-about utterances, so that what we say turns out to be in some degree spontaneous after all. We can, of course, learn what we want to say 'by heart', but this would almost certainly involve a written version as a mnemonic device. In direct contrast to mentally rehearsed, or even learned, speech is the brilliant piece of repartee that could not possibly have been anticipated: its brilliance partly lies in the fact that it is instantaneous. Spontaneity, then, covers a spectrum of speech events from the instantaneous remark to the learned recital. The non-spontaneous end of this spectrum consists of speech with a high degree of rehearsal, most often based on writing. In an early influential discussion of the spontaneity factor Abercrombie

(1965) coined the term 'spoken prose' to encompass all forms of reading aloud from written material, including verbatim recitation, as in news bulletins, for example. It is debatable whether this last category can really count as a speech style. We hear spoken language, but only as a reproduction of a written script. More interesting as a type of spoken writing is dramatic dialogue, where the relationship between speech and writing is more subtle and complex: this topic is the subject of Chapter 11. Speech styles range from the highly rehearsed, such as stand-up comic routines, via the pre-planned, as in a more formal interview, to the properly spontaneous end of the spectrum.

Broadcast interviews provide an interesting context for speech that might be called quasi-spontaneous, since those being interviewed will be more or less aware of likely topics and questions in advance. The level of forward planning and preparation of answers will depend on the nature of the interview. For example, a high level of rehearsal is likely in interviews with politicians concerning specific news stories or with entertainers plugging a particular event. In-depth interviews, covering a wider range of personal issues, may involve less predictably focused questions, though the format and tenor of such interviews will be well known to the participants. Interviews of this kind are conducted by Jeremy Isaacs for BBC Television's *Face To Face* series and I have chosen three of these to exemplify quasi-spontaneous speech. The participants were comedian and writer Ben Elton, actor Ian McKellen and Martin Bell, broadcaster and current member of parliament. These interviews stick fairly closely to the same format, an encounter of approximately forty minutes in which the interviewer is never seen and most of the time the interviewee's face is in full close-up on the screen. The defining criterion of these interviews is that only the interviewer asks questions. This factor of non-reciprocity is heightened by the format just described.

The discourse of these interviews is, then, a non-reciprocal series of contextual rejoinders. One way of looking at the textual quality of such interviews is to focus on the amount and type of ellipsis in these contextual rejoinders. For this purpose I transcribed the interviews and classified all the responses. One general quality was noticeable for all three interviews: there were hardly any overlaps between question and answer, or between answer and subsequent question. In other words, the interviews were virtually interruptionless. Even though both interviewer and interviewees showed some false starts and lapses in performance, this lack of overlaps and interruptions creates a very different texture from spontaneous informal conversation and, indeed, from political interviews where interruptions are often bluntly ill-mannered. A further general quality differentiated one of the interviewees from the other two. Bell's answers were generally succinct in comparison with those of Elton and McKellen who were more expansive in their responses. Consequently, the interviewer asked Bell twice as many questions, adding supplementaries within a topic to prompt further answers.

My classification of the rejoinders has three categories. First, there are non-elliptical responses. Where the rejoinder is a direct answer, it may shun ellipsis by repeating the material of the question or using pronominal substitution or both:

> JI: Do you wear that white suit every day?
> MB: I wear it every day when I'm on duty.

Quite often, however, the non-elliptical response evades or even invalidates the question:

> JI: How would you describe yourself now?
> BE: I don't try and describe myself . . .

Sometimes the response is not a direct answer to the question at all, but creates an oblique answer by means of implicature:

> JI: You fitted in easily there? (at grammar school)
> IM: I was an absolutely dreadful head boy . . .

The initial rejoinder does, on many occasions, lead into further elaboration that may well answer the question directly in the end. A total of 61 per cent of all the responses were non-elliptical in the ways illustrated here.

My second rejoinder category is the yes/no response that ellipts the whole of the question. Of all responses 25 per cent fell into this category. It can be considered stylistically significant that not one of them was 'bare'. Each interviewee supplements his answer every time. McKellen invariably uses coordination to do so:

> JI: Was that a busy time for you?
> IM: Yes [it was a busy time for me], and I had thought at that time I was going to act.

The other two interviewees do not use this additive construction, but simply juxtapose further information:

JI: Do you miss war reporting?

MB: No [I don't miss war reporting], I never enjoyed being shot at.

Within this category I have also included adverbial rejoinders to yes/no questions, which in effect take into account the whole of the question. For example, when Ben Elton is answering questions about his role as master of ceremonies at a venue for new or aspiring stand-up comedians, the following exchange takes place:

JI: Did you gong people off?

BE: Occasionally [I gonged people off], because they were dying.

Again, none of these adverbial rejoinders was unaccompanied by a supplementary sentence or clause. An unqualified yes, no or adverbial would not be appropriate in an interview where cooperative revelation of ideas and opinions is the whole point of the exercise.

About 14 per cent of all rejoinders fell into my third category, elliptical responses not involving a qualified yes, no or adverbial. Most of these were responses to *wh*-questions, as in this example:

JI: What was destroyed?

IM: Er, a normality [was destroyed].

Here a clause element, the predicate of the antecedent clause, is omitted. Sometimes, however, whole clauses or clause complexes are involved in the ellipsis:

JI: When did you realize that Bosnia was going to mean something much more to you?

MB: I think [I realized that Bosnia was going to mean something much more to me] in the first week.

The highly abbreviatory effect of such ellipsis is underlined by this kind of expansion. Judging by the high incidence of non-elliptical rejoinders, we might speculate that these interviewees took fewer opportunities to abbreviate their responses in this way because of the interview format itself. However, a correlation between ellipsis in contextual rejoinders and level of formality would need to be investigated by surveying large amounts of data in settings of varying formality.

Exercise 9.1

The particular interview format of *Face To Face* provides a useful point of comparison between individual interviewees, since they are all at some stage asked the same one or two questions about their parentage. Set out below are the transcripts of this sequence for Martin Bell, Ben Elton and Ian McKellen respectively. Compare the level of ellipsis in each interviewee's responses. To what extent do their answers reflect what I have told you about their overall patterns of response?

JI: Where were you born?

MB: I was born in Redisham, Suffolk, the sort of high plateau of the blessed corner of England.

JI: Who was your father?

MB: My father was a remarkable man, a farmer, a writer . . .

JI: Where were you born?

BE: Er, I was born in Lewisham hospital in south east London and, er, went home to our house in Catford.

JI: Who are your parents?

BE: Well, my mother is now retired, but she was an English teacher . . . and my father was a lecturer in physics . . .

JI: Where were you born?

IM: Er, [ ] in the hospital in Burnley in Lancashire . . .

JI: Who were your parents?

IM: My mother, Marjorie Sutcliffe [ ] from Cheshire where she'd met my father, Dennis McKellen. They'd met probably going to church.

Number of participant speakers

The next major factor in categorizing speech styles is the number of participant speakers. As Table 9.1 makes clear, the basic contrast is between speech by a single speaker and speech by more than one participant speaker. The premise of this split is that, regardless of formality or level of rehearsal, speech involving more than one speaker will have characteristics that are excluded from monologue, such as turn-taking and rejoinder sequences. Furthermore, where rehearsal is minimal or absent and there is no written basis, conversation is natural. Conversation is deemed natural, not just because it is unrehearsed, but also because it is the commonest way for people to communicate and interact with each other. It is the interactive nature of dialogic speech that is highlighted by the analysis of contextual rejoinders and other exchanges. Yet this attention to interactivity and turn-taking can obscure an interesting issue with regard to the number of participant speakers in conversation. It is an issue that Abercrombie addresses as well as anyone in his seminal discussion of the topic:

> Under 'conversation' I would include all those linguistic occasions when there is the opportunity to give and take; when it is understood that, at least in theory, there is more than one active participant, however long one of the participants may go on for. (1965: 2)

While the dialogic potential of conversation is rightly signalled by the notion of 'give and take', Abercrombie prompts the question of whether long turns are in effect monologic. Is there an optimum turnover of participants in a conversation below which dialogue can no longer be said to be taking place? If the possibility of give and take becomes very remote, then a long turn may be indistinguishable from a monologue with a designedly passive audience. Speakers who 'hog the floor' and won't allow others 'to get a word in edgeways' are monologuists in spirit, if not by Abercrombie's definition.

Broadcast discussion programmes which grant individual speakers uninterrupted turns provide useful examples of the interplay between monologic and dialogic speech within conversational settings. One such programme is BBC Television's *Question Time*, in which topical questions from members of the audience are addressed by guest panellists. The format is fairly standard. A questioner from the floor is invited by the programme's chair, David Dimbleby, to put a question. Dimbleby then briefly clarifies the question and invites the first panellist to answer. A discussion of the Home Secretary Jack Straw's role in the extradition proceedings against General Pinochet is initiated in precisely this way, as the following transcript (from the programme on 10.12.98) shows:

Q: Was Jack Straw's decision brave and ethical or was he passing the buck to Spain?

DD: The decision, of course, to allow General Pinochet to go before the magistrate tomorrow for possible extradition to Spain. Francis Maude, was it a brave and ethical decision?

Note the ellipsis of any linking verb in Dimbleby's elaboration, such as '[This was] The decision, of course . . .' or 'The decision [was], of course . . .'. This enhances cross-speaker cohesion by putting his comment in apposition with the questioner's. Francis Maude, a Conservative politician, knows that Dimbleby's question is an invitation to speak at length on the topic, so his initial 'No', which presupposes the whole of the question, would be inappropriate, if left bare:

> FM: No [it was not a brave and ethical decision]. I think it was a cowardly decision really . . .

There follows from Maude a quite lengthy rehearsal of the Conservative line that the Home Secretary has given in to left-wing pressure and that, in any case, Chile is now a democracy friendly to Britain. As Maude is concluding this stage in his argument, Dimbleby tries to ask a supplementary question. There is some overlap and resulting indistinctness here, which I indicate with underlining:

> FM: If the Chileans are ready to draw a line under their past, then I don't think, see that it's our business to second guess them . . .
>
> DD: Did the Pinochet . . .
>
> FM: Well let me finish the point.

Maude is agitated because his legitimate monologic turn has been interrupted. Variants of 'Let me finish' or 'I let you have your say, now you let me have mine' are very common on such programmes. However, as what he goes on to say demonstrates, he is also anxious to air the second stage of his argument:

> FM: The people of Northern Ireland who have suffered terribly in the last thirty years, they have been ready to draw a line under the past, and sickening though it is, we've been ready to see convicted murderers, people who've, who've convicted, committed horrible murders in the very recent past, as part of the price of drawing the line, we've been prepared to see them, er, er, being released back into society . . .

Other Conservative politicians at the time made a similar link between the Pinochet issue and the release of prisoners in Northern Ireland, so this particular line of argument can be seen to be an agreed Conservative tactic for deploring an aspect of the Northern Ireland peace process under the guise of talking about something else: it can be brought to people's attention as part of 'drawing a line under the past'. At this stage it seems as though Maude could continue this monologue indefinitely, so Dimbleby interrupts. Maude has had his allotted monologue and concedes to engage in a dialogic exchange with further overlaps and lapses:

FM: And that's <u>caused terrible, that's caused</u> . . .

DD: <u>So it's not to do with the law</u> in your view, the decision's political, not legal.

FM: Well I think in Jack Straw's case it is political, yes, it absolutely is. He's given way to political <u>pressure and and</u> . . .

DD: <u>But if it was</u> the legal decision, what would, what would the decision be in your view?

FM: That's a matter for the law, I mean, for the courts. I don't know, I'm a politician.

Note that, as contextual rejoinders, Maude's replies are not immediately elliptical. His first response does use ellipsis to re-emphasize his view, however: 'Well I think in Jack Straw's case it is political, yes, it absolutely is [political]'. His second reply contains a delayed contextual ellipsis that refers back to Dimbleby's question: 'I don't know [what the decision would be], I'm a politician'. Earlier I made the point that political interviews are often characterized by interruptions. Although part of a wider discussion, this exchange has some of the qualities of a political interview, with a media figure firing questions at a politician. Maude resorts to a rather lame and self-contradictory response, denying the commonly acknowledged and practised role of Home Secretaries in judicial affairs:

DD: But he says he's operating as a lawyer effectively, as the Home Secretary. It's a quasi-legal, quasi-legal decision.

FM: But that's a cop-out, David.

The above transcripts exemplify a pattern of possibly semi-rehearsed monologic turns alternating with 'give and take' exchanges. On this evidence we can suggest that the concept of face-to-face monologue is most applicable in fairly specific discourse settings where the status of a particular speaker rules out any possibility of exchange, such as a formal lecture, a sermon, a judge's summing up. Elsewhere the takers of long conversational turns, as this panellist shows, may be monologuists at heart, but Abercrombie's criterion seems to hold good: long turns may be monologic, but they are not monologues.

Exercise 9.2

Like many live debate shows, *Question Time* includes an element of audience (Aud) participation. Here is a transcript of a later stage in the same debate where members of the audience are brought into the discussion. Are there any elliptical features here or are the gaps entirely a matter of performance lapse and normal non-fluency?

DD: Do you agree, do you agree with Francis Maude? (pointing to a member of the audience)

Aud 1:   I agree with Francis Maude. I think that to capture or to kidnap, erm, a gentleman like <u>Pinochet</u> . . .

Another panellist: <u>Gentleman</u>?

Aud 1:   a gentleman like Pinochet landing on our shores, landing on our shores voluntarily, er, is amazing, particularly when his own country want him back and that, as has been said, is now a proper democratic country and they should be given the chance to . . . Can I just have, make another point <u>Mr Dimbleby, why didn't</u> . . .

DD: <u>But stick to, stick</u> . . .

Aud 1:   Why don't we arrest the communist leaders of China, the communists who come from Russia, or why didn't we arrest the Japanese, er, er, Emperor who was here <u>the other week</u>?

DD: <u>Do you agree</u> with him? (pointing to another member of the audience)

Aud 2:   No I don't, and 70 per cent of the people of Chile said they wanted him tried and they wanted him tried in Europe. And if the people of Chile want that, I think that's a very important . . . (audience applause).

Discussion of Exercises

Exercise 9.1

The most interesting point of comparison between the way individual interviewees respond to the same questions is how closely their answers reflect their predominant style across the whole interview. Martin Bell and Ben Elton both provide non-elliptical answers. They repeat, rather than omit, the propositions embodied in the questions, 'I was born in . . .', 'My father was . . .', though Elton chooses not to repeat 'My parents were . . .' by individuating his mother and father immediately. These replies reflect the higher incidence of non-elliptical responses from Bell and Elton across the whole interview compared with Ian McKellen whose proportion of elliptical rejoinders is much greater. Here are McKellen's answers to the key questions with elliptical gaps indicated:

JI: Where were you born?
IM: Er, [I was born] in the hospital in Burnley in Lancashire . . .
JI: Who were your parents?
IM: My mother, Marjorie Sutcliffe [was] from Cheshire where she'd met my father, Dennis McKellen. They'd met prob-ably going to church.

McKellen's answers avoid redundant repetition but they also avoid asserting the propositions in the questions. This is particularly noticeable in his second answer where he avoids 'My mother was . . .' by ellipsis and 'My father was . . .' by shifting to how and where his parents met. The interviewer in clearly not satisfied with this, since he immediately follows up with: 'What did your father do?' McKellen, as if chastized for not having given the 'right' information, replies, non-elliptically: 'He was a civil engineer . . .'.

Exercise 9.2

The discourse structure of live debate shows is an interesting one in terms of the number of participant speakers and the status of the audi-ence. Where there is a set of panellists who do most of the talking, the audience is passive for much of the time, witnessing the exchanges of the panellists rather like the audience of a play overhears the exchanges of actors on stage. However, unlike most plays, some members of the audience become active participants in the debate. On the programme *Question Time* this audience participation is kept fairly orderly through the chair, who invites contributions. Even so, people do shout out or interrupt, though on this occasion it is another panellist who responds with incredulity to the opinion of an audience member: 'Gentleman?'. It is difficult to know whether to count such interjections as genuine contextual rejoinders or not. There is no straightforward recoverability, as there would be in the following exchange:

A: General Pinochet is a gentleman.
B: [Is he a] Gentleman?

However, there is a cohesive relation between the audience member's statement and the panellist's interjection, even though a contextually recoverable expansion is inappropriate. Compare this with the clear-cut contextual rejoinder that the second audience member uses to assert her opinion:

DD: Do you agree with him?
Aud 2: No I don't [agree with him] . . .

The extent of ellipsis in this kind of rejoinder seems to grade the strength of the reply. A fully ellipted 'No' is much less vehement than a non-elliptical 'No I don't agree with him'. The actual reply 'No I don't' falls somewhere between.

Most of the gaps here, as with other instances of natural conversation, stem from interruptions and other features of normal non-fluency, such as false starts and repetitions. While much conversational repetition is likely to be a kind of lapse in performance, it is worth noting that, as with other styles of language, it can be used as a rhetorical device. There are two possible instances in this extract. The first audience member says: 'a gentleman like Pinochet landing on our shores, landing on our shores voluntarily'. The repetition here supports the effect of emphasizing 'voluntarily' when the speaker gets to it. The second member of the audience to speak says: 'they wanted him tried and they wanted him tried in Europe'. In this case the repetition is a common rhetorical formula for reinforcing the point being made.

CHAPTER 10

SPORTS COMMENTARY

The language of sport is a much broader topic than that addressed in this chapter. Sport is spoken and written about in a wide variety of contexts from casual pub debate to highly technical instruction manuals. Each of these ways of speaking and writing about sport is influenced by the full range of stylistic factors and not just its subject or theme. Even what is unequivocally 'reportage' shows considerable variation, not only from sport to sport, but, most relevantly here, between spoken and written accounts. Aspects of function and modality related to the eye-witness immediacy of play-by-play reportage give spoken sports commentary a quite different quality from most written sports reports. There is, however, one linguistic feature common to the language of sport in all its guises: its specialist vocabulary. Much of this is specific to individual sports, though some is generic. Most sports have referees and penalties, for example, though only some have fouls, while others have code violations. In any case, we would expect to hear and read such generic and specific lexical items in all contexts where sport is referred to. Once we begin to focus on broadcast sports commentary, however, features exclusive to speech can be identified. Linguists are particularly interested, for example, in what Ferguson, in his influential paper on sports commentary (1983), calls 'the prosodic pattern' of sports announcer talk, including variations in speed, volume and the intonational movement of the voice in relation to reported sporting action. Such prosodic features are closely related to the characteristic grammatical patterns of broadcast sports commentary that are the main topic of this chapter and will be noted where appropriate in what follows.

Two types of commentary

In her treatment of sports announcer talk Holmes makes a useful distinction between the 'play-by-play description' that constitutes commentary on the sporting action, and 'colour commentary', a term for 'the more discursive and leisurely speech with which commentators fill in the often quite long spaces between spurts of action' (1992: 277). One fairly reasonable hypothesis is that the description of action sequences would be characterized by a more abbreviated speech style, as commentators try to capture events instantaneously, while the discursive and leisurely speech between actions would allow for more expansive, less abbreviated language. If this is the case, the incidence of ellipsis is likely to be a marker. Commentary on fast-moving action sports is the obvious context for revealing such a contrast, so it is worth looking at commentary on a slower-paced sport to see if differences occur. For this purpose I have chosen commentary on the 1998 British Open Golf Championship. The first extract is a piece of conversational 'colour commentary', involving two presenters, following the completion of the 12th hole by the golfer, Tiger Woods:

> A: Tony, I'll tell you something, Tiger Woods is a real rebel, you know, isn't he? Cos he has a cheese and pickle sandwich this afternoon, and yesterday he used the ladies loo instead of the gents at the 11th.
> B: Well, you know, I didn't know that.
> A: What's he gonna do tomorrow?
> B: I just don't know what I'm going to say to that. You know, I suppose it was convenient.
> A: Russell Black from Westerhope Golf Club was the green keeper at the 11th yesterday and he spotted Tiger trying to force the door on the gents by the 11th green, realized it was occupied and so he looked over his shoulder, hoping no-one would see, and he slunk into the ladies. (BBC Radio 5, 17.7.98)

This piece of trivial banter, designed to fill in the quite considerable spaces between golfing action, is quite carefully structured in comparison with wholly spontaneous conversation. The register is colloquial, signalled by contracted verb forms like 'isn't' and 'don't' and a sprinkling of more casual forms, such as 'cos' and 'gonna'. The turn-taking is very orderly, however, and there are no interruptions. The syntax is more or less fully realized, though there is a lapse in performance in the final bit of narrative. From the context it is clear that the subject of 'realized it was occupied' is Tiger, but the structure of the sentence doesn't match this intended meaning. One sport-specific term involves a conventional ellipsis, in that it is customary to refer to a hole on a golf course by its number alone: 'the 11th [hole]'.

Compare this background filler with commentary by a single presenter on a spurt of action that took place a few minutes later, when the golfer, Jesper Parnevik, putted at the 10th hole:

> With his black upturned cap peak showing for all to see the advertising on the front, the double advertising, settles over it. He's gonna have to hit this quite hard. Fires it up the hill. He's got a good weight on it. Oh, very good effort! (BBC Radio 5, 17.7.98)

Within this bit of play-by-play commentary, it is significant that the two actions are described by subjectless clauses: '[He] settles over it', '[He] fires it up the hill'. Given that Parnevik has not been mentioned by name by the previous commentator, these ellipses have a fairly distant antecedent, but absolute explicitness gives way to other stylistic considerations here. A further sentence-initial ellipsis occurs in the commentator's assessment of the shot: 'Oh, [it's a] very good effort!'. In his survey of American sports commentary, Ferguson notes two categories of 'simplification'. One is the widespread absence of sentence-initial material, which he terms 'prosiopesis'. His examples are very similar to those noted above. Either the subject pronoun is deleted, as in: '[He] pops it up', or subject pronoun plus copular BE, as in: '[It's] a bloop single'. Ferguson provides a neatly comprehensive rationale for this kind of sentence-initial ellipsis that is worth quoting in full:

> It seems likely, however, that prosiopesis in SAT (sports announcer talk) serves to 'index the moment' as nonleisurely (you have to speak rapidly and concisely), informal (you mustn't sound too bookish), exciting (like the attention-getting language of headlines or advertising copy), and vignette-quality (like captions of pictures). (Ferguson 1983: 159)

The background banter illustrated earlier does not have this rationale of indexing the moment. Although it may exhibit informal characteristics and present anecdotal material that may have a vignette-like quality, the element of urgency is absent. Ellipsis is, at least in part, the mechanism by which the two variants of sports commentary are differentiated.

Exercise 10.1

The following is an extract from television commentary on the same Open Golf Championship. Indications of the picture shot are given in block capitals. Make a note of any ellipses and the way they characterize play-by-play description. Is there any part of the extract that could be called colour commentary?

> PARNEVIK MEASURING HIS SHOT AT THE EDGE
> OF THE GREEN
> Parnevik at the 11th. Looks as if he's going to putt this. He's used his, er, this club many times.
> PARNEVIK WITHDRAWS FROM TAKING HIS SHOT
> Just, just people on the hill. Voices carry with the wind behind. They don't perhaps realize it on occasion. Parnevik seems to love this championship, he's played so well the last couple of years.
> PARNEVIK PLAYS HIS SHOT SUCCESSFULLY
> That for a four.
> CUT TO SCOREBOARD
> Alphabetical scores for you. (BBC1 TV, 17.7.98)

Football commentary

The second category of simplification noted by Ferguson is the deletion of copular BE from the middle of a sentence, usually after the name of a player, as in his example: 'McCatty [is] in a tough spot' (Ferguson 1983: 160). This is similar to the last example I referred to in the discussion of Exercise 10.1: 'That [is] for a four'. The effect of copular BE deletion is to produce telegraphic strings typical of much play-by-play description. However, as we saw in Chapter 5, telegraphic ellipsis operates on a much wider array of elements than copular BE or even other lexical verbs, producing sentences of fairly indeterminate structure that rely on situational factors for resolution. Even a brief extract from a football commentary offers an example of this type:

> Cesar Sanpaolo then loses possession to Deschamps. Desailly [ ] to Leboeuf, who certainly doesn't seem overawed by the occasion. (BBC Radio Five Live, 12.7.98)

In the situational context of listening to football commentary we can readily understand the telegraphic expression marked in this extract. A reasonable expansion would be: 'Desailly [passes the ball] to Leboeuf'. Two things are borne out by this example. First, the understood elements far exceed copular BE or any other lexical verb. Secondly, the linguistic context doesn't support the proposed expansion. One might assume that the immediately preceding sentence is not a sufficiently wide linguistic context and that the thread of discourse runs further back. In order to test this theory, here is a transcript of the previous minute's commentary:

> Lizarazu to take the throw in, twenty five yards over the half way line, nearside, French left. Thrown to Djorkaeff, back to Lizarazu. Then he's a little careless. Knocked away by Leonardo.

It is significant that what is being thrown to Djorkaeff, given back to Lizarazu and knocked away by Leonardo, is never mentioned, so situationally determined is the subject of these verbs. Most interesting is the lack of verb in '[ ] back to Lizarazu'. In a text where contextual ellipsis was operating, the verb would be anaphorically cued as 'thrown', as in: '[The ball is] thrown to Djorkaeff and [thrown] back to Lizarazu'. Here, the context of situation blocks that expansion, since Djorkaeff is not allowed to handle the ball. The listener to this commentary assumes, rightly, that Djorkaeff gets the ball back to Lizarazu by legitimate means: 'given', 'passed', 'kicked' are situationally acceptable. The similar verb-lessness, with the ball as object this time, of 'Desailly [ ] to Leboeuf' gives a formulaic quality to this phrasing. The context of situation supports our understanding that Desailly has passed the ball to Leboeuf, with the telegraphic structure of the sentence providing a syntactic framework for that understanding.

To get a feel for how ellipsis, and particularly telegraphic ellipsis, operates within commentary on a fast-moving sport whose action is sporadically, though usually briefly, interrupted, let's examine a more sustained extract from the same radio commentary on the 1998 World Cup Final. I have marked probable ellipsis sites throughout:

> France [ ] building down the right. In the area [ ] Guivar'ch and also Djorkaeff. And Roberto Carlos does not manage to avoid [ ], and then kicks the corner flag over. That'll have to be a yellow card for dissent. The linesman over on the far

side has given a corner kick to France. This has to be a yellow card. I know it's the World Cup Final, but that has to be a yellow card and it hasn't been shown to him. That was the clearest gamesmanship [ ] you could ever see on a football pitch, or rather clearest dissent [ ] you could ever see on a football pitch. [ ] Emmanuel Petit with a French corner over on the right and [ ] a header from Zidane. Zidane's there to score off the post. Zinedine Zidane scored the very first goal in the stadium at the start of the year. That's his first goal in the World Cup. The papers today said this would be le grand trois de Zidane. Zidane [ ] wearing Platini's number ten responds. It's France one, Brazil nil. (BBC *Radio Five Live*, 12.7.98)

One of the features of this commentary that struck me most forcefully is unfortunately lost in this kind of transcription, namely, its prosodic pattern. The speed of the commentary seems very quick and this is reinforced by other prosodic features, such as rhythmic patterning, pitch variation, emphatic stress and intonation. These features would require very detailed analysis to relate them precisely to the syntactic structure of the text, but good examples are the way the commentator uses emphatic stress and heavy falling intonation to give point to repeated assertions about Roberto Carlos's offence or repetitions of Zidane's name at the time the goal is scored.

A closer look at the overall structure of this piece of commentary reveals a direct correlation between play-by-play description and telegraphic syntax. Most of the action is captured by sentences with initial or telegraphic ellipsis: 'France [is] building down the right. In the area [is] Guivar'ch and also Djorkaeff. [This is] Emmanuel Petit with a French corner over on the right and [there's] a header from Zidane'. The central section of this text, in which Roberto Carlos commits an offence and the commentator calls for a yellow card three times, is expressed in more or less fully realized syntax. Even in the thick of such action, there is space for colour commentary of sorts. While the corner kick is being set up, the commentator has time to express his opinion further: 'That was the clearest gamesmanship [that] you could ever see on a football pitch, or rather clearest dissent [that] you could ever see on a football pitch'. The parallelism of this pronouncement is reinforced by matching reduced relative clauses. Later, incidental information about the goal scorer also uses a reduced relative clause: 'Zidane [who is] wearing Platini's number ten responds'. Ellipsis of this kind is not particularly significant to the speech style of sports announcer talk as such. It provides a kind of background level of ellipsis against which the stylistically significant telegraphic structures occur. I have marked one further gap in this bit of commentary, which occurs in the sentence: 'And Roberto Carlos does not manage to avoid [ ], and then kicks the corner flag over'. This constitutes play-by-play description of Roberto Carlos conceding a disputed corner, then kicking over the corner flag in disgust. The fact that the player has actually given the corner away is not reported. On this occasion there is no elliptical design to this gap nor is it an idiosyncratic nonrealization of the normally mandatory direct object of 'avoid'. A break in the intonation pattern suggests that it is actually a lapse in performance. The commentator is about to say something like 'avoid [letting the ball go for a corner]', but events overtake him as Roberto Carlos kicks the flag over, so he abandons this and describes the more consequential action for the listener. This kind of discontinuity is surprisingly rare, given the sometimes hectic pace of the action and the speed at which the commentary has to flow to keep up with it. In fact, the utterance is more significant for describing action without using telegraphic syntax than for its lapse in performance.

Exercise 10.2

Here is a transcript of the television commentary for the same sequence of play as the radio commentary discussed above. Identify any ellipses and suggest possible expansions. Compare the differences between this commentary and the one for radio: how do insights about ellipsis inform your comparison?

> In the middle Guivar'ch and Djorkaeff. Karembeau, Thuram.
> The two Real Madrid colleagues there again in contention.
> And Roberto Carlos lets the ball, oh he's kicked the flag in
> his annoyance at the decision. A corner's been given, but
> that was dissent by Roberto Carlos. Moroccan referee de-
> cides to have a quiet word. Petit will take the corner for
> France. Karembeau's there, Desailly is there, Leboeuf is there.
> Oh and that's a goal with Zidane, Zinedine Zidane, a header
> from the corner. France have scored first in the World Cup
> Final and it's Zidane, his first goal of the World Cup. And
> what a time to get it, twenty-seven minutes gone, the corner
> taken by Emmanuel Petit, and Zidane gets his head onto
> that, and Taffarel is nowhere. He beat the defender in the

air. And the man who scored the first goal ever in the Stade de France when it was opened at the beginning of the year against Spain scores the first goal for France in the World Cup Final against Brazil. (BBC1 TV, 12.7.98)

Horse race commentary

Golf is a relatively leisurely-paced sport with clearly forecastable breaks in play that commentators can be prepared to fill. Football offers much longer stretches of fast-moving, continuous action whose breaks in play are unexpected, such as the aftermath of a goal or injury to a player. Even so, as we have seen, elements of colour commentary, however brief, can be prepared and inserted at opportune moments. Some sports, however, consist of single 'spurts of action' that require possibly quite brief, but entirely unbroken, stretches of commentary. The sprint races in athletics or the downhill ski run are cases in point, as is the horse race, particularly over short distances on the flat.

In this final section I want to look more closely at the commentary on a single horse race. The prosodic pattern of horse race commentary is often commented upon by listeners and viewers. Although there is variation between individuals, the increase in tempo and pitch of the commentator's voice as the race progresses to its climax is characteristic of horse race commentary in general. This prosodic pattern is also fairly well documented by linguists. For example, Holmes plots the intonation contour of a New Zealand race caller's drone and notes that the 'race caller's pitch rises by about an octave during the race, and drops rapidly back to the initial pitch after the finish' (Holmes 1992: 281). Routines, formulaic utterances and specialist vocabulary also give much to the typical speech style of horse race commentary. Here, I am particularly interested in the type and distribution of elliptical expressions across a single race commentary. Given the incidence of telegraphic structures we have seen to typify play-by-play description in other sports, we can reasonably expect that commentary on such a concentrated piece of sporting action will also be characterized by telegraphic syntax.

The race at Newmarket, whose commentary I transcribed (Channel 4 TV, 29.9.98), was given by a single commentator and lasted little more than a minute, yet the commentary runs to some three hundred words. Rather than give a full transcript, my approach here will involve some fairly simple micro-statistics about the distribution of syntactic structures together with selective illustration. I first divided the text of the commentary into 'separate syntactic entities'. This deliberately vague term serves to remind us that the text is spoken and its syntax is signalled by intonation patterns and pitch movements, not punctuation. Although one or two syntactic boundaries had to be decided upon in a slightly *ad hoc* way, I was surprised at how 'neat' the text turned out to be. Some separate syntactic entities were fully realized sentences, such as:

> Through on the inside with a big rush goes Imperial Beauty.

The most notable feature of this sentence is the inversion of normal modern English word order. The 'subject, verb, adverbial' sequence is perfectly reversed here, allowing the most salient fact, the horse's name, to be placed in a prominent position at the end of the information unit. Far from being fully realized, some separate syntactic entities were extremely telegraphic, simply identifying a horse by name:

> [ ] Subeen.

In the television football commentary, discussed in Exercise 10.2, such identifications are surrounded by moments of silence, while play continues. Here they are part of a fairly hectic recital of the horses' positions in the race, that mixes full and elliptical syntactic structures:

> It's still, er, Miss Universe by a length. [Then it's] Subeen. Flanders in the yellow [is] in pursuit.

Filling the gap for such minimal utterances is also open to alternatives here. My assumed ellipsis site treats this example as an abbreviated caption for a moving picture, with an expansion that indicates some form of deictic sentence. However, the analysis that treats them as subjects whose predicates are supplied visually is also applicable and would yield expansions like: 'Subeen [comes next]'. The BE deletion of the next sentence is much more surely located: 'Flanders in the yellow [is] in pursuit'.

The text of the commentary consists of thirty-six separate syntactic entities. On the basis of analytical distinctions like those above, 53 per cent are elliptical structures and 47 per cent are fully realized expressions. This breakdown suggests that, while the urgency of the race requires a high level of abbreviated commentary, this has to be grounded in more explicit comment to maintain clarity for those following the race. This is borne out by the even distribution of elliptical and non-elliptical expressions throughout the commentary. The opening is quite typical in this respect:

> [ ] Getting away for a Group One contest. And Imperial Beauty [ ] a bit slow to stride. Early pace goes for Miss Universe with Optional running fast.

Here the picture of the horses leaving the starting box is captioned with a sentence-initial ellipsis for immediacy: '[They're] Getting away for a Group One contest'. Characteristic BE deletion identifies the slow start of one of the favourites. The next sentence, using a racing formula, 'pace goes for', makes clear who the early leaders are.

Most of the nineteen elliptical syntactic structures can be classified into the three categories illustrated so far, as follows: sentence-initial ellipsis, 32 per cent; BE deletion, 37 per cent; single nominative phrases, 16 per cent. One further example of BE deletion is worth singling out, as it also involves syntactic inversion:

> Pressing hard [is] Subeen.

The combination of displaced word order and ellipsis produces a quite distinct prosodic pattern that gives emphasis to the horse's name.

There were three further telegraphic structures that did not fall into these categories. For example, at one point the commentator identifies a horse with the phrase: 'the light colour to the black cap'. The rider of this horse is wearing a black cap with light trim and the commentator's compressed phrase pinpoints the horse as quickly as possible for the viewer. The syntax of this is uncertain, either as single noun phrase or truncated clause, but its formulaic compression is typical of the speech style of the commentary as a whole.

Within both elliptical and fully realized syntactic structures there occurred one further type of abbreviatory device typical of sports announcer talk. On several occasions the commentator uses a number alone to indicate the place of a horse: 'in second [place]', 'for third [place]'. This is directly comparable with the convention for identifying golf holes that I noted earlier. However, one interesting example in the race commentary extends this to a less obvious phrase in the following sentence:

> And it's a blanket [ ] for third.

Here the deleted head noun is not a conventionally determined term like 'hole' or 'place'. The audience needs to know the full phrase, 'blanket finish', in order to understand its abbreviated nature. There may be an interesting pointer to how language change occurs in this. It is possible that 'a blanket' will become more widely known as an absolute term for a tight finish, in which case it will no longer be perceived as an ellipsis of a larger expression. In due course, that definition will be added to the entries for 'blanket' in the dictionaries of the future, no doubt defined in relation to 'blanket finish', the term from which it is derived.

Discussion of Exercises

Exercise 10.1

Ferguson's notion that abbreviated sports announcer talk has an affinity with the captions of pictures is much more compelling in the case of television commentary, where it can be seen as a kind of oral caption for the picture on the screen. This is particularly appropriate to the first and last comments in this extract, whose label-like quality is reinforced by the fact that they do not describe actions. Their function is presentational, as these possible expansions suggest:

> [Here is] Parnevik at the 11th.
> [Here are the] Alphabetical scores for you.

These can be seen as variants of Ferguson's prosiopesis, even though they incorporate slightly different elements. The next comment is more directly descriptive of the picture:

> [It] Looks as if he's going to putt this.

When Parvenik stands back from taking his shot, the commentator provides a reason:

> Just, just people on the hill.

This expression is very close to a properly situational ellipsis, since it can only be expanded, by reference to the picture, with a fairly indeterminate paraphrase:

[Parvenik has interrupted his shot] Just, just [because of] people on the hill.

There is then a space in the action until the golfer takes his shot. This is filled with extraneous comment, first related to the reason for Parvenik's withdrawal, then of a background type:

Voices carry with the wind behind. They don't perhaps realize it on occasion. Parnevik seems to love this championship, he's played so well the last couple of years.

Interestingly, this stretch of commentary has no ellipsis. It is, in effect, colour commentary. The idea that play-by-play description alternates with colour commentary at the level of larger discursive units within a sports commentary may be more appropriate to radio than television and to some sports more than others. Here the switch from one to the other happens across fairly small units of textual organization. The switch back to play-by-play description is marked by an abrupt return to abbreviated style. As Parvenik sinks his putt, the commentator says:

That [is] for a four.

The relationship between syntax and type of sports commentary is confirmed, with ellipsis figuring as a significant marker of stylistic variation.

Exercise 10.2

Comparing the television and radio commentaries for the same sequence of play raises interesting issues about the overall linguistic style required and supported by the different media. Clearly, we always have to acknowledge that some differences may be due to the personal choices of individual commentators. Compare, for example, the attitude to Roberto Carlos's offence. Whereas the radio commentator calls repeatedly for a yellow card, the television commentator is more matter of fact:

A corner's been given, but that was dissent by Roberto Carlos. [The] Moroccan referee decides to have a quiet word.

Evaluative comments and asides are bound to show individually motivated variation, but it is clear that both commentators have also done the same 'homework' and possibly rehearsed bits of colour commentary.

Both mention that Zidane scored the first goal in the new French national stadium, though the television commentator gives a slightly different version of the same facts:

> And the man who scored the first goal ever in the Stade de France when it was opened at the beginning of the year against Spain scores the first goal for France in the World Cup Final against Brazil.

Again, what is more significant stylistically is the lack of ellipsis in this function of commentary.

In the play-by-play description there are also similarities, for example in the familiar BE deletion structure:

> In the middle [are] Guivar'ch and Djorkaeff.
> The two Real Madrid colleagues [are] there again in contention.
> The corner [is] taken by Emmanuel Petit.

However, there are also fundamentally different stylistic demands made by television commentary, some of which are signalled by different kinds of ellipsis. Most notably, the incidence of single proper names, spoken as separate tonal entities and often surrounded by substantial pauses, is unique to the television commentary: 'Karembeau [ ], Thuram [ ]'. Clearly, a radio commentator would make little sense if he merely nominated the player with the ball. Without the picture the string of players' names would be wholly inexplicit, elliptical in the stylistic, as well as the linguistic, sense. Expanding these minimal utterances is problematical. If they are seen as features of a truncated narrative, then they must be the subjects of sentences whose predicates are supplied visually, as in: 'Karembeau [has the ball], Thuram [receives the pass]'. If they are more like spoken captions for moving pictures, nominative rather than dynamic, then they are best seen as fragments of some form of deictic sentence, such as '[That's] Karembeau, [That's] Thuram'. Strings of telegraphically unattached names of players seem to be most made use of when events on the pitch are unspectacular, as in this piece of build-up play.

The television description of the Roberto Carlos offence confirms that the event was so sudden and unexpected that commentators were surprised into making lapses of performance:

> And Roberto Carlos lets the ball [ ], oh he's kicked the flag in his annoyance at the decision.

161

Again, we can see that the commentator was about to say something like '[go for a corner]', but abandoned this to cover the more interesting event. Goals, the most important events of all, have to be reported explicitly and even with a picture the television commentator is very explicit:

> Oh and that's a goal with Zidane, Zinedine Zidane, [with] a header from the corner.

There is, however, an additional kind of commentary that is unique to television: the instant replay. Barely has the commentator had time to confirm that a goal has been scored, when he must re-narrate the event as it is shown from a succession of camera angles:

> And what a time to get it, twenty-seven minutes gone, the corner [is] taken by Emmanuel Petit, and Zidane gets his head onto that, and Taffarel is nowhere. He beat the defender in the air.

There is one interesting narrative shift here. At first the action is revisited in the present tense: 'Zidane gets his head onto that, and Taffarel is nowhere'. As commentary moves from description to evaluative replay, the tense shifts to the past: 'He (Zidane, of course) beat the defender in the air'. This goal is already history.

In general, we can say that many of the actions supplied by television pictures tend to be realized verbally by the radio commentary, though not in a very exact manner. Radio commentators have to be selective in a different way, since they cannot possible report every action or event, despite their ability to talk non-stop with an amazingly sustained coherence. On the other hand, while it is the television commentator's job to identify players on screen without laboriously telling viewers what they can see for themselves, it is clear from this data that commentary on television often does just that.

CHAPTER 11

DRAMATIZING DIALOGUE

When we visit the theatre and become involved in the action of a play as it unfolds before us, we engage with the speech of the characters on stage. Regardless of its dramatic effectiveness or literary merit, the quality of that speech is distinctly odd in its modality. It is apparently spontaneous, yet it has been not just rehearsed but committed to memory. The writing it is derived from is in its turn modally strange, since it has been specifically written to be memorized and spoken as if it hadn't been written in the first place. These are aspects of the modality factor that I introduced in Chapter 9, as they pertain to the subtle and complex relationship between spoken dialogue and scripted speech. This chapter explores the role of ellipsis in the way dramatic dialogue is written in relation to spoken and speakable language. First, however, it looks at the elliptical structures that help to orchestrate and facilitate the enactment of that dialogue.

Stage directions

The general relationship between speech and writing has been extensively written about. The structuralist tradition of linguistics has particularly focused on substance, the way the graphic medium of writing relates to the phonic medium of speech. Of particular relevance here are the paralinguistic and non-verbal communication systems that accompany spoken language. As we have seen in other chapters, aspects of paralanguage, such as intonation, accent and tempo, play a significant part not only in the meaning of speech but in the style whereby that meaning is conveyed. Non-verbal gestures and facial expressions also play a vital role in face-to-face communication, reinforcing and, sometimes more significantly, contradicting verbal meaning. The written medium can convey some paralinguistic features by means of punctuation, the use of capitals and underlining to suggest prosodic pattern, volume and emphasis. But, more subtle shifts in voice tone and tempo, as well as non-verbal communication, have to be spelled out in writing.

The most explicit way that dramatists can handle paralanguage and non-verbal communication is usually covered by the term 'stage directions', which tends to mean all the bits of a playscript that are not actual dialogue. Stage directions vary in amount and explicitness from the minimal to the voluminous, depending on a range of factors, such as historical period, dramatic genre and, of course, the individual playwright, so that generalizations are hard to make. Looking at the stage directions of one play by a modern dramatist does, however, allow us to classify some of their functions. For this purpose I have chosen Harold Pinter's play *A Night Out* (1960).

The first category of stage directions serve the purpose of identifying the setting of a scene, as in the following selection:

> *A coffee stall by a railway arch.* (p. 48)
> *The lounge of* MR KING'S *house.* (p. 58)
> *The* GIRL'S *room.* (p. 74)

Note that these are all detached noun phrases, whose structure and function as telegraphic fragments are similar to those we have encountered in a range of literary and non-literary texts in other chapters. Here they serve as introductory headings and subheadings within the overall discourse of the play as written text which is reflected in an expansion along the lines of: '[The scene is] A coffee stall by a railway arch'.

The next category of stage directions, and the most prevalent, are those which describe the movements and actions of characters around the stage, their use of props, their physical interaction with other characters:

> ALBERT *walks through the railway arch across to the bench.*
> (p. 54)
> KEDGE *and* BETTY *are dancing.* (p. 58)
> *She turns on the gas fire and lights it.* (p. 75)

These are all structurally complete sentences. Although their function is directive, their form is rarely imperative. Their verbs are mainly simple present tense with some present progressive forms. Unlike the imperative form, this present tense description or narration ensures the explicit identification of characters essential to performance. Pronominal reference is only used where it is unambiguous. Some directions of this type may indicate non-verbal communication:

RYAN *nods and smiles*. (p. 58)

A third category of stage direction more closely associates non-verbal gestures and expressions with what the characters are saying:

ALBERT (*touching his forehead*): No, I feel a bit ... you know ... (p. 55)
GIRL (*struggling*): What are you doing? (p. 82)

In Pinter's play the structure of this category of stage direction is invariably a present participle with or without attachments. These are best analysed as reduced subordinate clauses, either adverbial: '[as he is] touching his forehead', or relative: '[who is] struggling'. The reduced relative clause is readily attached to its antecedent: 'GIRL ([who is] *struggling*)'. However, adverbial clauses need to be attached to some main clause. This reminds us that the convention for setting out dramatic dialogue globally omits a verb of saying at each turn, so the main clause is in effect: 'ALBERT [SAYS]', to which the elliptical subordinate clause is attached:

ALBERT [SAYS] ([as he is] *touching his forehead*)

This analysis is borne out by the fourth category of stage direction, which indicates the paralinguistic features of a character's speech, as well as possible facial expressions and other gestures:

KEDGE (*brightly*): I'm listening, Mr. King. (p. 68)
ALBERT (*quietly, intensely*): Sit down. (p. 82)

Tone of voice, tempo, volume and other features that are signalled by the prosodic pattern of speech are indicated here by adverbs of manner. By definition, these adverbs qualify verbs, in this case the verbs of saying that are conventionally ellipted in the presentation of dramatic dialogue. How these adverbs are realized by the paralanguage of any particular actor is just one aspect of the larger challenge of interpreting all categories of stage direction in performance. Lexical and syntactic properties of the dialogue itself also suggest particular types of spoken delivery. Together, written dramatic dialogue and stage directions constitute a playscript that can be compared to the score of a piece of music. It allows for repeated performances of what is recognizably the same work, but depends on the individual interpretations and talents of those performing it on any particular occasion.

Exercise 11.1

Dramatists of some earlier periods, for example, Elizabethan and Jacobean, were fairly sparing with their stage directions, most of which do little more than get characters to enter and exit appropriately. Specific identifiers of setting may not be provided for many scenes and, if necessary, the setting is established in the dialogue. Directions indicating nonverbal communication and paralanguage are mostly lacking. In this case the dialogue is more or less the whole 'score'. Here is a piece of dialogue from Shakespeare's *Othello*, Act 3, Scene 3. From your reading of the text add some 'Pinteresque' stage directions. To what extent does the explicit expansion of any ellipses support your provision of such directions?

> *Exeunt Desdemona and Emilia.*
> OTHELLO: Excellent wretch! Perdition catch my soul
> But I do love thee; and when I love thee not
> Chaos is come again.
> IAGO: My noble lord . . .
> OTHELLO: What dost thou say, Iago?
> IAGO: Did Michael Cassio,
> When you wooed my lady, know of your love?
> OTHELLO: He did, from first to last. Why dost thou ask?
> IAGO: But for the satisfaction of my thought;
>   No further harm.
> OTHELLO: Why of thy thought, Iago?
> IAGO: I did not think he had been acquainted with her.
> OTHELLO: O, yes, and went between us very oft.
> IAGO: Indeed! (1603: 97–8)

Dramatizing conversation

From the examples we have looked at so far in examining the relationship between paralinguistic and other non-verbal aspects of speech and their representation in writing, it is clear that we cannot divorce substance from structure. When we turn to what are generally recognized as the structural properties of language, such as vocabulary and syntax, it further becomes clear that differences between spoken and written language at this level cannot be divorced from function and discursive context.

Where vocabulary is concerned, we can consider the types of words that occur and their distribution. The concept of core and non-core vocabulary is helpful in the first respect. Core vocabulary is common to all registers of spoken and written language, while non-core words are likely to occur in some varieties but not others. For example, words that are non-core by virtue of being slang are associated with speech, whereas non-core words that are learned or technical are more likely to occur in writing. The second consideration, distribution, can be approached purely as a matter of frequency, but the concept of density is additionally helpful. Lexical density measures the ratio of individual content words to the overall number of words in a particular text. Spoken language is generally characterized as lexically less dense than written language: for a discussion see Halliday (1994: 55–8). As we have seen from examples in earlier chapters, spoken language contains many lapses in performance, false starts and the like which involve repetition, most frequently of small function words, so lower lexical density is to be expected.

Where syntax is concerned, previous chapters have already illustrated and analysed examples from a fairly wide range of speech and writing. These have revealed trends in difference across the two mediums that are widely reported in contrastive studies. Spoken utterances are organized paralinguistically in ways that often appear quite awkward when transcribed. Syntactic boundaries within chains of, mainly paratactic, structures are not always readily discerned. Overlaps, false starts and other lapses confuse analysis, but, unless they are chronic or affect audibility, do not seem to receive much attention from participants in speech events. Written sentences are usually signalled by punctuation marks that regulate their syntactic organization and make it more transparent. While writing tends to use a wider variety of hypotactic structures, the number of major syntactic boundaries within an orthographic sentence is generally smaller than the equivalent stretch of speech, making the structure of writing easier to discern.

What implications do these rather crudely drawn, but generally attested, contrasts have for writers of dramatic dialogue? Rather than answer this question in the abstract, it is useful to discuss it with reference to some examples, with ellipsis as the common focus, as always. First, let's remind ourselves of what 'natural' dialogue is like with a further example of transcribed speech. This sample is from the beginning of a chance encounter I recorded between two old acquaintances who had not met for some years:

A: I seem to recognize that person as well.
B: Hello!
A: Hello, <u>how are you</u>?
B: <u>I didn't recognize</u> the sight of you. Yeah I'm great. How are . . . I'm fine <u>thanks, yes</u>
A: <u>Good, good</u>.
B: You're looking well.
A: Yeah, oh, I'm doing OK, yeah.

In presenting this brief sample of spontaneous conversation, I have underlined those parts where both speakers were talking at the same time. Overlaps of this kind are very common, go unnoticed by participants and do not seem to hinder communication, as long as simultaneous monologuing doesn't set in. Overlaps aside, the conversation is quite 'clean'. Speaker B does abandon one structure for another with 'How are . . . I'm fine thanks, yes'. Otherwise, the exchange is lapse free and the contextual rejoinders are orderly. The most striking quality here is the entirely formulaic nature of the exchange. In terms of Jakobson's dominant function theory, mentioned in Chapter 8, this is 'phatic' language, whereby contact is opened and sustained by means of almost ritual turns with very low information load and a high degree of personal orientation between addresser and addressee. Whatever communicative qualities are discerned here, the above speech is unlikely to be mistaken for a piece of dramatic dialogue, though the routines of phatic language are often parodied and exaggerated for comic effect in contemporary playscripts and comedy sketches.

Natural speech is variously characterized as transient, urgent or instantaneous, qualities which are related to its function as the primary order communication medium. In discussions of orality and literacy the primacy of speech is generally acknowledged. As far as the species is concerned, the emergence of writing is relatively recent. In the individual the ontogenetic inevitability of speech stands in contrast with a writing system that is unnatural and sometimes never acquired. Writing may be derived from speech, but, apart from transcription, it is not speech written down. Writing has qualities of its own, such as preservability, reflectiveness and editability, which are related to its function as a secondary order communication medium.

Speech, as the primary medium, provides the model for dramatic dialogue, which has, at least some of the time, to be speech-like. Most modern dramatists want to convey the naturalness and spontaneity of speech to some extent and may indicate this in their stage directions and by structured false starts and overlaps. However, as Short notes, the concept of normal non-fluency is really inappropriate for dramatic dialogue, since 'if features normally associated with normal non-fluency do occur, they are perceived by readers and audience as having a *meaningful* function precisely because we know that the dramatist must have included them *on purpose*' (1996: 177, original italics). On the other hand, because the writing of dramatic dialogue can be revised and reworked, it may be refined away from the contours of natural speech where this is considered to be dramatically appropriate. However, if it becomes too writing-like, it will cease to be credible when spoken as if it had not been written in the first place. This next extract, from Christopher Fry's play *Venus Observed*, demonstrates the challenge posed by the relationship between speech and writing for playwrights working in the non-realist medium of verse drama:

> JESSIE: Is everybody safe?
> DUKE: Safe: I'll not say
>   'As houses', considering what goes on,
>   But as safe and suffering as health can be.
> HILDA: It's a fortunate thing that providence
>   Was in her friendly mood tonight
>   And kept you out of Galileo's lap.
> DUKE: Not she. She saw two souls there, happily occupied
>   At the narrow end of the telescope,
>   Two star-loving minutiae, male and female,
>   Perpetua and my unoffending self:
>   And instantly shot out a vituperative
>   Tongue. (1950: 90)

There is something slightly incongruous about the language of this dialogue. The Duke has suffered a disastrous house fire. Jessie and Hilda, having seen the flames from a distance, have just arrived to make enquiries. Their conversation has the semblance of real talk. For example, both the Duke's replies begin with elliptical contextual rejoinders. The first has a straightforward expansion: '[Everybody is] Safe'. The second, 'Not she', is an abbreviated way of saying, 'She was not in her friendly mood tonight', that is both formulaic and rather mannered. Even so, we can say that Fry is attempting to be speech-like in this respect. The incongruity may be seen to stem from the lexical density of non-core words, such as 'vituperative', 'Galileo's lap' and 'minutiae' as well as the way some core words are combined in rather odd ways: 'as safe and suffering as health can be'.

The syntax of the Duke's second turn also offers a clue to the oddity of the dialogue. It has a basic coordinate structure: 'She saw two souls there and instantly shot out a vituperative tongue'. Without intervening material, coordination of predicate verb phrases can be recognized without ellipsis of the subject in the second conjunct. However, between these two coordinates is a fairly large amount of qualifying material: 'happily occupied at the narrow end of the telescope, two star-loving minutiae, male and female, Perpetua and my unoffending self'. Vocabulary and phraseology aside, the insertion of such material is much more suited to written language where the reader can rescan, if necessary, to pick up the overall structure of the sentence and confirm the subject of the second conjunct. In speech, this is much harder and the same information would have been presented in a different way. At the very least the subject of the second conjunct would have been reiterated explicitly: 'and she instantly shot out a vituperative tongue'.

In his study of odd talk and dramatic discourse Simpson concentrates on the incongruities between how characters choose to communicate and the context in which they are doing so, rather than the structural features I have looked at. For him, dramatic odd talk is epitomized by the irrational and anti-realist dialogue of the Absurdist school of theatre. Even so, his remarks about the continuity between speech and dramatic dialogue are relevant here: '. . . while everyday speech and drama discourse are not homologous modes of communication, they are none the less parallel, and expectations about well-formedness in everyday speech form the benchmark against which aberrant and incongruous discourse can be measured.' (Simpson 1998: 41). By the benchmark of everyday speech Fry's characters speak aberrantly, though not because they use weird non-sequiturs or spout total nonsense. Neither can the dimension of social class provide a full account, though the intention to parody upper class speech may be at work. The lexical and syntactic features I noted above suggest that the source of incongruity is the literate nature of Fry's dialogue: it is too writing-like to pass for everyday speech. This is not in any sense an absolute criticism of Fry's dramatic idiom which, though it is far from surreal, makes no pretence of capturing the realities of natural conversation. Fry prefers to explore a self-consciously poetic mode of theatrical expression.

Exercise 11.2

At the other end of the spectrum from Fry is the attempt to make dramatic dialogue as speech-like as possible. Look carefully at the following brief example of realist dialogue, from Trevor Griffiths's play *Oi For England*, and identify the types of ellipsis the writer uses to capture the feel of spoken exchange:

> LANDRY: Wanna come?
> FINN: No, it's all right.
> LANDRY: 'Ya gonna do?
> FINN: Mooch. Nowt.
> LANDRY: Story of our lives.
> FINN: Yeah. (1982: 31)

Dramatic monologue

To conclude this chapter, I want to look at a further, and perhaps more obvious, example of odd dramatic talk: the monologue. In Chapter 9 I made the distinction between audienced and audienceless monologue, suggesting that the modality of the latter was more complex. Both types occur in drama. Some characters do overtly address audiences, but others talk to themselves merely in the presence of an audience which, in the complex structure of dramatic discourse, they do not 'know' is there. This second type of monologue is usually known as soliloquy and, as we saw in discussing the passage from *Othello*, is meant to reveal the private thoughts of a character to the audience rather than to other characters in the play. Othello's soliloquy in that example was very brief, but other, more famous Shakespearean soliloquies, such as those of Hamlet, are much longer. They trace the logic, such as it is, of Hamlet's 'antic disposition' in finely modulated blank verse. Marvellous though they are, these soliloquies make little attempt to create an impression of Hamlet's inner speech. As we saw in Chapter 5, psycholinguistic impressionism in the representation of interior monologue was a much later development.

One possible intermediate step between Shakespearean soliloquy and modernist stream of consciousness is the so-called dramatic monologue, especially those by Robert Browning. Most of Browning's dramatic monologues are poems in which an individual character speaks aloud to a specific addressee who is implicated in the text, even if not overtly named. Although these audienced monologues are not soliloquies as such, the way they expose the inner thoughts and psychology of their personae is clearly influenced by the true dramatic soliloquy. One of Browning's poems, *Soliloquy of the Spanish Cloister* (1842), is a witty and psychologically penetrating acknowledgement of this influence. It has the primary ingredients of a dramatic monologue, since a specific addressee is apparently being spoken to:

> Gr-r-r – there go, my heart's abhorrence!
>   Water your damned flower-pots, do!
> If hate killed men, Brother Lawrence,
>   God's blood, would not mine kill you! (Jack (ed.)
>   1970: 376)

However, the title of the poem alerts us to the fact that this could hardly be spoken aloud and that the dramatic monologue is actually interior monologue. Browning is revealing the inner speech of his persona, a monk whose hatred of a fellow member of the community knows no bounds. The interiority of this monologue is confirmed in later passages where the protagonist refers to Brother Lawrence in the third person:

> Oh, those melons! If he's able
>   We're to have a feast! So nice!
> One goes to the Abbot's table,
>   All of us get each a slice.
> How go on your flowers? None double?
>   Not one fruit-sort can you spy?
> Strange! And I, too, at such trouble
>   Keep them close-nipped on the sly!

Here Browning is beginning to use the telegraphic structures that we saw Joyce making so much of in his representation of Bloom's inner speech in *Ulysses*: 'Oh, those melons!', 'So nice!', 'None double?', 'Strange!' The usage is limited and unsystematic and surrounded by the archaic phraseology Browning adopts for his character. Nevertheless, Browning is attempting to capture the abbreviated linguistic structures of talking to oneself.

One of the most striking depictions of such egocentric speech is Samuel Beckett's play *Krapp's Last Tape* (1958). Unlike Browning's poem this is a dramatic monologue in the theatrical sense, since it accompanies staged action. Furthermore, it was written long after the example of Joyce's representation of interior monologue had been available to be learned from by other writers. Given Beckett's early association with Joyce, as his secretary, it is possible to see Krapp's speech style as theatrical stream of consciousness in the Joycean tradition. Although *Krapp's Last Tape* is a play for a single character, its monologic voice has two aspects, since Krapp both speaks and hears himself speaking on tape, so there is a rapport between Krapp's present and former self. In this extract he is recording his responses to a tape from his past:

> KRAPP: Just been listening to that stupid bastard I took myself for thirty years ago, hard to believe I was ever as bad as that. Thank God that's all done with anyway. (*Pause*) The eyes she had! (*Broods, realizes he is recording silence, switches off, broods. Finally.*) Everything there, everything, all the – (*Realizes this is not being recorded, switches on.*) Everything there, everything on this old muckball, all the light and dark and famine and feasting of . . . (*hesitates*) . . . the ages! (*In a shout*) Yes! (*Pause*) Let that go! Jesus! Take his mind off his homework! Jesus! (*Pause. Weary*) Ah well, maybe he was right. (*Pause*) Maybe he was right. (*Broods. Realizes. Switches off. Consults envelope.*) Pah! (*Crumples it and throws it away. Broods. Switches on.*) Nothing to say, not a squeak. What's a year now? The sour cud and the iron stool. (*Pause*) Revelled in the word spool. (*With relish.*) Spooool! Happiest moment of the past half million. (1958: 62)

Representing the thoughts of fictional characters in dramatic monologue is to make an 'outer' psycholinguistic impression of 'inner' speech. Recalling Vygotsky's characterization of inner speech quoted in Chapter 5 as 'disconnected and incomplete', we can expect to find some of the features of Bloom's interior monologue in Krapp's speech. But the dramatic situation here is more complex in that Krapp is not just soliloquizing but recording his thoughts on tape. He is compiling a kind of oral diary, so we could also look for features characteristic of diary entries. Krapp's monologue is also the dramatic equivalent of 'free direct speech' in prose fiction. The identity of the character and the fact of his speaking are not in doubt for the audience, so there is no uncertainty in this freeness. Yet, because this text is also a blueprint for staged action, the speech is paradoxically 'unfree', overtly so to the reader and covertly to a theatrical audience, since Beckett provides meticulously detailed indicators of non-verbal communication and paralinguistic features in his stage directions, as in this sequence:

> Everything there, everything on this old muckball, all the light and dark and famine and feasting of (*hesitates*) . . . the ages! (*In a shout*) Yes! (*Pause*)
> Let that go! Jesus! Take his mind off his homework! Jesus!

The liberal use of exclamation marks further serves to indicate the vehement tone of Krapp's speech. The stage directions themselves are similar in structure and function to those of Pinter's categorized earlier. However, given that only one character is involved, the subject is regularly omitted: '[Krapp] *Broods, realizes he is recording silence, switches off, broods*'. In this way stage directions take on some of the elliptical quality of the monologue itself. Beckett seems to want to hint at the egocentric rapport between Krapp's speech and action through the language of his stage directions. In this extract the most telling example is Beckett's use of ellipsis in: '*Broods. Realizes* [he is recording silence]. *Switches off.*' The lack of an objective clause after the verb captures in abbreviated form the nature of Krapp's realization, while referring back to the earlier full version of the same stage direction. It is as if Beckett is saying: 'Krapp knows what he realizes: if you have been paying attention, director, actor, reader, so will you'.

The way in which Beckett indicates the orality of what Krapp actually says is a clear reminder that this is 'outer speech' and not just a projection of interior monologue for a theatre audience. For example, there is some normal non-fluency, though this lapse in performance has a dramatic function connected with the taping process: 'Everything there, everything, all the –'. When Krapp switches on to record this, he elaborates upon it, as speakers do when repeating themselves: 'Everything there, everything on this old muckball', before picking up the discontinued structure: 'all the light and dark and famine and feasting of . . .'. Other orality features include vocal interjections like 'Pah!' and the phonic play of 'Spooool' which Krapp savours with delight.

Structural ellipses reinforce not only the fragmentary and desultory nature of egocentric speech, but also its obliqueness to the overhearer. As with inner speech, the speaking subject is implicit and this is most obviously realized by sentence-initial ellipsis: '[I've] Just been listening to that stupid bastard I took myself for thirty years ago, [it's] hard to believe I was ever as bad as that', '[I] Revelled in the word spool'.

These sentences particularly support the idea that Krapp's tapes are oral diary entries.

Many of the other orthographically separated utterances in Krapp's monologue are oblique either because, as with inner speech, the topic and situation are givens to the egocentric speaker, or because some topic is mentioned without an adequately explicit comment. Obviously, in a short extract of this kind there are references to earlier parts of the text and this accounts for some of the obscurity. But even in such cases structural gaps show how much the egocentric speaker takes for granted. Take, for example, the exclamation: 'The eyes she had!' There are earlier references to the striking eyes of a woman, of which this is one:

> Not much about her, apart from a tribute to her eyes. Very warm. I suddenly saw them again. (*Pause*) Incomparable! (p. 58)

We might reasonably assume that Krapp is revisiting this tribute in his thinking aloud, but the structural isolation of the noun phrase, 'The eyes she had!', means any expansion can only be speculative: 'The eyes she had [were incomparable]!', or, to reinforce the exclamatory form: '[How incomparable were] The eyes she had!' Here the single noun phrase is understood as the topic of an unexpressed predicate. However, it is the overall grammatical indeterminacy of this phrase that is the chief characteristic of such telegraphic strings in the representation of egocentric speech.

Discussion of Exercises

Exercise 11.1

This passage begins the famous exchange in which Iago manipulates Othello into thinking that his wife, Desdemona, has been unfaithful. Desdemona has just been pleading the cause of Michael Cassio with Othello. A typically brief stage direction, mixing English and Latin, removes her and her maidservant from the scene: '*Exeunt Desdemona and Emilia*'. Othello's first remarks have to be read as addressed to the departed Desdemona. The only other character on stage is Iago and they are clearly not meant for him. The abbreviated exclamation, 'Excellent wretch!' is Othello's oxymoronic valuation of Desdemona and not a castigation of himself, something the following expansion shows: '[Thou art an] Excellent wretch!' We have, then, a mini–soliloquy meant for the audience only. In a film it would be best done as voice-over, so an appropriate stage direction would be along the following lines:

> OTHELLO (*aside, musingly*): Excellent wretch! Perdition catch my soul
> But I do love thee; and when I love thee not
> Chaos is come again.

Iago interrupts these thoughts with his address: 'My noble lord'. The way this is broken off by Othello's response suggests another indicator of paralanguage:

> OTHELLO (*startled*): What dost thou say, Iago?

Othello replies to Iago's question about Cassio with an elliptical rejoinder: 'He did [know of my love]'. The ellipsis itself is likely to have a paralinguistic correlation, an emphatic stress on 'did' followed by a slight pause before 'from first to last'. Iago's next turn twice takes account of Othello's question 'Why dost thou ask?' At this point Iago wants to appear indifferent, so a stage direction could be added:

> IAGO (*casually*): [I ask] But for the satisfaction of my thought;
> [I ask for] No further harm.

This second remark is ironic for the reader or the audience, of course, since we know that harm is the first thing on Iago's mind. Othello's next question picks up the elliptical thread of discourse:

> Why [dost thou ask for the satisfaction] of thy thought, Iago?

Iago's reply is subordinate to the whole of Othello's question:

> [Because] I did not think he had been acquainted with her.

The word 'think' could be subject to emphatic stress here to play on the idea of Iago's supposed ignorance. Othello seemingly cannot see where this is leading. His 'yes' confirms Cassio's acquaintance with Desdemona. The naive way he offers Iago further ammunition could be signalled with a stage direction:

OTHELLO (*openly positive*): O, yes [he was acquainted with her], and went between us very oft.

Iago's 'Indeed!' may then be delivered with an exaggerated falling intonation, betokening an irony he this time wants Othello to detect. Othello does so and the manipulation continues.

Exercise 11.2

Griffiths's play about racism in Manchester is a fine example of socialist realism in contemporary drama. In this brief exchange two members of a skinhead band part company after a rehearsal. A race riot rages outside. As with the Fry play, there is a social class dimension, but here it is the opposite end of the social scale, the disaffected urban underclass. Linguistically, this social class dimension interacts with regional dialect features with the result that non-core lexical items, such as 'mooch' and 'nowt', are markers of casual, non-standard speech. Griffiths also suggests pronunciations associated with colloquial speech by orthographic means: 'wanna', 'ya', 'gonna'. Most of all, though, it is the syntactic reduction of the dialogue that signifies the speech style of the characters. All of Landry's turns have sentence-initial ellipsis: '[Do you] Wanna come?', '[What are] 'Ya gonna do?', '[That's the] Story of our lives'. Note that in '[What are] 'Ya gonna do?' the reduction is indicated by a punctuation mark before 'Ya'. The clipped, telegraphic style is reinforced by Finn's monosyllabic contributions. 'Mooch. Nowt' is particularly interesting as a kind of compound ellipsis, since it only makes sense with the following expansion: '[I'm gonna] Mooch. [I'm gonna do] Nowt'. Griffiths's dramatic dialogue not only derives from a spoken mode, but attempts to represent that mode in a way that indicates how it might be said. Although it is no more speech written down than any other fictional dialogue, it is much more likely to be heard as speech that was not written down in the first place than Fry's verse. The dramatic purposes of the two playwrights are, of course, poles apart and the contrast in dialogic expression is a reflection of that.

CHAPTER 12

THE CONATIVE TURN

This chapter looks at the way ellipsis helps to characterize those kinds of non-literary writing whose focus is on the addressee, the recipient of the message. The conative turn of language underpins a range of functional styles from the abbreviated formulas of written instructions to the often obliquely gapped messages of advertising. After some discussion of the conative turn in general terms I will illustrate and analyse linguistic examples from these functional styles with a specific focus on the types of ellipsis that contribute to their overall stylistic quality.

In Chapter 8, I suggested that, given the multifunctional nature of language events, a functional approach to style has to relate to the dominant function of a text. The best-known schema for establishing this dominant function is that of Jakobson, mentioned there and elsewhere in this book, who relates a set of 'constitutive factors' of speech events to a corresponding set of functions (1960: 353). Of the six constitutive factors outlined by Jakobson, the relevant one here is 'orientation towards the addressee', an orientation which determines the corresponding conative function. The term 'conative', with its etymology in a Latin word whose semantic field is that of attempt and effort, implies the function of language to get things done or, more precisely, to get others to do things. In his very useful collation of functional approaches, Leech sees this as part of the goal orientation of language as a whole: '. . . a "function" presupposes some kind of orientation towards a goal. For example, we use language conatively *in order* to influence the addressee in some way . . .' (1987: 77). The notion of influencing the addressee nicely extends the conative dimension as illustrated by Jakobson, who focuses on its imperative or commanding aspect. One functional schema for language that Leech doesn't incorporate in his survey is that of Kinneavy, who similarly extends the conative turn. Kinneavy's schema is clearly influenced by Jakobson in the way he correlates a set of basic communicative factors with a corresponding set of functions. He renames the addressee 'decoder' (Kinneavy 1971: 19) and goes on to elaborate a set of discourse aims in which a focus on the decoder corresponds to the 'persuasive' function.

On the basis of these insights we have to recognize that the conative turn is itself multifunctional or at least bifunctional. On the one hand, the conative function, in Jakobsonian terms, is the language of command and 'finds its purest grammatical expression in the vocative and imperative' (Jakobson 1960: 355). On the other hand, according to Kinneavy, a focus on the addressee results in persuasive language, typically advertising and political propaganda. The conative turn, then, has both an instructive and a persuasive dimension. Leech's notion of 'influencing the addressee in some way' covers both dimensions. The decoder of a recipe, for instance, is clearly influenced by its message, but has no need to be persuaded to follow its instructions. Similarly, an advertisement may well influence its addressees but commanding them to buy a product is unlikely to be very persuasive, something most advertisers know and don't do or only do obliquely. It is likely, therefore, that instructional language will be overtly imperative, since its readers are willing instructees. Persuasive language, however, is likely to disguise its underlying motive by mitigating the imperative form in some way or avoiding it altogether.

Telling language

The language of instruction is something most of us respond to on a daily basis. We spend quite a lot of time doing what we're told. We might do so in an unthinking, more or less automatic way, out of a sense of social conformity when falling into line at a 'Queue here' notice, for our own safety when we 'Mind the gap', or to avoid breaking the law when obeying a 'Stop' sign. However, the instructive language that is the subject of this section is the kind we consciously turn to when we want to know what to do and how to do it: recipes, manuals, guidelines and the like. The only obvious thing that much of this instructional language can be guaranteed to have in common is a predominance of subjectless imperative verbs. Recall that in Chapter 2 subjectless imperatives were ruled out as a type of ellipsis on normative grounds. The omission of the subject is so common that I suggested commands with the subject expressed would be the stylistically marked form. Certainly, the subjectlessness of imperatives in instructional language is the norm. The nonrealization of subjects reflects a tacit contract between the addresser and the addressee, a willingness to be told.

Apart from this common grammatical feature, we might expect the language of instructions to be quite variable across different domains of subject and purpose. Within a particular field, however, there is also likely to be a high level of conformity to modes of presentation and linguistic convention. Indeed, some types of instructional language have such distinctive text conventions that they are subgenres in their own right. One such type is the cookbook recipe. There are two essential elements in the format of a recipe: a list of ingredients and a set of directives. There may be peripheral elements, such as notes about the origin or character of the dish, which vary from cookbook to cookbook, but the essential elements vary very little across a wide range of recipes.

Lists of ingredients, like lists for other purposes and in other contexts, have only one consistent structural characteristic as pieces of discourse: they consist of syntactically unrelated, self-contained items. The physical proximity of these items is rather different from the juxtaposition of paratactic structures which embodies a grammatical and often cohesive relation. Depending on the purpose of the list, the linguistic structure of individual items will vary. Shopping lists and lists of ingredients are invariably noun phrases, whereas 'to do' lists are mainly verb phrases. Here is a typical list of ingredients, from the cookbook *Sainsbury's Combined Recipes*, for a dish called 'Cauliflower Provençale':

3–4 tablespoons olive oil
1 onion, chopped
2 cloves garlic, chopped finely
625g chopped tomatoes
1 tablespoon finely chopped basil
4 tablespoons finely chopped parsley
50g breadcrumbs
25g black olives, pitted and chopped
1 large cauliflower, divided into florets
salt and pepper

(McFadden and Hillman 1992: 37)

The use of numerals and standard abbreviations for weights aside, there are one or two ways in which ingredient noun phrases are reduced that typify recipe lists. Noun phrases of quantity consistently omit 'of', as in this selection: '3–4 tablespoons [of] olive oil', '2 cloves [of] garlic, chopped finely', '50g [of] breadcrumbs'. Postmodifying phrases are the result of relative clause reduction: '25g black olives, [which have been] pitted and chopped', '1 large cauliflower, [which has been] divided into florets'. These ellipses effectively create predicative adjectives and adjective phrases and it is worth asking why these are applied in some cases, whereas in other noun phrases an attributive adjective is applied, as in: '4 tablespoons finely chopped parsley'. It is possible that the noun phrases with attributive adjectives imply that the ingredient comes ready bought in that form, in contrast with ingredients that have to be actively prepared. For example, tinned chopped tomatoes are frequently used in cooking, whereas it is likely that an onion would be chopped by the person preparing the meal. This suggests that a more explanatory expansion of the relative clause gap would be, for example: '1 large cauliflower, [which you have] divided into florets'. In effect, even within the list of ingredients, the reader is being told what to do, as befits the instructive dimension of the conative turn.

The set of directives that tell us how to make these ingredients into Cauliflower Provençale are chiefly characterized by two syntactic features: subjectless imperatives and contextually elided direct objects. I have marked the gaps created by this kind of ellipsis in the following text:

> Heat 2 tablespoons of the oil in a pan and gently fry the onion until translucent. Add 1 clove garlic, the tomatoes, basil, 1 tablespoon parsley and season [ ] with salt and pepper. Simmer [ ] for 20–30 minutes until thick, stirring occasionally.
>
> In a bowl, mix the breadcrumbs, olives, remaining parsley and garlic. Season [ ] with pepper and then add 1–2 tablespoons olive oil to bind the mixture together. Place the cauliflower florets in a greased ovenproof dish.
>
> Pour the tomato mixture around the cauliflower and top [ ] with the olive mixture.
>
> Bake [ ] on the top shelf of a preheated oven, 180C, 350F, Gas Mark 4, for 40–50 minutes.

The main verb in every orthographic sentence of the above set of directives is a subjectless imperative, from 'Heat' through to 'Bake'. This imperative is the first word in each sentence with one exception: 'In a bowl, mix the breadcrumbs, olives, remaining parsley and garlic', which begins with a preposed adverbial element before the imperative 'mix'. This preposed adverbial effectively ensures that the reader does not begin to mix the breadcrumbs etc. into the simmering tomato mixture by mistake.

The second grammatical feature, contextually ellipted direct objects, is the most significant marker of recipe style. These ellipses are particularly interesting because, being contextual, they should be fairly strictly recoverable from antecedent text. However, a careful look shows that this is not the case. What, for example, is the object of 'Simmer' in: 'Simmer [ ] for 20–30 minutes' or 'Bake' in: 'Bake [ ] on the top shelf of a preheated oven'? In neither case is there a unique antecedent. An adequate expansion has to supply some globally cohesive element, such as: 'Simmer [this mixture] for 20–30 minutes' or: 'Bake [the entire dish] on the top shelf of a preheated oven'. Even if we suggest that the gaps are filled by pronominal reference, as in: 'Simmer [it] for 20–30 minutes' or: 'Bake [it] on the top shelf of a preheated oven', a strategy I employed on a similar example in Chapter 3, the problem remains as to how the reader understands the reference for such pronouns and the gaps they fill. Brown and Yule (1983: 175–6) address this problem with some insight. Discussing a similar example, they note that a strict indexing of ellipsis to a specific textual antecedent breaks down. They suggest that readers expand gaps of this kind pragmatically, by filling the gap as approximately as possible on the textual evidence available together with what is known of the real world. Returning to the problem in referential terms at a later point, they add that the reader has to 'associate changes of state with the referent and to carry them (or some of them) through the discourse' (p. 202). This is a reasonable characterization of reader strategy. It can be readily applied to similar gaps: season [everything in the pan] with salt and pepper', 'Season [the mixture] with pepper'. The other constituent object ellipsis may be strictly contextual: 'Pour the tomato mixture around the cauliflower and top [the cauliflower] with the olive mixture'. However, even here the antecedent may be a more generalized referent, associated with further changes of state, such as: 'top [everything] with the olive mixture'.

That such pragmatic inferencing of ellipted direct objects may be unduly demanding for inexperienced readers is not lost on those who write cookbooks for children. Such objects tend to be realized in the text by nouns or unambiguous pronominal reference. A recipe for peanut butter sweets from the *Children's Quick and Easy Cookbook* is typical. In the following extract I have underlined those objects which would have been omitted from an adult recipe:

> Melt the butter in a saucepan. Mix <u>it</u> in a bowl with the brown sugar, peanut butter, and icing sugar. Spoon <u>the mixture</u> into the baking tray and spread <u>it</u> out evenly. Press <u>it</u>

down firmly on top with a palette knife. Break the chocolate into a bowl and add the butter. Stir <u>them</u> over a saucepan of simmering water until they melt. (Wilkes 1997: 90)

Here, for example, 'Spoon <u>the mixture</u>' makes explicit a 'change of state' referent of the kind Brown and Yule suggest is pragmatically implied by the ellipsis of the adult recipe.

Exercise 12.1

At the beginning of this section I suggested that we might expect the language of instructions to vary from one subject to another, apart, that is, from using subjectless imperatives. To test this out, here is an extract from a set of guidelines for a walk in The Cheviot Foothills, taken from the Ordinance Survey manual *Walker's Britain* (1982). Compare the incidence of ellipsis and other instructional features in this guideline with those of recipe style.

> **Energetic** A solitary walk through contrasting country-side; some exposed moorland – avoid in poor visibility or bad weather. Superb views to the Tweed Valley and Scottish border country. Moorland, valley, farmland; 2 climbs.
> **Start** Wooler, signposted from the A697; frequent buses.
> **Parking** in Wooler.
> 1. From the Market Square walk up Ramsey's Lane. After about 0.5 km its name changes to Common Road. Almost at the last house on this lane turn left on to a rough track to Waud House Farm.
> 2. At the farm a stile by a gate leads to open country. Cross and turn sharply right to climb a small hill ahead on gradually improving path. Pass ramparts of a prehistoric settlement. (1982: 278)

Selling language

Advertising comes in a wide variety of forms: printed in newspapers, magazines and on billboards, usually with a mixture of pictorial and linguistic elements; broadcast on radio in a combination of voice, music and other sounds; broadcast on television and in the cinema with the potential to use a whole range of linguistic, pictorial and sound elements in an inventive way. The language associated with these very different forms of advertising is clearly influenced by the demands and constraints of different media, but it is still useful to think of advertising in generic terms as a subcategory of persuasive discourse. While the focus here is on advertising, it is worth remembering that the 'product' associated with persuasive discourse isn't always goods and services, but sometimes attitudes, opinions or beliefs. Even in the case of adverts, the exhortation isn't always to buy in any straightforward sense. Like other forms of persuasive discourse, one of the main purposes of adverts is to lodge the identity of the product in the memory, rather than make an instant sale, however much selling is the ultimate goal.

The conative turn in its persuasive dimension maintains a sharp focus on the recipient of the message that excludes the possibility of give and take, one of the primary features of ordinary conversation. This discrepancy is explored with some insight by Robin Lakoff, who suggests that the defining quality of persuasive discourse is its 'nonreciprocity'. She notes that ordinary conversation is fully reciprocal with all participants having 'the same conversational options' (1982: 27). Persuasive discourse, on the other hand, is a decidedly one way affair, where the express intention of one participant is to change the behaviour or, in the case of adverts, buying habits of others. Only the persuader is linguistically active. Many advertisers, conscious of this nonreciprocal dimension to their discourse, attempt to engage their audience in quasi-reciprocal communication. A clever example of this is the advert for the Ssangyong Korando, a four-wheel-drive vehicle (see Figure 12.1). Above a picture, which shows a gleaming silver model of the car with a suited young man turning his head to stare at it, is the headline:

WHAT DO YOU THINK YOU'RE LOOKING AT?

The aggressive street language not only addresses the staring man but also the target audience of the advert, presumably youngish, monied males like the one in the picture. The headline invites a suitable response, which the body copy of the advert provides. The headline has a double meaning, of course. Apart from being an aggressive rhetorical question, it also asks if the addressee is curious about the vehicle and wants to know more. The rest of the advert assumes that this is the case. Beneath the picture is the following body copy:

Figure 12.1

A new in-your-face 4×4. A muscle-flexed body aggressively styled around the legendary thrust of Mercedes-Benz designed 2.9 diesel or 2.3 petrol power. Want to take it further? Take a look at the 4×4 you've been waiting for.

This body copy effectively answers the headline question, so the first two orthographic sentences can be seen as contextual rejoinders which presuppose part of the question:

> [You're looking at] A new in-your-face 4×4. [You're looking at] A muscle-flexed body aggressively styled around the legendary thrust of Mercedes-Benz designed 2.9 diesel or 2.3 petrol power.

The metaphoric domain of the description is in keeping with the headline question and the implied target audience: this vehicle is 'in-your-face' and has a 'muscle-flexed body'. Its style is aggressive, its thrust legendary and its power guaranteed by its pedigree design. This is a vehicle for the street-credible, physically fit, sexually assured lad about town. If you aren't such a person, then owning this vehicle just might help you to be mistaken for one. The implied interaction between advert and audience is reinforced with the colloquial follow-up: '[Do you] Want to take it further?' The sentence-initial ellipsis here is appropriate to the street-casual rapport. The question is again ambiguous: an in-your-face challenge plays off against an invitation to find out more. The final imperative, 'Take a look at the 4×4 you've been waiting for', is mitigated by the jangling internal rhyme. A telephone number in large print beneath the body copy makes an actual response possible, but a command to call is relegated to the standing details at the very bottom of the page.

Exercise 12.2

Compare the advert just discussed with the one for Panasonic Digital Video Cameras (see Figure 12.2). Here the headlines and body copy appear together immediately below a picture of a male hand clasping one of the cameras, marked 'Actual size'. The headlines and body copy are reproduced below:

> The world's smallest digital video camera.
> Easy to get to grips with.
> You've got to hand it to Panasonic for producing the NV EX1B, the world's smallest digital video camera with a 2.5 inch colour screen. But don't let its compact size deceive you. Packed with the latest digital technology means it produces superb sound and picture, with near broadcast quality. It's also compatible with PCs for editing. Thankfully though, it's remarkably easy to use. And amazingly it's shown above

Figure 12.2

at actual size, so what you see is what you get. Be one of the
first to get your hands on one and call us on 0990 357 357.

Look carefully at how this advert addresses and engages with its readers.
Note any significant differences from the previous advert in terms of
ellipsis and other structural patterns that relate to its overall style.

Persuasion without conation

Body copy which engages with or otherwise directly addresses the advert's audience, however imaginatively, is frequently supplanted by a more indirect approach in which the visual image dominates and text is reduced both in amount and structure. Neither headline nor body copy make any attempt to address the reader, so markers of the conative function, imperatives and second-person pronouns, disappear. Accomplished examples of this kind are the twin adverts for the Minolta Vectis camera (see Figures 12.3 and 12.4). In both cases the silver casing of the camera is foregrounded against the torso of a black model. The grey background suggests a studio setting that disassociates the image and the camera from the usual holiday snaps that accompany many adverts for cheaper cameras, film and printing services. In the male version, the hand of the model holds the camera so that it is entirely offset by his body, the eye of the camera being exactly where his nipple would be. The headline here is:

Stainless steel and ebony.

In the female version the hand of the model holds the camera slightly away from her body to allow an unbroken view of her bikini-clad torso. The model's skin is sensually enhanced with water droplets. In this case the headline is:

Stainless steel and bronze.

The body copy for both adverts is identical:

The new Vectis 300. The Advanced Photo System sophist-icate. Encased in silky smooth, sensual, yet strong, stainless steel. With 3× power zoom, the Vectis 300 sets the scene. A steal at around £260.

Of the five orthographic sentences only one is fully realized with a finite verb: 'With 3× power zoom, the Vectis 300 sets the scene'. The idea of 'setting the scene' is coyly ambiguous, of course, referring not only to the camera's capability but to the prestige of owning one, and suggesting the intimate encounter hinted at by the accompanying image. The other four orthographic sentences are variously incomplete. The first two are detached noun phrases, introducing, pointing to the

Figure 12.3

product: '[This is] The new Vectis 300. [This is] The Advanced Photo System sophisticate'. The use of this last word is sophisticated in itself. As a postposed adjective it can mean 'sophisticated', as in: 'The sophisticated Advanced Photo System'. However, it is also a noun, meaning 'a sophisticated person'. This opens up the possibility that 'The Advanced Photo System sophisticate' refers to the person in the picture, an attractive

189

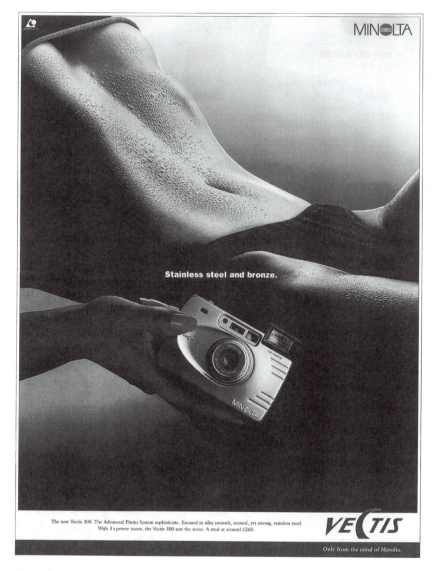

Figure 12.4

ambiguity for an advertiser. The other two sentences can be seen as truncated clauses with initial ellipsis: '[It's] Encased in silky smooth, sensual, yet strong, stainless steel', '[It's] A steal at around £260'. The first is notable for its string of alliterative adjectives, all with highly positive connotations, of course. The second uses a common advertising ploy, suggesting that something expensive is in fact cheap, and does so with the slang expression 'a steal'. As Cook notes in his helpful treatment of ellipsis in advertising, the use of ellipsis goes beyond the brevity principle of reducing text for economic reasons to imply a relationship of informality and shared knowledge between advertiser and reader: '. . . ellipsis – a formal, textual phenomenon – has a discourse function, in that it creates an atmosphere of proximity and intimacy' (Cook 1992: 172). Since various types of ellipsis are common features of ordinary reciprocal conversation, their use in adverts lends that colloquial quality to this nonreciprocal discourse. These twin adverts cleverly exemplify the way persuasively indirect discourse creates the atmosphere Cook refers to with a sophisticated mix of luxury product and sexual promise that image and elliptical text combine to offer.

Discussion of Exercises

Exercise 12.1

In some ways the overall structure of this extract from a book of guided walks is not dissimilar from a cookbook entry. The sections headed 'Energetic', 'Start' and 'Parking' amount to a list of ingredients and preparatory information, while the 'recipe' for the walk consists of a set of numbered instructions. The ingredients and preparatory information for the walk are presented in elliptical syntax. Sentence-initial ellipses characterize many of the main syntactic units: '[This is] A solitary walk through contrasting countryside', '[there is] some exposed moorland', [There are] Superb views to the Tweed Valley and Scottish border country', '[there are] frequent buses'. There is also the more obviously telegraphic list: 'Moorland, valley, farmland; 2 climbs'. Even within this preliminary information there is an overt command: 'avoid [ ] in poor visibility or bad weather'. Note the direct object ellipsis that is a major feature of recipe style. Although this is not a 'change of state' referent, it is ambiguous: are we being told to avoid the solitary walk altogether or just the exposed moorland bit of it? Bad weather no doubt makes the moorland dangerous, but, as superb views are a highlight, perhaps poor visibility rules out the whole walk.

The instructions for the walk itself are firmly within subjectless imperative mode: 'walk up Ramsey's Lane', 'turn left on to a rough track', 'turn sharply right'. Note again the omission of a direct object in 'Cross [the stile]'. In this case the gap is contextually recoverable and unambiguous. Within this instructional framework, however, there are frequent shifts into a descriptive mode, which is untypical of recipes, in such sentences as: 'After about 0.5 km its name changes to Common Road', 'At the farm a stile by a gate leads to open country'. These are required by the very different purpose for which the instructions are written and the circumstances in which they are being followed, capturing the ongoing features of the route from the walker's point of view.

One other elliptical feature remains to be noted: the omission of structure words at phrase level in, for example, 'on [a] gradually improving path' and '[the] ramparts of a prehistoric settlement'. This kind of omission is not applied systematically and many comparable structure words are realized throughout the text. Such gaps, then, are not a consistent means of linguistic economy, but they do reinforce the overall stylistic impression of abbreviation that written instructions often achieve in their aim to be concise and directly accessible for the addressee to whom they are orientated. To some extent the analysis of this text suggests that instructions do vary according to subject and purpose. On the other hand, it is also clear that, when combined with subjectless imperatives, certain abbreviatory devices, particularly direct object ellipsis, are characteristic of a wider instructional genre.

Exercise 12.2

As I noted in relation to the Ssangyong Korando advert, the nonreciprocal nature of persuasive discourse is often mitigated by addressee-orientated colloquial language. To some extent reciprocity is being simulated to create the right persuasive atmosphere. The headlines of this Panasonic advertisement appear to hold out the possibility of open-ended engagement with the reader. The first, a detached noun phrase, amounts to a title: 'The world's smallest digital video camera'. The second headline, with its sentence-initial ellipsis, '[It's] Easy to get to grips with', puns on its literal meaning ('easy to handle') and its idiomatic meaning ('easy to understand'), in order to draw in the potential purchaser. However, the body copy does not fulfil this initial engagement. Directly addressing the reader does not automatically create quasi-reciprocal text. This becomes clear when we itemize the imperative and second-person pronoun structures:

> You've got to hand it to Panasonic . . .
> But don't let its compact size deceive you.

. . . so what you see is what you get.

Be one of the first to get your hands on one and call us on 0990 357 357.

By using contracted forms and other markers of casual or colloquial discourse, such as 'Thankfully though' and 'And amazingly', this text achieves a superficially chatty tone, but, as the isolated structures above show, the address to the reader is fundamentally conative in the instructive sense. The reader is told what to think, what not to think and what to do. Unlike the car advert, the command to call is promoted to the body copy and reinforced by a rather urgent use of imperative BE: there is no simulated reciprocity here. Likewise, the body copy has no significant ellipsis to engage the reader in filling the gaps. Goldman's comments, though specifically about television advertisements, are enlightening in this respect:

> Using ambiguity and ellipsis as advertising strategies is high-risk, but can also bear huge dividends. If viewers do not try imaginatively to resolve the ambiguity or fill in the ellipsis, then the ad flops. The up side is equally obvious: viewers are much more likely to make a cognitive investment in a product sign if they have actively 'worked through' the puzzle. (1992: 201)

Using Goldman's terms, we can see that the Ssangyong Korando advertisement is high risk to the extent that it engages the reader with ambiguity and ellipsis. By comparison, the Panasonic advert makes no attempt to promote cognitive investment through problem-solving.

CHAPTER 13

NARRATIVE VOICES, NARRATIVE GAPS

In this chapter I will be trying to show how different authors represent the narrative voice in prose fiction and how that voice can interact and overlap with other voices in the text. As in other chapters, I will be focusing on ellipsis, its incidence and its absence, as a touchstone for our understanding of how such representations are achieved. But there is another sense of gap that is worth bearing in mind here. In my introduction I quoted a recommendation for a novel which was deemed to be 'elliptical'. I suggested it would be worth exploring the extent to which ellipsis as a figure of syntax was indicative of this rather more elusive stylistic quality. One of the things which is likely to render a novel elliptical is a narrative gap, in which something inexplicit is left for the reader to speculate about. For example, in May Sinclair's *The Life and Death of Harriett Frean* (1922), a modernist treatment of Victorian repression, the child Harriett deliberately disobeys her parents and goes for a walk down the forbidden Black's Lane. She comes to a neglected house:

> It was not like the houses people live in; there was something queer, some secret, frightening thing about it. The man came out and went to the gate and stood there. *He* was the frightening thing. When he saw her he stepped back and crouched behind the palings, ready to jump out. (p. 18)

The inexplicit nature of the text leaves the reader uncertain as to what happened. Did the man expose himself sexually to the girl or really threaten her at all? Certainly, the reaction of Harriett's parents and the repressive guilt they engender in the girl seem to confirm the seriousness of the incident. Later we learn:

> They must have known all the time about Black's Lane; Annie, the housemaid, used to say it was a bad place; something had

happened to a little girl there. Annie hushed and reddened and wouldn't tell you what it was. Then one day, when she was thirteen, standing by the apple tree, Connie Hancock told her. A secret . . . Behind the dirty blue palings . . . She shut her eyes, squeezing the lids down, frightened. (p. 24)

The speculation aroused by the first passage is intensified by this later revelation, but in a very vague way. It is noteworthy that this further inexplicitness is reinforced by actual gaps in the text, creating telegraphic strings: 'A secret [ ]. Behind the dirty blue palings [ ]'. The reader has to fill these gaps on the basis of inferences or implicatures of the kind I explored briefly in Chapter 2 together with whatever clues the structures themselves afford. Such syntactic gaps at what can be called the micro-level of syntax may well be indexical at the macro-level of a fiction's overall narrative design. In Sinclair's novel the gaps suppress detail for the reader in a way that mirrors the thematic repression of the main character's progress through life. This overlap or coincidence between ellipsis and narrative gap, especially in idiosyncratic fictional worlds like that of Laurence Sterne's *The Life and Opinions of Tristram Shandy* (1767), is further explored in the next section in relation to the narrative voices most fiction employs.

Narrative voices

There are two basic narrative voices in prose fiction: first-person and third-person. Second-person narratives are not impossible, but their occurrence is both rare and comparatively recent in the history of fiction. Edna O'Brien's novel, *A Pagan Place* (1971), which traces a girl's upbringing in rural Ireland, sustains a second-person narrative throughout:

One day your father had a pitchfork raised to your mother and said I'll split the head of you open and your mother said And when you've done it there will be a place for you. And you were sure that he would and you and your sister Emma were onlookers and your sister Emma kept putting twists of paper in her hair, both to curl it and pass the time. (p. 21)

This use of the second person normally implies a focus on the addressee and it is just possible to read this text as a narrator, who must clearly know the girl very well, telling her the story of her childhood from an omniscient point of view. However, this discourse dynamic is strained, if not made impossible, by passages like the following:

> But even praying your mind wandered. You thought about your mother and Aunt Bride and what they might be discussing. (p. 71)

This level of introspection suggests that narrator and addressee are one and the same. The whole text can then be seen as egocentric speech in which the narrator recalls and recounts to herself the events of her childhood. On the other hand, there is very little of the elliptical impressionism characteristic of interior monologue, the use of telegraphic structures, truncated sentences and the like. The syntax, predominantly paratactic, linking together chains of coordinate clauses, orders the narrative voice's self-reflections coherently, without the dislocations and ellipses associated with inner speech. The discourse ambiguity and the textual uncertainty that sustains it probably account for the relative rarity of this narrative voice in fiction, though it is worth noting that the second person is a common poetic voice which may even be considered favoured in lyric poetry.

First-person narratives are related by a textual 'I'. This 'I' is most often a named character in the story, such as, for example, Sasha Jensen, in Jean Rhys's *Good Morning, Midnight* (1939), who gives an account of her own bleak existence in Paris. Occasionally, the first-person narrator is closely identifiable with the author. Perhaps the most famous example of this is Marcel Proust's *Remembrance of Things Past* (1913–27). This vast multi-volumed novel explores the power of memory to evoke a past that is in many ways the author's own. Its first-person narrator is called 'Marcel', which in itself invites the reader to assume the novel is quasi-autobiographical. Referring to the identity of Marcel in his commentary on the novel, Michel-Thiriet asks: 'Is he Proust himself? The incidents he relates are often so closely based on Proust's own life that it is tempting to think he must be Proust . . .' (1989: 292). However, he goes on to note that Proust himself stated clearly that the book was definitely not an autobiography. Proust asserted the distinction between the actual person who is or was the author and the narrator of a particular text, in this case the first-person narrator, Marcel. Where author and narrator have much in common, the search for parallels and sources can be a fascinating one, as Michel-Thiriet's book proves. In most cases, however, an unsophisticated equation of the person of the author with the 'I' of the text can be very misleading.

The term 'third-person narrative' implies at least two things. First, that the story is being related by some third party who is not involved as a character in the narrative. That third-person narrator is omniscient about the story's events and is able not only to report the actions and dialogue of characters but also to reveal their thoughts. For example, May Sinclair's *The Life and Death of Harriett Frean* (1922) is a kind of fictional biography in which the main character's thinking on the conduct of her life is subtly revealed under the control of Sinclair's carefully structured narrative. The other main implication of third-person narrative is that all the characters are referred to in the third person. Characters can, of course, refer to themselves in the first person through dialogue and projections of their thoughts, but these are all, to some extent, filtered through the third-person narrator's voice. The extent and degree to which characters are allowed to perceive and report on events through their own eyes is, in Genette's treatment (1980: 189), referred to as 'focalization'. Subtle shifts and overlaps between narrative voice and character focalization are often a source of narrative gaps, especially in modernist fiction.

Laurence Sterne's *The Life and Opinions of Tristram Shandy* (1767), a mock autobiography of its eponymous protagonist, is often cited as the first modernist novel and a major influence on later experimental fiction. It is full of idiosyncratic tricks, graphological oddities and linguistic playfulness as well as digressions, diversions and tales within tales. These techniques create narrative gaps, some of which are literal and physical: not only are sentences, paragraphs and stories broken off but their incompleteness is signalled by strings of asterisks, whole paragraphs of dashes and even blank, and sometimes black, pages. Much of this is for comic or satiric effect, especially in relation to bawdy indiscretions of act and word, but it also manifests a larger rationale for the fictional enterprise which is spelled out by Tristram, the narrator, himself:

> Writing, when properly managed, (as you may be sure I think mine is) is but a different name for conversation: As no one, who knows what he is about in good company, would venture to talk all; – so no author, who understands the just boundaries of decorum and good breeding, would presume to think all: The truest respect which you can pay to the reader's understanding, is to halve this matter amicably, and leave him something to imagine, in his turn, as well as yourself. (p. 127)

The narrator, then, has a deliberate policy of creating gaps. Sometimes Tristram explicitly invites the reader to fill those gaps, as when, for example, he calls upon the reader to describe the 'concupiscible' widow Wadman, with whom his uncle Toby has fallen in love: a page is left blank for the reader to do so (p. 450). On other occasions a gap is created by Sterne's habit of having his narrator fail to finish a sentence on grounds of decorum. Referring to the gossip about his accidental circumcision at the drop of a faulty window sash, when he was five years old, Tristram notes:

> . . . in a week's time, or less, it was in every body's mouth,
> *That poor Master Shandy* ★ ★ ★ ★
> ★ ★ ★ entirely. (p. 418)

The reader is invited by the asterisks to imagine the exact wording of the rumour. It is just about possible to do this on the basis of events described earlier in the narrative, so this narrative gap is to some extent contextually supported rather than relying solely on the reader's fantasy. Such a strategy combines a fairly strict form of ellipsis with reader inference: structural omission at the sentence level coincides here with a narrative gap. The gap is a kind of contrived lapse in performance, asterisked into the text to tease the reader for comic effect.

Exercise 13.1

Here is an extract from another first-person narrative, Jean Rhys's novel *Good Morning, Midnight* (1939), set in Paris in the 1930s. In it the narrator, Sasha, returns to her room, slightly drunk. She reads a note from a painter from whom she has bought a picture and decides to unwrap the painting there and then. Comment on any features of the narrator's vocal style that seem significant to you. To what extent does she create narrative gaps that leave the reader 'something to imagine'?

> I unroll the picture and the man standing in the gutter, play-ing his banjo, stares at me. He is gentle, humble, resigned, mocking, a little mad. He stares at me. He is double-headed, double-faced. He is singing 'It has been', singing 'It will be'. Double-headed and with four arms . . . I stare back at him and think about being hungry, being cold, being hurt, being ridiculed, as if it were in another life than this.

This damned room – it's saturated with the past . . . It's all the rooms I've ever slept in, all the streets I've ever walked in. Now the whole thing moves in an ordered, undulating procession past my eyes. Rooms, streets, streets, rooms . . . (1939: 91)

Mimesis and diegesis

At this stage a useful distinction can be made between two terms that have their roots in classical rhetoric: mimesis and diegesis. Their historical significance as well as their usefulness in discussing the representation of narrative voices is fully outlined by Rimmon-Kenan (1983: 106–16). Mimesis can, simplistically, be equated with imitation: narratives imitate events, including speech events. This imitation is essentially a linguistic illusion. However, as Rimmon-Kenan notes, 'the representation of speech comes closest to pure mimesis', because language, ultimately, can only imitate itself (p. 108). By contrast diegesis indicates a declarative report of events, including speech events, which does not attempt to imitate them. The linguistic illusion, that characters are speaking, rather than a narrator writing, is minimized.

First-person narratives are, in an overarching sense, mimetic. They purport to represent the narrative voice of a single character who is the main focalizer through which all events are perceived and recorded. Clearly, this narrator can report the actions and speech of other characters in a diegetic manner. Nevertheless, such diegesis is subject to what we might call the mimetic consistency of the first-person narrator. The two narratives we have looked at tend to confirm this. The elaborate and loquacious idiosyncrasy of Tristram Shandy's narrative voice is maintained, despite the numerous and sometimes lengthy digressions and diversions, across the best part of six hundred pages. The very different voice of Sasha Jensen is likewise consistently represented in all its anxiety and unease.

Third-person narratives are, in the same overarching sense, diegetic. The third-person narrator reports and describes the actions and dialogue of the story's characters. We expect this anonymous narrative voice also to be consistent: it is subject to what we might call the diegetic consistency of the third-person narrator. The most obvious way in which this consistency might be violated is for the narrator to switch languages, but radical diegetic inconsistency can also be achieved by shifts in code or style. As with so many experimental narrative techniques, James Joyce provides us with an archetypal example in the section of *Ulysses* known as 'Oxen of the Sun' (1922: 366–407). Here the third-person narrative voice begins in mock Anglo-Saxon alliterative style:

> Before born babe bliss had. Within womb won he worship.

Through a series of shifts Joyce takes us on a chronology of English prose styles with parodies of, among others, the Bunyan of *The Pilgrim's Progress*: 'But was young Boasthard's fear vanquished by Calmer's words? No, for he had in his bosom a spike named Bitterness which could not by words be done away.' The section ends with a drunken concoction of dialect and slang. The effect of such diegetic shifts is, intentionally, to draw attention to the manner in which the narrative is being unveiled rather than its story content.

When it comes to reporting the speech of fictional characters, the third-person narrator has a number of options on the deigetic–mimetic continuum. One is to maintain diegesis fairly strictly. Speech is simply another kind of action to be reported, as in this example:

> Billy spoke vehemently about his sister's lost career opportunities.

This reports the fact that speech has happened and even indicates its manner and content in minimal terms. Calling this form a 'narrative report of speech acts', Leech and Short note that 'the narrator does not have to commit himself entirely to giving the sense of what was said, let alone the form of words in which they were uttered' (1981: 323). If the narrator wants to give more detail in reporting what a character says, but does not wish to indicate its style or tone, then indirect speech can be used:

> Billy said that his sister should have been a model and that they had wanted her to model for Pepsodent toothpaste, but his mother would not hear of it. He explained that somebody at the church had told her that models were loose ladies and that if a girl got her picture taken, it turned her into a floozy.

Indirect speech of this kind retains what might be called diegetic control of what the character says: the voice is still that of the narrator rather than the character. If, on the other hand, the narrator wants to represent the flavour of a particular character's spoken language with regard to style or tone, then an element of mimesis has to be used. The most common option here is direct speech in which the third-person narrator 'quotes' what the character says. This is the option William Kennedy actually chose in his novel *Ironweed*:

> 'Well she shoulda, goddamn it, she shoulda,' said Billy. 'They wanted her to model for Pepsodent toothpaste, but Mama wouldn't hear of it. Somebody over at church told her models were, you know, loose ladies. Get your picture taken, it turns you into a floozy.' (1983: 183)

Note that Kennedy, in representing colloquial American speech of a particular era, uses orthographic conventions to simulate pronunciation, as in 'shoulda', markers of casual speech, such as expletives 'goddamn it' and 'you know', and introduces vocabulary suggestive of time and place, such as 'floozy'. Note also the characteristically colloquial sentence-initial ellipsis, '[If you] Get your picture taken', which, significantly, I expanded in my more diegetic version of Billy's speech.

The overarching diegetic voice of third-person narrative, then, allows for the introduction of more or less mimetic representations of its characters' speech. A similar continuum of representation also applies to what characters are thinking. Leech and Short (1981: 337) identify points on this continuum ranging from 'narrative report of thought acts', a bare diegetic report that thought processes have taken place, to 'free direct thought', a quasi-mimetic impression of a character's interior monologue. As we saw in Chapter 5, the use of such free direct thought was a radical technique of modernist writers like Joyce to try to capture in writing the way thought is structured. The passage we looked at in that chapter consisted entirely of interior monologue. It was clear that reduced and telegraphic structures were the syntax of choice for this exclusively mimetic representation of thought. Here, it is useful to look at another passage from *Ulysses* in which the diegetic third-person narrative alternates and contrasts with mimetic free direct thought. In this extract Leopold Bloom is going out to get something for breakfast, leaving his wife Molly dozing in bed:

> On the doorstep he felt in his hip pocket for the latchkey. Not there. In the trousers I left off. Must get it. Potato I have. Creaky wardrobe. No use disturbing her. She turned

> over sleepily that time. He pulled the hall door to after him
> very quietly, more, till the footleaf dropped gently over the
> threshold, a limp lid. Looked shut. All right till I come back
> anyhow. (1922: 54)

The passage begins with the outer diegetic voice of the third-person
narrator:

> On the doorstep he felt in his hip pocket for the latchkey.

This reports Bloom's action in standard third-person past tense narrative
mode. His thoughts on not having his key and the possibility of disturbing
his wife while retrieving it are then presented in the typically telegraphic
style that we noted in Chapter 5:

> [The latchkey's] Not there. [It's] In the trousers I left off. [I] Must
> get it.
> [A] Potato I have. [The key's in the] Creaky wardrobe. [There's]
> No use disturbing her. She turned over sleepily that time.

This inner mimetic voice is essentially first-person and present tense.
It attempts to simulate the abbreviated immediacy of Bloom's interior
monologue with a string of mainly predicate structures which my expansions fill out with subjects and auxiliary elements. The desultory
nature of inner speech is nicely reflected in Bloom's mental aside about
the hole in his pocket, 'Potato I have', which intrudes upon his main
line of thought. The ellipsis of the indefinite article is compounded
by the syntactic inversion of 'I have [a] potato'. We could, of course,
understand this literally to mean that Bloom has discovered a potato in
his pocket, something which is possible though slightly unlikely. Alternatively, we can infer, as I have, that Bloom is mentally noting a hole in
his pocket. This meaning depends on a culturally based inferential gap,
since it relies on knowing that 'potato' is a colloquial term in a number
of regional varieties of English for holes in socks, gloves and pockets.

The last sentence, 'She turned over sleepily that time', seems to be a
return to past tense narrative, but is in fact a continuation of Bloom's
reflections: the previous time he called to her, she was obviously still
dozing. Third-person narrative report returns with the next sentence:

> He pulled the hall door to after him very quietly, more, till
> the footleaf dropped gently over the threshold, a limp lid.

Note the more expansive syntax and the metaphoric characterization of the footleaf as 'a limp lid', features that seem designed to tell us that this is the diegetic narrator here. The last two sentences revert to the truncated structures of inner speech:

[The door] Looked shut. [It'll be] All right till I come back anyhow.

The past tense of the first sentence gives us some pause, since we would expect the mimetic immediacy of Bloom's thought, as he inspects the door, to be in the present: 'Looks shut'. However, this can be explained as one of those occasions where an ellipsis coincides with a narrative gap. Although the text doesn't say so, we have to assume that Bloom has already turned away from the door. The past tense reflects the fact that he is recalling to himself that the door looked shut, as he walks off to cross the street, which is the next event the narrative reports.

Exercise 13.2

In her novel, *The Weather in the Streets* (1936), Rosamond Lehmann alternates diegetic and mimetic voices in respect of the actions and thoughts of her main character, Olivia Curtis. Examine the following passages, paying particular attention to the distribution of third-person narrative and first-person inner speech. To what extent does Lehmann employ ellipsis as a contrastive marker? In the first passage, Olivia and her sister are awaiting news of their father who is seriously ill and being visited by the doctor upstairs:

> Kate got up and lit the lamp, Olivia poked the fire. They looked out. With the increase of light in the room the darkness without had grown suddenly complete, uncompromising. It's night. Mother's been away too long, I want her to come . . . Draw the curtains. No. The waiting car won't let us . . . They sat down again. (p. 51)

In the second passage, towards the end of the novel, Olivia is at a party:

> Jasper kissed her hand with old-world courtesy, gazed deeply beneath his brows upon her, said intensely: 'Yes . . .' nodding his head with slow and cryptic significance. But soon he passed on. I can't be bothered tonight and nor can he. He's other fish to fry. Fresh, palpitating young virgins to

mould and subjugate. I'm in a black dress, drab and sober, unalluring; an old stager with a totally undistinguished walking on part. (p. 362)

The ambiguous voice: free indirect speech and thought

In the novels looked at in the previous section we saw texts which make a fairly clear distinction between a diegetic third-person narrative voice and a mimetic first-person interior monologue. As well as differences in person and tense, contrasts in syntactic structure pointed up this distinction, especially in the the case of Joyce, who employed a high amount of sentence-initial and telegraphic ellipsis to create a very distinctive brand of free indirect thought. Exposing the thought processes of a character in this way allows for very sharp and unambiguous focalization: there is no doubt that the character's perception of events is being presented and not the narrator's. Even at this level of differentiation, however, we saw that some sentences, such as 'She turned over sleepily that time', can appear deceptively to mark a shift back from free indirect thought representation to the diegetic narrative voice. Uncertainty arises on the basis of quite subtle differences in detail, such as tense markers or deictic expressions. Much earlier in this chapter I noted that such shifts between narrative voice and character focalization are often exploited in modernist fiction. The most subtle means for such exploitation is the interplay between free indirect speech and free indirect thought. In this final section I want to illustrate this interplay in operation by discussing a brief, but more or less perfect, example.

Earlier in the chapter I illustrated the diegetic–mimetic continuum as it related to representing spoken dialogue by contriving different versions of the same piece of fictional speech. One of the versions was indirect speech:

> Billy said that his sister should have been a model and that they had wanted her to model for Pepsodent toothpaste, but his mother would not hear of it. He explained that somebody at the church had told her that models were loose ladies and that if a girl got her picture taken, it turned her into a floozy.

This can easily be converted into free indirect speech by removing the superordinate clauses of saying:

His sister should have been a model. They had wanted her to model for Pepsodent toothpaste, but his mother would not hear of it. Somebody at the church had told her that models were loose ladies and that if a girl got her picture taken, it turned her into a floozy.

Seeing the two versions in proximity highlights some of the effects of free indirect speech. Since the text no longer specifies that a character is speaking, the voice becomes ambiguous. It is possible that this is not a character's voice, but the third-person narrator's. Unlike free direct speech, the past tense system of indirect speech reinforces this diegetic possibility. The ambiguity may even be more complex: perhaps some sentences are the third-person narrative voice and others are the indirectly reported thoughts of a character. If my fairly crude contrivance can create these uncertainties, in the hands of a consummate writer the interplay of free indirect speech and thought is a major vehicle for irony and ambiguity.

May Sinclair was one of the finest English novelists of the late Victorian and early modernist periods. Her involvement in the suffragette movement and what would now be called psychiatric social work prior to the First World War is reflected in novels which explore, among other things, the psychology of female repression in a patriarchal society, something we looked at briefly in the introduction to this chapter with extracts from *The Life and Death of Harriett Frean* (1922). The novel traces its protagonist from cradle to grave, exposing both the mechanisms and the consequences of her repressive socialization. For example, in an early scene the girl Harriett goes without her tea at a school treat because her mother thinks the used plate Harriett has been given means that her daughter has already eaten. Harriett says nothing at the time, but at home later the mistake comes out. Harriett's mother is pleased and tells her:

'Well, I'm glad my little girl didn't snatch and push. It's better to go without than to take from other people. That's ugly'.

Harriett's felt response is conveyed as follows:

Ugly. Being naughty was just that. Doing ugly things. Being good was being beautiful like Mamma. She wanted to be like her mother. Sitting up there and being good felt delicious. And the smooth cream with the milk running under it, thin and cold, was delicious too. (p. 15)

Cleverly, Harriett's thoughts begin with a single detached word: '[ ] Ugly'. The telegraphic structure appears to herald a piece of Joycean free direct thought. The tense of the next sentence, however, marks it as free indirect thought. This is reinforced by the ellipsis that follows, if we assume it is contextually recoverable: '[Being naughty was] Doing ugly things'. We still seem to be witnessing Harriett's thoughts with: 'Being good was being beautiful like Mamma'. The next sentence demonstrates the real effectiveness of the free indirect mode. 'She wanted to be like her mother' may be a free indirect version of Harriett's thought: 'I want to be like my mother'. Equally, focalization may have shifted: this could be the third-person narrator's voice offering us an explanation of Harriett's behaviour. Perhaps the choice of 'mother' rather than 'Mamma' tips it towards the latter. We seem to be back with Harriett's perceptions with the final two sentences:

> Sitting up there and being good felt delicious. And the smooth cream with the milk running under it, thin and cold, was delicious too.

However, if these are read as narrator comments rather than the free indirect representation of Harriett's thoughts, they take on an ambiguously ironic quality. Self-sacrificial virtue makes Harriett feel like the cat who got the cream. Just as a thin, cold milk runs beneath that cream, the implication is that something psychologically thin and cold underpins the Victorian value. The free indirect mode, ambiguous between speech and thought lets both meanings linger in the text. Genette's aphorism is particularly appropriate in this respect: 'Narrative always says less than it knows, but it often makes known more than it says' (1980: 198).

Discussion of Exercises

Exercise 13.1

In *Good Morning, Midnight* the first-person narrator, Sasha Jensen, wanders the streets of Paris, sits in cafés and bars, goes to the cinema, getting by in a present that constantly triggers memories of her past. The narrative is for the most part in the present tense. Even past events, as they invade Sasha's memory, are mostly rehearsed in the present tense which allows the past and the present to interact in an apparently seamless way. The narrative voice maintains a vivid presence, as if Sasha is giving a running commentary on her life, both as it happens and is remembered, as here: 'I unroll the picture and the man standing in the gutter, playing his banjo, stares at me'. She might almost say 'stares at me in recognition', since the string of complements she uses to describe the figure in the picture could easily be applied to Sasha herself: 'gentle, humble, resigned, mocking, a little mad'. But Sasha is also 'a woman on the verge of a nervous breakdown'. Her own disintegration is ironically mirrored in her drunken vision of the man with the banjo, who is 'double-headed, double-faced'. At this point Rhys employs reduced syntax to telegraph Sasha's thought: '[He appears] Double-headed and with four arms'. Throughout the book Rhys uses sets of three dots to indicate pauses, shifts and gaps in Sasha's thinking. Sometimes these are little more than an extended punctuation mark, suggesting a slightly longer pause in the 'stream of consciousness', as the first set in this extract: '. . . I stare back at him and think about being hungry, being cold, being hurt, being ridiculed, as if it were in another life than this'. The next set marks a temporal shift in Sasha's thinking, a transition from present to past triggered by the abject figure in the picture and the redolence of the room itself: 'This damned room – it's saturated with the past . . . It's all the rooms I've ever slept in, all the streets I've ever walked in.' The final set, attached to the telegraphic alternation of rooms and streets, represents an indeterminate ellipsis, as Sasha's thoughts run out: 'Now the whole thing moves in an ordered, undulating procession past my eyes. Rooms, streets, streets, rooms [. . .]'. This extract, ending with what amounts to a communicative lapse, concludes a whole section of the book. There is a genuine sense here that the narrator has created a narrative gap that leaves the reader something to imagine, for now at any rate. This is the kind of gap that Iser sees as central to his theory of reader response:

> Whenever the reader bridges the gaps, communication begins. The gaps function as a kind of pivot on which the whole text–reader relationship revolves. Hence the structured blanks of the text stimulate the process of ideation to be performed by the reader on terms set by the text. (1978: 169)

Rhys's novel is full of such structured blanks. They stimulate the reader, as Iser suggests, into engaging with the text, to bridge the gaps both at the micro-level between the sentences of Sasha's thought and on the larger scale between her present and past life. However, structured blanks are also an important technical means of characterizing the narrative voice of a lonely and desperate woman.

Exercise 13.2

Rosamond Lehmann's novels are best known for their accomplished exploration of individual female development in the context of romantic and sexual relationships. In this respect her novel, *The Weather in the Streets* (1936), is a sequel to *Invitation to the Waltz* (1932) in which the same protagonist, Olivia Curtis, is depicted as a seventeen year old. Although not renowned as an experimental novelist, Lehmann clearly writes in ways that acknowledge the narrative techniques of more high-profile modernists, such as Joyce. In *The Weather in the Streets* she complicates an apparently anonymous third-person narrative by moving in and out of the interior monologue of her main character. As in the previously discussed passage from Joyce, diegetic reporting and description is in the third-person past tense:

> Kate got up and lit the lamp, Olivia poked the fire. They looked out. With the increase of light in the room the darkness without had grown suddenly complete, uncompromising.

Although the implied perception of the night is that of the sisters, the narrator retains diegetic control. With the shift to free direct thought, however, it is Olivia who becomes the focalizer, the sensibility through which events are perceived, though this is not signalled by any superordinate clause of thinking:

> It's night. Mother's been away too long, I want her to come . . . Draw the curtains. No [Don't draw the curtains]. The waiting car won't let us [Draw the curtains] . . .

The mimesis of Olivia's thought is achieved in the first-person present tense with a few contracted forms that help to differentiate it from the main narrative. There are, however, no telegraphic strings of the kind that characterize Bloom's interior monologue. Ellipsis, such as it is, is contextual. The 'No' negatively takes into account the whole of the previous proposition: '[Don't draw the curtains]'. The idea that they cannot draw the curtains until the doctor has left in the car that awaits him is conveyed by the same contextually supported ellipsis. The last sentence returns to third-person diegesis: 'They sat down again'.

It is fair to say that Lehmann is not attempting the radical representation of inner speech that Joyce achieved. Olivia's thoughts are clearly differentiated from diegetic narrative and simulated to some extent, but their syntax is more typical of casual spoken language than Joycean interior monologue. The second passage tends to confirm this. Third-person narrative reporting ends with: 'But soon he passed on'. There is an abrupt switch to the first-person present tense of Olivia's thoughts. The coordination reduction of the first sentence is characteristic of conversational style rather than inner speech: 'I can't be bothered tonight and nor can he [be bothered tonight]'. The next ellipsis is a sentence-initial omission of an existential marker: '[There are] Fresh, palpitating young virgins to mould and subjugate'. The final gap is a coordination reduction disguised by the orthography and the paratactic omission of a conjunction: 'I'm in a black dress, drab and sober, unalluring; [and I'm] an old stager with a totally undistinguished walking on part'. Undoubtedly, the parataxis and coordination reductions, as well as the contracted forms, are successful in differentiating Olivia's thoughts from the overarching narrative voice. Lehmann convincingly sustains this diegetic–mimetic distinction throughout the novel, even though Olivia's interior monologue is more representative of casual conversational turns than inner speech.

CHAPTER 14

ELLIPSIS AND COMPRESSION
IN POETRY

Definitions of poetry which avoid circularity are notoriously difficult to devise. Those which invoke design features, such as stanzaic form, metrical pattern and rhyme, exclude vast amounts of modern poetry written in so-called 'free verse'. Perhaps the only criterion that applies to all written poetry is its fixed shape on the page. The lineation of a poem, the physical disposition of its words and phrases, decided upon by the poet, is maintained, no matter how many different editions and typesettings the poems appears in. This consistency can be seen as the most rudimentary form of what van Peer calls 'typographic foregrounding', a minimal sign that something is poetry. He notes: 'Written or printed poetry presupposes in our culture a typographic lay-out which must be deemed deviant *vis-à-vis* our everyday (as against our literary) expectations' (1993: 50). Yet this deviance, in van Peer's terms, from everyday norms does in fact extend to our literary expectations. Compare, for example, the very different treatment of prose fiction. The lineation of a novel can vary considerably from one edition to another, depending on such things as typeface and page size. This might seem a rather superficial way of distinguishing poetry from other literary and indeed non-literary genres, but it captures an aspect of linguistic control and responsibility that is exclusive to poetry. It also serves to underline the fact that very few other poetic features are exclusive to poetry in the same way. This is no less true of compression in language, though its manifestation in poetry, the main topic of this chapter, is its best exemplification.

Expansiveness versus compression

The idea of compression in poetry may be related to the more general meaning of the word. Compression denotes greater density, especially when it is achieved by squeezing a large amount of material into a more compact form. By analogy, compressed poetic language condenses a large amount of meaning into fewer words than ordinary or, to use Mukařovský's term referred to in Chapter 8, 'standard' language. If there are fewer words, then presumably at least some of them have been omitted in ways that fall into the categories of ellipsis outlined in this book, creating structural gaps in the poetic text. We might reasonably expect, then, the linguistic feature ellipsis to be a significant exponent of the poetic quality compression.

Before looking at examples of compression in poetry, it is worth asking what its opposite might be like, poetic language that is, let's say, expansive. It is tempting to associate expansion, my term for filling in elliptical gaps, with the poetic quality expansiveness. Could it be that an expansive poetic language would take up fewer opportunities for ellipsis, would expand potential gaps and therefore be, among other things, more repetitive structurally and rhetorically? The poet I most associate with expansiveness as I conceive it, a linguistically expanded rhetorical largess, is Walt Whitman. Accordingly, I scanned through the original edition of *Leaves of Grass* (1855), some 120 pages of poetry. On almost every page there were examples of 'expansiveness', of which the following are only two:

> What do you think has become of the young and old men?
> And what do you think has become of the women and children? (p. 30)

> The pleasures of heaven are with me, and the pains of hell are with me. (p. 44)

In each of these examples Whitman chooses not to take up opportunities for ellipsis which in ordinary, let alone compressed, language would be the norm. Both examples involve a coordinate structure in which the second conjunct could be reduced, as my brackets indicate:

> What do you think has become of the young and old men?
> And [what do you think has become] of the women and children?

> The pleasures of heaven are with me, and the pains of hell [are with me].

The removal of this material would, of course, change the rhetorical shape of the lines and destroy the effect of one of Whitman's most

211

distinctive poetic devices, emphatic repetition. The avoidance of elliptical compression gives second and subsequent repetitions of the same linguistic material an insistence that makes the reader, and the listener for that matter, take note of both its meaning and its rhetorical significance. The cumulative impact of this device is particularly noticeable when it involves multiple repetitions, as the following rather more sustained example shows:

> The law of the past cannot be eluded,
> The law of the present and future cannot be eluded,
> The law of the living cannot be eluded. . . . it is eternal,
> The law of promotion and transformation cannot be eluded,
> The law of heroes and good-doers cannot be eluded,
> The law of drunkards and informers and mean persons cannot be eluded. (p. 102)

The multiple repetitions create a syntactic and rhetorical frame made up of the first part of the subject noun phrase 'The law of . . .' and the whole of the predicate verb phrase 'cannot be eluded'. This frame allows for significant variants in the postmodifying material of the noun phrase to be inserted, creating a litany so typical of *Leaves of Grass* that its use by other writers is likely to be deemed Whitmanesque. The linguistic economy and communicative efficiency that an ordinarily elliptical version of this passage would afford is overridden by Whitman's poetic intentions and their stylistic realization. Such poetic language is confirmed as expansive because it expresses meaning in far more words than 'standard' language is likely to use: superfluity is part of the rhetorical design.

The antidote to Whitmanesque expansiveness is to be found in the poetry of Emily Dickinson. Dickinson's life was entirely contemporaneous with Whitman's and they are the two greatest American poets of the nineteenth century, but there commonality seems to end. Whitman was a much more public and politically involved figure whose life experiences, such as being a volunteer nurse in the American Civil War, are reflected in his poetry, which at first he published himself. Dickinson, on the other hand, led an eccentrically reclusive life and nearly all her poems remained unpublished till after her death. Where the expansiveness of Whitman's poetic language seems to correlate with his public persona, the compression of Dickinson's poetry may be seen to reflect her socially circumscribed life.

In her study of the language of Dickinson's poetry Miller gives the following usefully comprehensive definition of compression:

> More a quality of language than a particular use of it, compression denominates whatever creates density or compactness of meaning in language. It may stem from ellipsis of function words, dense use of metaphor, highly associative vocabulary, abstract vocabulary in complex syntax, or any other language use that reduces the ratio of what is stated to what is implied. (1987: 24)

The phrasing 'ellipsis of function words' suggests a rather minor role for syntactic reduction, but Miller adjusts this impression with later discussion of 'recoverable deletion', in my terms contextual ellipsis, and 'nonrecoverable deletion' which coincides with my categories of nonrealization and inferential gaps (pp. 28–30). The elements of compression listed by Miller operate integrally in Dickinson's poetry. Nevertheless, it is possible to focus on the structural gaps in Dickinson's poetic language and in particular the way they help to compact meaning within brief, self-contained lyric poems. To that end, here is the text of poem 543 from *The Complete Poems*:

> I fear a Man of frugal speech –
> I fear a Silent Man –
> Haranguer – I can overtake –
> Or Babbler – entertain –
>
> But He who weigheth – While the Rest –
> Expend their furthest pound –
> Of this Man – I am wary –
> I fear that He is Grand – (1960: 265)

The overall appearance of a Dickinson poem can be somewhat disconcerting with its liberal use of initial capital letters and especially its spray of dashes which do not necessarily mark conventional syntactic boundaries or natural breaks. In this case such surface features present no problem, because the poem itself is fairly straightforward and accessible in meaning. Lines three and four of the first stanza do delete recoverable function words, though this is slightly complicated by Dickinson's word order inversions, as this reconstitution shows:

> I can overtake [a] Haranguer
> Or [I can] entertain [a] Babbler

Here the lack of articles has the effect of suggesting that 'Haranguer' and 'Babbler' are proper names, known individuals who can be dealt with, in contrast to the anonymity of 'a Man of frugal speech' and 'a Silent Man'. The first two lines of the second stanza present an ambiguous gap that is also more fundamental to the meaning of the poem:

> But He who weigheth [ ] – While the Rest –
> Expend their furthest pound –

This may be taken as a strictly contextual ellipsis, in which case the gap is cataphorically resolved:

> But He who weigheth [his furthest pound] – While the Rest –
> Expend their furthest pound –

Clearly, in the context of this poem, 'his/their furthest pound' is a metaphor for verbal expenditure, so the gap could be seen as inferential, implying an appropriately metaphoric expansion:

> But He who weigheth [his words] – While the Rest –
> Expend their furthest pound –

This not only fits in with the metaphor, but allows the gap to imply the proverbial stricture to 'weigh one's words carefully before speaking'. The ellipsis effectively compresses both meanings into the one expression.

Exercise 14.1

Here is another of Emily Dickinson's brief, intensely felt lyrics. Fill out any syntactic gaps you discern in order to clarify the structure of the poem. Relate your expansions to its meaning as a whole. This one is number 729 in *The Complete Poems*:

> Alter! When the Hills do –
> Falter! When the Sun
> Question if His Glory
> Be the Perfect One –

Surfeit! When the Daffodil
Doth of the Dew –
Even as Herself – Sir –
I will – of You – (p. 358)

The compression of imagism

Emily Dickinson developed poetic techniques of compression in a unique and consummately skilful way, as our reading and discussion of two quite brief poems were able to show. She did so in a relatively single-handed way and certainly not as part of a poetic school of writers with their own aims and agenda, as was the case with the so-called imagist poets. In London, in the years immediately preceding the First World War, a small group of writers and artists, fronted, sometimes reluctantly and not without internal dispute, by Ezra Pound, forged the aesthetic doctrine known as imagism and tried to write poems according to its tenets. These principles were first published in 1913 and subsequently elaborated and explained, especially by Pound himself. Imagism was, among other things, a reaction against what was seen as the superfluous verbiage of Victorian and Georgian verse which, in the terminology of this chapter, might be glossed as 'badly written expansiveness'. Accordingly, one of the tenets of imagism was: 'To use absolutely no word that does not contribute to the presentation' (Pound 1918: 3). Although this is quite vague and Pound's follow-up comments target superfluous adjectives, it has the potential to be a recipe for compression and the ellipsis which helps to achieve it at the syntactic level. In this section we shall be looking at some imagist poems to see if this is the case.

The archetypal imagist poem is short and presents one or two visual images, usually without comment or explanation. The following poem, 'Yoshiwara Lament', by Amy Lowell, an American poet who played a significant part in publishing the early imagist anthologies, is a good example of this:

Golden peacocks
Under blossoming cherry-trees,
But on all the wide sea
There is no boat. (Jones (ed.) 1972: 89)

The structural hallmark of this, as of many other brief imagist poems, is the lack of finite clause elements, in this case in the first clause. This is probably best seen as a sentence-initial reduction of existential marker plus finite verb:

> [There are] Golden peacocks
> Under blossoming cherry-trees.

This expansion reinforces the presentational nature of the text, which points the reader to a rich visual image. The principle of using no super-fluous words is being realized by the omission of these finite elements, but the effect is more than just syntactic economy. On the page the text 'Golden peacocks' meets the reader's eye first and the image it creates is more immediately there in the mind's eye too. The lines are structurally ambiguous and a main verb ellipsis site is also possible:

> Golden peacocks [ ]
> Under blossoming cherry-trees.

The gap is not contextually recoverable and so invites the reader to supply an action verb in an open-ended way: is it 'stand', strut' or 'preen' perhaps? Note that the first ellipsis site implies a state and the second an action, but the image itself does not commit the reader either way.

Because of the apparent simplicity of this technique, the omission of relatively few and sometimes quite minor words, it is difficult to gauge how radical a shift in the grammar of poetic language it was at the time. Certainly the use of 'incomplete' sentences was recognized as a charac-teristic feature of imagist poetry and overtly parodied to comic effect by its detractors. Influenced by the prevailing orientalism of the time, Lowell's poem also fulfils another aspect of imagist doctrine, the notion of 'direct treatment'. The images are presented directly, without overt explanation. Paradoxically, this usually results in an indirection typical of Japanese verse forms, such as *haiku* and *tanka*. Poems become more or less cryptic because inferential gaps are left for the reader to fill. Here the poem is a lament because the absence of a boat signifies the failure of someone to return. The vividness of the peacocks, perhaps a gift of the one who is absent, is a foil to the lamenter's misery.

The imagist movement was relatively short lived. Apart from differ-ences in aesthetic stance and disputes over publishing practice, the advent of the First World War had a devastating impact on its major personal-ities. Some, like T. E. Hulme, were killed in action. Others, like Pound himself, were psychologically damaged by grief and guilt. Richard Aldington, another founder member of Pound's imagist circle, also fought in the trenches and recorded his experiences in poetic form. *Picket*, one of his more obviously imagist war poems, begins with a single, spatially isolated line:

Dusk and deep silence . . .

Again the presentational principle is realized by detached, telegraphic phrases that can be seen to delete deictic and finite elements:

[It is] Dusk and [there is] deep silence . . .

This indefinite scene is peopled in the next group of lines:

Three soldiers huddled on a bench
Over a red-hot brazier,
And a fourth who stands apart
Watching the cold rainy dawn.

This scene is essentially present. Any thought that 'huddled' might be simple past tense narrative is dispelled by the present tense 'stands' in the later relative clause. What the text lacks are markers of this present as main clause elements. These can, of course, be filled in:

Three soldiers [are] huddled on a bench
Over a red-hot brazier,
And [there is] a fourth who stands apart
Watching the cold rainy dawn.

The differences, as text, are small, but their significance, though subtle, is substantial: the expanded lines now describe rather than present. The next group of lines provide a contrast for this bleak human scene:

Then the familiar sound of birds –

This verbless clause acts as a heading, presents the list that follows:

Then [there is] the familiar sound of birds –
[The] Clear cock-crow, [the] caw of rooks,
[The] Frail pipe of linnet, the 'ting! ting!' of chaffinches,
And over all the lark [is]
Outpiercing even the robin . . .

Note the lack of definite articles in the noun phrases and the absence of finite verb elements, allowing these linguistic representations of sound to remain in an indefinite present. The still quality of the poem up to this point, as of a photograph, becomes cinematic in the final two lines:

> Wearily the sentry moves
> Muttering the one word: 'Peace'. (Jones (ed.) 1972: 57)

Here the sentry's movement is given a finite verb form and the scene is at last active. Overall the structural ellipses of the poem serve the imagist principle of presentation without superfluous words. To the extent that such ellipses reduce the ratio of what is stated to what is implied, they are an exponent of compression in poetic language. The presentation of images, however, is a rather different motivation from the presentation of cryptically encoded argument in the manner of Emily Dickinson. Indeed, imagism is often criticized because it makes sustained poetic argument unlikely, if not impossible.

Exercise 14.2

Below is the text of one of the most celebrated imagist poems, Ezra Pound's 'The Return'. It is generally noted for its vivid imagery and dynamic free verse rhythms. To what extent is the poem an example of compressed poetic language? Are there any elliptical gaps in the text that contribute to this? Can the poem be said to put forward an argument in any way?

> See, they return; ah, see the tentative
>> Movements, and the slow feet,
>> The trouble in the pace and the uncertain
>> Wavering!
>
> See, they return, one, and by one,
> With fear, as half-awakened;
> As if the snow should hesitate
> And murmur in the wind,
>> and half turn back;
> These were the 'Wing'd-with-Awe',
>> Inviolable.
>
> Gods of the winged shoe!
> With them the silver hounds,
>> sniffing the trace of air!

Haie! Haie!
     These were the swift to harry;
These the keen-scented;
These were the souls of blood.
Slow on the leash,
         pallid the leash-men! (1975: 39)

Compression in translation

Another of the imagist tenets was summed up by the catchphrase 'direct treatment of the thing'. Again, this rather vague principle can be seen as a pointer to presentational rather than explanatory modes of expression, realized by relatively simple syntactic structures linked by coordination and juxtaposition, some of which will be non-finite and/or elliptical, compressing rather than expanding upon the meaning of the original. Nowhere is this direct treatment better exemplified than in imagist translations of Classical and Chinese poetry, particularly Pound's *Cathay* (1915), a cycle of poems from the Chinese, and *Homage to Sextus Propertius* (1917), an idiosyncratic selection from the Latin lyrics of Propertius. These and other imagist translations were controversial because the directness of their treatment was particularly focused on the English of the translation rather than the language of the original, signalling a move away from crib-like literal interpretation. Some scholarly and critical opinion dismissed such translation as mere paraphrase, but a modernist approach to creative translation was established in which the quality of the translation as a poem in its own right was of major importance.

The highly acclaimed versions of a selection from Ovid's *Metamorphoses* by the late Ted Hughes can be seen to exemplify this approach to translation in contemporary terms, compressing the erudite and the colloquial into a sustained narrative voice. Because Hughes's *Tales from Ovid* are narrative rather than lyric, the predominant syntactic vehicle is the simple past tense, though he occasionally adopts the immediacy of present tense narrative, as in the first tale's account of Jove flooding the earth:

Now flood heaps over flood.
Orchards, crops, herds, farms are scooped up
And sucked down
Into the overland maelstrom. (1997: 21)

Hughes's direct treatment of things has, of course, many facets. Out-standing is a diction that ranges from technical terms to colloquial idioms to archaic dialect words. Carefully designed lineation also highlights meaning for the reader's eye. Most relevant to this chapter, though, is the use of structural ellipsis to give a presentational quality to narrative detail. These facets integrate perfectly in the following passage, which describes the goddess Hunger:

> In shape and colour her face was a skull, blueish.
> Her lips a stretched hole of frayed leather
> Over bleeding teeth. Her skin
>
> So glossy and so thin
> You could see the internal organs through it.
> Her pelvic bone was like a bare bone. (p. 89)

Here everyday, even casual, vocabulary, such as 'blueish', and 'stretched hole', stands alongside the clinical diction of 'internal organs' and 'pelvic bone'. The clever lineation of:

> Her skin
> So glossy and so thin

places the most salient word 'skin' in prominence and creates a tem-porary shift to full end-rhyme. This play on sound takes place in the context of a larger syntactic pattern achieved by the ellipsis of verb elements. This brief passage consists of four orthographic sentences with the same basic structure, 'her x was/were y', plus various attachments, such as adverbial phrases. In the first and last sentences the verb is realized, but in the middle two it is omitted:

> Her lips [were] a stretched hole of frayed leather
> Over bleeding teeth. Her skin [was]
>
> So glossy and so thin
> You could see the internal organs through it.

Although the sentences are not coordinated, the ellipsis is in effect an example of gapping, since recoverable verbs central to each structure are deleted. The subtle but important stylistic effect of this verbal ellipsis is to move, however fleetingly, from tensed description to, in imagist terms, direct presentation. Hughes employs this technique throughout the *Tales from Ovid* to move temporarily from the dynamic of narrative to the photographic of vivid images.

Exercise 14.3

Here is another brief extract from Hughes's *Tales from Ovid* which begins the story of the hero Hercules and his new wife Dejanira. Identify the elliptical sentence and suggest an expansion for it. Discuss the effect of this elliptical sentence as a way of presenting images.

> Hercules, the son of Jupiter,
> Was bringing his new bride home
> When he came to the river Evenus.
>
> Burst banks, booming torrent
> Where there had been a ford. (p. 151)

Discussion of Exercises

Exercise 14.1

This poem is in a long tradition of poetic expressions of devotion in which fantastic or impossible events are forecast before the devotee's love will waver. Poems in this tradition are most often concerned with declarations of courtly love for a human object of devotion. This poem can be interpreted as such an expression of devotion to another person, the 'Sir' of the second stanza, but it could also be one of Dickinson's less sceptical expressions of faith in a divine being. The poem is structured around a series of exclamations: 'Alter!', 'Falter!', 'Surfeit!'. Each of these protests at the idea that the poet will do anything of the sort and responds with an impossible condition on doing so. The first response has a recoverable gap:

> Alter! When the Hills do [alter].

However, the sense of the condition is only fully explicit if a main clause expressing the poet's intention is also supplied:

> Alter! When the Hills do [alter] – [I will alter].

This main clause is only quasi-recoverable by analogy with the pattern of the third response where such a clause is expressed. The gap is therefore strictly inferential. Although the second response is not elliptical itself, a similar clause, analogous with that of the third response, has to be inferred:

> Falter! When the Sun
> Question if His Glory
> Be the Perfect One – [I will falter]

The second stanza, which constitutes the third exclamation and response, clarifies the pattern of the previous two, but is highly elliptical in itself:

> Surfeit! When the Daffodil
> Doth [surfeit] of the Dew –
> Even as [she surfeits of] Herself – Sir –
> I will [surfeit] – of You –

These ellipses pull an anaphoric thread of discourse through the stanza which is ultimately tied to the initial exclamation. By this means the 'I' of the poem asserts that she will never have had enough of its addressee. The poem as a whole is a fine example of poetic compression in which meaning is concentrated into fewer words than would be required in 'standard' language. The deployment of fewer words is achieved by a symmetry of contextual and inferential gaps which exemplify the exponential relation between structural ellipsis and the density of its brief argument.

Exercise 14.2

One of the most frequently voiced criticisms of imagist poetry is that it is restricted to short, visually arresting presentations which inhibit sustained narrative or logical argument. The criticism would be more damaging if the imagists had claimed sustained narrative and logical argument among their goals. In any case, imagism was never a very pure doctrine and most imagist poets adapted its principles to suit the poetic project they were working on, making possible larger-scale works with narrative and discursive elements. But even with a short and relatively pure imagist poem, like Ezra Pound's *The Return*, it is possible to discern a hypothesis of sorts.

As an example of compressed poetic language, there are one or two crucial ellipses that are not fully contextual and require some degree of inference as well as a problematic cataphoric reference. Let's deal with the cataphoric reference first. Any piece of text which begins with an unsupported pronominal reference, such as 'they', will prompt the reader response 'who?'. Texts from advertisements to detective stories take advantage of the curiosity or suspense such pronouns arouse. In Pound's poem we learn a good deal about 'they' before we know who they are. And even when he tells us, Pound's elliptical sentence doesn't make the reference explicit, so we have to infer it to some extent:

[They are the] Gods of the winged shoe!

Once this cataphoric reference is resolved, then the first two sections can be read as giving information about these gods, how they are now, tentative, fearful, hesitant, and how they were, awesome, inviolable. But the two sections also assert that these gods are coming back and exhort us to see them, acknowledge their presence for ourselves.

The gods are accompanied, as they are often depicted on stone frieze work in classical architecture, by hunting hounds. Note their verbless presentation, characteristic of other imagist poems:

With them [are] the silver hounds,
      [who are] sniffing the trace of air!

The former glories of these hounds are paraded before the reader: they were 'swift to harry', 'keen-scented', 'the souls of blood'. The contrast with their present state has to be inferred from the next line's ellipsis:

[But now they are] Slow on the leash.

Their masters, the old gods, are also pale shadows of their former selves, as the final inverted line tells us:

pallid [are] the leash-men!

The poem presents, rather than argues a case for, belief in a pagan theological tradition. Its images assert the resurgent existence of the old gods of classical mythology who have been damaged and diminished by their neglect, particularly in the face of Christian doctrine. This hypothesis

is presented, not by logical argument, but in the compressed poetic
language of dynamically verbalized images.

Exercise 14.3

The opening of Hughes's story of Hercules and Dejanira effectively
follows a past tense narrative sentence with one which presents a vivid
image to the reader. The first stanza is entirely narrative with appropriately tensed verbs:

> Hercules, the son of Jupiter,
> Was bringing his new bride home
> When he came to the river Evenus.

The next sentence has no main verb. It gives us a sight of the river, as
if through Hercules' eyes:

> Burst banks, booming torrent
> Where there had been a ford.

The telegraphic structure of the first line, which constitutes a main clause
of sorts, can be minimally expanded to create a descriptive expression:

> [There were] Burst banks [and a] booming torrent
> Where there had been a ford.

Any suggestion that the perception of the river is Hercules' is lost in this
expansion. Focalization is restored to the narrator. It is interesting to
compare Hughes's version with a prose translation of this passage from
Ovid's *Metamorphoses* by Mary M. Innes:

> Jove's son, Hercules, was returning with his new bride to his
> native city, when he came to the raging waters of Evenus.
> The river was fuller than usual, increased by winter's rains,
> and it was impossible to cross the flood, with its swirling
> eddies. (1955: 206)

The structure of this version reflects its very different aim of providing
a full and fairly literal account of Ovid's original Latin. It maintains
narrative and descriptive modes with a verbally realized syntax: 'The

river was fuller than usual', 'it was impossible to cross the flood'. These perceptions and descriptions are the narrator's. Hughes gets round the distancing effect this creates between narrator description and the reader by compressing his translation into an image which is immediately there. This is partly achieved by the selection and fusion of detail but also by the elliptical syntax Hughes employs.

CONCLUSION

In one of the most important books about language by someone whose main academic interests lie outside linguistics George Steiner makes the very positive assertion that, 'Sustained grammatical analysis is necessary and cuts deep' (1975: 5). Steiner's motto constitutes a rationale for the approach to linguistics and stylistics adopted by this book. *Mind the Gap* has attempted to show the relevance of Steiner's assertion across a variety of language in use, spoken and written, literary and non-literary. In doing so I hope it has also demonstrated that grammatical analysis only cuts deep in relation to style when it is part of a textual exploration that takes into account wider communicative, literary and cultural factors. Such things as the extralinguistic setting of a speech event, the role of the listener or reader, the influence of genre and the part played by participant knowledge have all been touched upon briefly and their importance discerned in relation to the syntactic structure and stylistic quality of elliptical language.

Syntactic structure and stylistic quality have been the organizational principles of my approach, which has meant, as I signalled in my introduction, that this is, to some extent, 'a book of two halves'. The first half took a taxonomic approach to elliptical phenomena, resulting in a typology of sorts. Two points are worth noting. First, the typology makes some either/or decisions about phenomena that are inherently fuzzy. Cut-off points have been made in order to categorize features that may be more properly seen as falling on one or more continua. Such decisions are prompted by the natural flux of language in use, an example being some of the distinctions I have made between lapses in performance and ellipsis in spontaneous conversation. Secondly, such typologies are always ongoing, and so are open to addition and refinement. Nevertheless, the checklist presented in Chapter 7 is an analytical tool that could be used at least as the starting point for further textual investigation, to be elaborated upon in the light of new data or different theoretical perspectives.

The second half of the book was a demonstration and an assessment of ellipsis as an exponent of style, or more precisely, as one exponent in a complex of stylistic features that help to characterize specific types of language variation. Clearly, a wide range of other linguistic features figure in stylistic variation, from the more general, such as lexical choice, to the genre-specific, such as rhyme. I have tried to take into account how these features interact with the main focus of my enquiry in the characterization of functional and literary styles. Nor was the importance of non-elliptical gaps ignored in all this. Indeed, some of the more problematical issues for analysis arose in trying to differentiate some elliptical and non-elliptical gaps, particularly with regard to conversational implicatures and more globally discursive inferential gaps. There are theoretical positions available that would want to incorporate ellipsis as a syntactic figure with all its subcategories into a broader pragmatics of discourse, a global theory of gaps that goes well beyond a descriptive framework.

While the categorization of elliptical features presented here is very much informed by other, sometimes conflicting, treatments, it also reflects my own preferences in terms of both categorial focus and data selection. Perhaps the first of these is most noticeable in the attention given to telegraphic and other non-contextual forms of ellipsis that create sentence fragments in a wide range of genres from spoken sports commentary to imagist poetry. These forms are interesting linguistically because they challenge notions of sentencehood and 'syntactic closure' which have pervaded grammatical analysis at least since the advent of eighteenth-century prescriptivism. My approach, relating their structure to syntactically complete potential sentences, reflects the power of such notions. It may well be that telegraphic strings are best analysed without recourse to such expansions, but I have not found a way of doing so that provides similar insights about their communicative role. In this respect the comments of the linguist J. R. Ross are salutary. At the end of his vast and complex grammatical treatise, he concluded: 'All the proposals I have made should be regarded as being extremely tentative, for our present knowledge of syntax is ridiculously small' (1986: 291). While this may be unduly modest, coming from an acknowledged innovator in linguistic theory, it nevertheless prompts worthwhile caution about any particular linguistic certitude, even in respect of the descriptive approach presented in this book.

Similar issues arise with regard to my selection of examples. The totality of linguistic data in this book constitutes my mini-corpus of English. One positive aspect of that selection was my conscious decision to alternate and juxtapose, wherever appropriate and possible, spoken, written, literary and non-literary examples, both within and across chapters. This approach has highlighted, I hope in a positive way, the fact that stylistic diversity is at least as much about the manipulation of common linguistic resources as it is about generic or modal difference. With regard to the selection of such a corpus of texts by one person, however, some caution is needed. It is quite possible, for instance, that I may have chosen data to put my typology in the best light and to the exclusion of other, less advantageous data, even though I have not done so consciously. At the very least, particularly with regard to literary examples, the selection reflects my preferences for, and personal familiarity with, some texts over others and this needs to be taken into account when judging the general effectiveness of a particular stylistic analysis.

The concept of style has emerged as the most problematical concept of all. Style is easy to refer to, but much harder to define. With regard to ellipsis and its contribution to stylistic variation, Sperber and Wilson's comments both provide insight and imply the problem in a way that brings our textual exploration full circle:

> Choice of style is something no speaker or writer can avoid. In aiming at relevance, the speaker must make some assumptions about the hearer's cognitive abilities and contextual resources, which will necessarily be reflected in the way she communicates, and in particular in what she chooses to make explicit and what she chooses to leave implicit. (1986: 218)

Here style is both inherent in the very act of speaking or writing and a matter of conscious choice on behalf of the speaker or writer. As a syntactic exponent of style ellipsis is, accordingly, both a natural, even automatic phenomenon, and a deliberate means of 'leaving implicit'. Gauging the significance of the inevitable and the optional is a defining challenge for stylistic enquiry.

Although other ways of 'leaving implicit' are available to speakers and writers, this textual exploration has sought to investigate the extent to which ellipsis, a figure of syntax, is a vehicle for such implicitness, both natural and contrived. Implicitness as a stylistic quality has been found to coincide with patterns of ellipsis, among other things. While the exact nature of that coincidence remains, in some cases, elusive, minding the gaps has proved to be a positive strategy for exploring stylistic variation in texts. An understanding of ellipsis reveals how important what is not said or what is not written can be to the meaning of what is [ ].

BIBLIOGRAPHY

Abercrombie, D. (1965) *Studies in Linguistics and Phonetics*. Oxford: Oxford University Press.

Barthes, R. (1990) *S/Z*. Oxford: Blackwell.

Beaugrande, R. de (1980) *Text, Discourse and Process: Toward a Multidisciplinary Science of Texts*. London: Longman.

Beckett, S. (1958) *Krapp's Last Tape*, in Beckett, S. (1984) *Collected Shorter Plays*. London: Faber and Faber.

Blakemore, D. (1992) *Understanding Utterances: An Introduction to Pragmatics*. Oxford: Blackwell.

Blevins, J. P. (1994) 'Derived constituent order in unbounded dependency constructions', *Journal of Linguistics*, Vol. 30, No. 2: 349–409.

Bradford, R. (1997) *Stylistics*. London: Routledge.

Brenton, H. (1986) *Plays One*. London: Methuen.

Brown, G. and Yule, G. (1983) *Discourse Analysis*. Cambridge: Cambridge University Press.

Bunting, B. (1978) *Collected Poems*. Oxford: Oxford University Press.

Carter, R. and McCarthy, M. (1995) 'Grammar and the spoken language', *Applied Linguistics*, Vol. 16, No. 2: 141–58.

Carter, R. and Nash, W. (1990) *Seeing Through Language: A Guide to Styles of English Writing*. Oxford: Blackwell.

Chambers English Dictionary (1992) Seventh Edition: W. and R. Chambers Ltd.

Chomsky, N. (1965) *Aspects of the Theory of Syntax*. Cambridge, Mass.: The MIT Press.

Clark, H. H. and Clark, E. V. (1977) *Psychology and Language*. New York: Harcourt Brace Jovanovich.

Cook, G. (1992) *The Discourse of Advertising*. London: Routledge.

Crystal, D. (1980) 'Neglected grammatical factors in conversational English', in Greenbaum, S., Leech, G. and Svartvik, J. (eds), *Studies in English Linguistics*. London: Longman: 153–66.

Department for Education and Employment (1998) *The National Literacy Strategy: Framework for Teaching*. London: HMSO.

Dickens, C. (1837) *The Pickwick Papers*. Harmondsworth: Penguin (1986).

Dickens, C. (1853) *Bleak House*. W. W. Norton and Co. (1977).

Dickinson, E. (1960) *The Complete Poems* (edited by Johnson, T. H.). Boston: Little, Brown and Company.

Donleavy, J. P. (1965) *The Ginger Man*. London: Corgi.

Durrell, L. (1968) *Balthazar*. London: Faber.

Eliot, T. S. (1963) *Collected Poems*. London: Faber.

Emmott, C. (1997) *Narrative Comprehension: A Discourse Perspective*. Oxford: Oxford University Press.

Fabb, N. (1997) *Linguistics and Literature*. Oxford: Blackwell.

Fairclough, N. (1989) *Language and Power*. London: Longman.

Faulkner, W. (1929) *The Sound and the Fury*. London: Picador (1993).

Ferguson, C. A. (1983) 'Sports announcer talk: syntactic aspects of register variation', *Language in Society*, Vol. 12: 153–72.

Fish, S. (1980) *Is There a Text in This Class?*. Cambridge, Mass.: Harvard University Press.

Fowler, R. (1996) *Linguistic Criticism* (2nd edition). Oxford: Oxford University Press.

Fry, C. (1950) *Venus Observed*. London: Oxford University Press.

Gardner, W. H. (ed.) (1963) *Gerard Manley Hopkins: A Selection of His Poems and Prose*. Harmondsworth: Penguin.

Garnham, A. (1987) 'Effects of antecedent distance and intervening text structure in the interpretation of ellipsis', *Language and Speech*, Vol. 30, Part 1: 59–68.

Genette, G. (1980) *Narrative Discourse*. Oxford: Blackwell.

Goldman, R. (1992) *Reading Ads Socially*. London: Routledge.

Gramley, S. and Patzold, K.-M. (1992) *A Survey of Modern English*. London: Routledge.

Grant-Davie, K. (1995) 'Functional redundancy and ellipsis as strategies in reading and writing', *JAC: A Journal of Composition Theory*, Vol. 15, No. 3: 455–69.

Greenaway, P. (1988) *Drowning by Numbers*. London: Faber and Faber.

Greene, R. (1587) *The Carde of Fancie*, in *Shorter Elizabethan Novels*. London: J. M. Dent (1960).

Grice, H. P. (1975) 'Logic and conversation', in Cole, P. and Morgan, J. (eds), *Syntax and Semantics 3: Speech Acts*. New York: Academic Press: 41–58.

Griffiths, T. (1982) *Oi For England*. London: Faber and Faber.

Grossmith, G. and Grossmith, W. (1892) *The Diary of a Nobody*. Harmondsworth: Penguin (1965).

Gunter, R. (1963) 'Elliptical sentences in American English', *Lingua*, Vol. 12: 137–50.

Halliday, M. A. K. (1994) 'Spoken and written modes of meaning', in Graddol, D. and Boyd-Barret, O. (eds), *Media Texts: Authors and Readers*. Milton Keynes: Open University Press: 51–73.

Halliday, M. A. K. and Hasan, R. (1976) *Cohesion in English*. London: Longman.

Hampton, C. (1970) *The Philanthropist*. London: Faber.

Holmes, J. (1992) *An Introduction to Sociolinguistics*. London: Longman.

Holzman, M. S. (1971) 'Ellipsis in discourse', *Language and Speech*, Vol. 14, No. 1: 86–98.

Huddleston, R. (1984) *Introduction to the Grammar of English*. Cambridge: Cambridge University Press.

Huddleston, R. (1988) *English Grammar: An Outline*. Cambridge: Cambridge University Press.

Hudson, R. A. (1976) 'Conjunction reduction, gapping and right node raising', *Language*, Vol. 52: 535–62.

Hughes, T. (1997) *Tales from Ovid*. London: Faber and Faber.

Iser, W. (1978) *The Act of Reading*. London: Routledge.

Jack, I. (ed.) (1970) *Browning: Poetical Works*. Oxford: Oxford University Press.

Jakobson, R. (1960) 'Closing statement: linguistics and poetics', in Sebeok, T. A. (ed.), *Style in Language*. Cambridge, Mass.: The MIT Press: 350–77.

Jespersen, O. (1949) *A Modern English Grammar. Part 7: Syntax*. London: Allen and Unwin.

Johnson, B. S. (1973) *Christie Malry's Own Double-Entry*. New York: New Directions (1985).

Jones, P. (ed.) (1972) *Imagist Poetry*. Harmondsworth: Penguin.

Joyce, J. (1922) *Ulysses* (edited by Rose, D.). London: Picador (1997).

Kennedy, W. (1983) *Ironweed*. New York: The Viking Press.

Kinneavy, J. L. (1971) *A Theory of Discourse*. Englewood Cliffs, NJ: Prentice-Hall.

Klein, E. and Stainton-Ellis, K. (1989) 'A note on multiple VP ellipsis', *Linguistics*, Vol. 27: 1119–24.

Kress, G. (1979) 'The social values of speech and writing', in Fowler, R., Hodge, B., Kress, G. and Trew, T. (eds), *Language and Control*. London: Routledge: 46–62.

Kress, G. and Hodge, R. (1979) *Language as Ideology*. London: Routledge.

Lakoff, R. (1982) 'Persuasive discourse and ordinary conversation', in Tannen, D. (ed.), *Analyzing Discourse: Text and Talk*. Washington, DC: Georgetown University Press: 26–42.

Leech, G. (1987) 'Stylistics and functionalism', in Fabb, N., Attridge, D., Durant, A. and McCabe, C. (eds), *The Linguistics of Writing: Arguments between Language and Literature*. Manchester: Manchester University Press: 76–88.

Leech, G. and Short, M. (1981) *Style in Fiction: A Linguistic Introduction to English Fictional Prose*. London: Longman.

Lehmann, R. (1932) *Invitation to the Waltz*. London: Virago Press (1981).

Lehmann, R. (1936) *The Weather in the Streets*. London: Virago Press (1981).

Levinson, S. C. (1983) *Pragmatics*. Cambridge: Cambridge University Press.

Levy, D. (1996) *Billy and Girl*. London: Bloomsbury.

Lyons, J. (1977) *Semantics* (Vol. 2). Cambridge: Cambridge University Press.

Matthews, P. H. (1981) *Syntax*. Cambridge: Cambridge University Press.

McFadden, C. and Hillman, J. (1992) *Sainsbury's Combined Recipes*. London: Reed International Books.

Meyer, C. F. (1995) 'Coordination ellipsis in spoken and written American English', *Language Sciences*, Vol. 17, No. 3: 241–69.

Michel-Thiriet, P. (1989) *The Book of Proust*. London: Chatto and Windus.

Miller, C. (1987) *Emily Dickinson: A Poet's Grammar*. Cambridge, Mass.: Harvard University Press.

Montgomery, M., Durant, A., Fabb, N., Furniss, T. and Mills, S. (eds) (1992) *Ways of Reading: Advanced Reading Skills for Students of English Literature*. London: Routledge.

Mukařovský, J. (1964) 'Standard language and poetic language', in Garvin, P. L. (ed.), *A Prague School Reader on Esthetics, Literary Structure, and Style*. Washington, DC: Georgetown University Press: 17–30.

Nash, W. and Stacey, D. (1997) *Creating Texts: An Introduction to the Study of Composition*. London: Longman.

O'Brien, E. (1971) *A Pagan Place*. Harmondsworth: Penguin.

Oostdijk, N. (1986) 'Coordination and gapping in corpus analysis', in Aarts, J. and Meijs, W. (eds), *Corpus Linguistics II: New Studies in the Analysis and Exploitation of Computer Corpora*. Amsterdam: Editions Rodopi: 177–201.

Ordinance Survey (1982) *Walker's Britain*. London: Guild Publishing.

Ovid, *Metamorphoses* (translated by Innes, M. M.). Harmondsworth: Penguin (1955).

Pinter, H. (1960) *A Night Out*, in Pinter, H. (1968) *A Slight Ache and Other Plays*. London: Methuen.

Pound, E. (1915) *Cathay*, in Pound, E. (1975) *Selected Poems*. London: Faber.

Pound, E. (1917) *Homage to Sextus Propertius*, in Pound, E. (1975) *Selected Poems*. London: Faber.

Pound, E. (1918) 'A retrospect', in Eliot, T. S. (ed.) (1968), *Literary Essays of Ezra Pound*. New York: New Directions: 3–14.

Pound, E. (1975) *Selected Poems*. London: Faber.

Pound, E. (1987) *The Cantos*. London: Faber and Faber.

Proust, M. (1913–1927) *Remembrance of Things Past* (trans. by Moncrieff, C. K. S. and Kilmartin, T.). Harmondsworth: Penguin 1983.

Qian, Z. (1995) *Orientalism and Modernism: The Legacy of China in Pound and Williams*. Durham, NC, and London: Duke University Press.

Quirk, R., Greenbaum, S., Leech, G. and Svartvik, J. (1985) *A Comprehensive Grammar of the English Language*. London: Longman.

Rhys, J. (1939) *Good Morning, Midnight*. Harmondsworth: Penguin (1969).

Rhys, J. (1968) *The Wide Sargasso Sea*. Harmondsworth: Penguin.

Rimmon-Kenan, S. (1983) *Narrative Fiction: Contemporary Poetics*. London: Routledge.

Ross, J. R. (1986) *Infinite Syntax*. Norwood, NJ: Ablex Publishing Corporation.

Sadock, J. M. (1974) 'Read at your own risk: syntactic and semantic horrors you can find in your medicine chest', *Chicago Linguistics Society Papers*, Vol. 10: 599–607.

Selders, D. (1995) *Artwork: Discourse Processing in Machine Translation of Dialog*. New Mexico State University: http://crl.nmsu.edu/Research/Projects/artwork

Shakespeare, W. (1603) *Othello*. London: Methuen (1972).

Shklovsky, V. (1917) 'Art as technique', in Lodge, D. (ed.) (1988), *Modern Criticism and Theory*. London: Longman: 15–30.

Short, M. (1996) *Exploring the Language of Poems, Plays and Prose*. London: Addison Wesley Longman.

Simpson, P. (1998) 'Odd talk: studying discourses of incongruity', in Culpeper, J., Short, M. and Verdonk, P. (eds), *Exploring the Language of Drama: From Text to Context*. London: Routledge: 34–53.

Sinclair, J. (1988) 'Compressed English', in Ghadessy, M. (ed.), *Registers of Written English*. London: Pinter Publishers: 130–5.

Sinclair, M. (1922) *The Life and Death of Harriett Frean*. London: Virago Press (1980).

Sperber, D. and Wilson, D. (1986) *Relevance: Communication and Cognition*. Oxford: Blackwell.

Stainton, R. J. (1994) 'Using non-sentences: an application of relevance theory', *Pragmatics and Cognition*, Vol. 2, No. 2: 269–84.

Steinberg, D. D. (1993) *An Introduction to Psycholinguistics*. London: Longman.

Steiner, G. (1975) *After Babel: Aspects of Language and Translation*. Oxford: Oxford University Press.

Sterne, L. (1767) *The Life and Opinions of Tristram Shandy*. Harmondsworth: Penguin (1967).

Tannen, D. (1992) *You Just Don't Understand: Women and Men in Conversation*. London: Virago Press.

Taylor, T. J. and Toolan, M. (1984) 'Recent trends in stylistics', in Weber, J. J. (1996) *The Stylistics Reader: From Roman Jakobson to the Present*. London: Arnold: 87–91.

Thomas, A. L. (1979) 'Ellipsis: the interplay of sentence structure and content', *Lingua*, Vol. 47, No. 1: 43–68.

Thomas, A. L. (1987) 'The use and interpretation of verbally determinate verb group ellipsis in English', *International Review of Applied Linguistics*, Vol. 25, No. 1: 1–14.

Thomas, D. (1963) *Miscellany One*. London: J. M. Dent.

Tilgals, K. and Gaunt, N. (1996) *The After Work Cookbook*. Sydney: Harbour Books.

Toolan, M. (1998) *Language in Literature: An Introduction to Stylistics.* London: Arnold.

Townsend, S. (1982) *The Secret Diary of Adrian Mole.* London: Methuen.

Trask, R. L. (1997) *A Student's Dictionary of Language and Linguistics.* London: Arnold.

van Peer, W. (1993) 'Typographic foregrounding', *Language and Literature,* Vol. 2, No. 1: 49–61.

Vygotsky, L. (1986) *Thought and Language.* Cambridge, Mass.: The MIT Press.

Wales, K. (1989) *A Dictionary of Stylistics.* London: Longman.

Wales, K. (1992) *The Language of James Joyce.* London: Macmillan.

Walker, A. (1983) *The Color Purple.* London: The Women's Press.

Walker, J. (ed.) (1997) *Halliwell's Film and Video Guide* (1997 Edition). London: HarperCollins.

Whitman, W. (1855) *Leaves of Grass: His Original Edition* (edited, with an introduction, by Cowley, M.). Harmondsworth: Penguin (1976).

Wilder, C. (1994) 'Coordination, ATB and ellipsis', *Groninger Arbeiten Zur Germanistischen Linguistik,* Vol. 37: 291–329.

Wilkes, A. (1997) *Children's Quick and Easy Cookbook.* London: Dorling Kindersley.

Wilson, P. (1997) *A Preface to Ezra Pound.* London: Longman.

Woolf, V. (1915) *The Voyage Out.* Harmondsworth: Penguin (1992).

INDEX

Abercrombie, D., 138, 143, 145
addressee, 122, 136–7, 178–9, 180,
    184, 192, 195
addresser, 122, 126, 136, 180
adverts, advertising, 8, 15, 20, 119,
    178–9, 183–93
Aldington, R., 216
    'Picket', 217–18
ambiguity, 2, 10, 44, 46, 47, 49–50,
    64, 68, 74, 100, 131, 188,
    190–1, 193, 196, 205, 206
anaphoric, 12, 38, 40, 42, 97,
    107–8, 153, 222

Barthes, R., 129
BE deletion, 152, 157, 158, 161
Beaugrande, R. de, 78
Beckett, S.,
    Krapp's Last Tape, 172–4
Blakemore, D., 32–3, 36
Blevins, J. P., 97
Bradford, R., 118, 119, 128, 129
Brenton, H.,
    Magnificence, 11–12
Brown, G., 182–3
Browning, R., 171
    Soliloquy of the Spanish Cloister, 172
Bunting, B.,
    Chomei at Toyama, 9–10

cataphoric, 38, 40, 41, 42, 43, 72,
    75, 98, 214, 223
Carter, R., 17, 56, 57, 58

Carter, R., 71, 124
Chomsky, N., 22–3, 25
Clark, E. V., 23–4
Clark, H. H., 23–4
cognition, 12, 18, 25, 109
cohesion, cohesive, 39–41, 42, 46,
    62, 75
compressed language, 15, 21, 73, 80,
    211, 223–4
conjunction reduction, 92–3
content words, 70
contextual ellipsis, 38, 43, 55, 62,
    82, 107, 133, 208, 213, 214
contextual rejoinders, 8, 10, 18, 20,
    23, 39–40, 45–50, 53, 58, 62,
    83, 95, 108, 139–41, 143, 145,
    147–8, 186
conventional ellipsis, 58–9, 109, 151
conversational implicature, 13, 32,
    36, 79, 114, 140, 227
Cook, G., 191
cooperative principle, 32, 79
coordination reduction, 39, 85–7,
    92, 94–7, 101, 103, 107, 112,
    209
Crystal, D., 28–9, 30, 31

decoder, 128, 178–9
defamiliarization, 121, 131
Department for Education and
    Employment,
    The National Literacy Strategy, 2, 7,
    9, 17

deviation, 26, 119–20
dialogue, 11, 13, 143, 145, 163, 165, 166, 167, 168, 177
diary entries, 65–6, 120, 123, 124, 173, 175
Dickens, C.,
  The Pickwick Papers, 77–8, 127, 132–3
  Bleak House, 127, 133–4
Dickinson, E., 212, 218
  'I fear a man of frugal speech', 213–14
  'Alter! When the hills do', 214–15, 221–2
direct object ellipsis, 41, 182, 191, 192
Donleavy, J. P.,
  The Ginger Man, 76, 86
Durrell, L.,
  Balthazar, 73

egocentric speech, 83, 137, 172, 174, 175
Eliot, T. S.,
  The Waste Land, 51, 53–4,
  'Portrait of a Lady', 57
e-mail, 25
Emmott, C., 12
encoder, 126
endophoric, 55
exophoric, 55, 62–3, 65, 110
explicature, 32–3, 36
explicitness, 28, 31, 37, 50, 164, 175

Fabb, N., 97
Fairclough, N., 36
false starts, 23, 24, 25, 34, 45, 62, 80, 110, 113–14, 137, 139, 148, 167, 169
Faulkner, W.,
  The Sound and the Fury, 29
Ferguson, C. A., 149, 151, 159
Fish, S., 128–30

focalization, 197, 199, 204, 206, 208, 224
Fowler, R., 29, 35
Fry, C., 171
  Venus Observed, 169–70

gapping, 97–9, 102–3, 108, 112, 114, 220
Garnham, A., 108–9
Genette, G., 197, 206
Goldman, R., 193
Gramley, S. and Patzold, K-M., 29
Grant-Davie, K., 129
Greenaway, P.,
  Drowning by Numbers, 13–14, 19
Greene, R.,
  The Carde of Fancie, 99
Grice, H. P., 32, 79
Griffiths, T.,
  Oi For England, 171, 177
Grossmith, G.,
  The Diary of a Nobody, 61, 65
Grossmith, W.,
  The Diary of a Nobody, 61, 65
Gunter, R., 38, 72

Halliday, M. A. K., 24, 25–6, 36, 39–40, 45, 47, 60, 167
Hampton, C.,
  The Philanthropist, 39, 46, 49
Hasan, R., 36, 39–40, 47, 60, 62, 95
headlines, 2, 71–3, 74, 75, 80, 184, 186
Hodge, R., 35
Holmes, J., 149, 156
Holzman, M. S., 36
Hopkins, G. M.,
  'The Windhover', 123
Huddleston, R., 29–30, 87, 89
Hudson, R. A., 93
Hughes, T.,
  Tales from Ovid, 219–21, 224–5

idiolect, 24, 126

implicitness, 17, 28, 31, 36, 64, 228

indefinite ellipsis, 27

inferential gaps, 13, 31–3, 110, 114, 202, 213, 214

interior monologue, 82–4, 171–4, 196, 202, 208–9

intersentential ellipsis, 38, 39, 45–51, 85, 86, 107

interviews, 139–42, 145–7

intrasentential ellipsis, 38, 39, 41–4, 85, 107

Iser, W., 207

Jakobson, R., 119, 122, 124, 168, 178–9

Jespersen, O., 71, 74

Johnson, B. S.,
    Christie Malry's Own Double-Entry, 99, 102–3

Joyce, J., 172, 173, 204, 208, 209
    Ulysses, 78, 81–4, 200, 201–3

Kennedy, W.
    Ironweed, 201

Kinneavy, J. L., 178–9

Klein, E., K., 107–8, 109

Kress, G., 24, 35

Lakoff, R., 184

lapses in performance, 22–6, 62, 110, 113, 139, 150, 155, 167, 198, 226

Leech, G., 29, 117, 134, 178, 200, 201

Lehmann, R.,
    The Weather in the Streets, 203–4, 208–9

Levinson, S. C., 32

Levy, D.,
    Billy and Girl, 108

Lowell, A.,
    'Yoshiwara Lament', 215–16

Lyons, J., 11

Matthews, P. H., 45, 62–3

maxims of conversation, 32, 79–80

McCarthy, M., 17, 56, 57, 58

metaphor, 10, 203, 214

metonymy, 33, 59

Meyer, C. F., 108, 109

Michel-Thiriet, P., 196

Miller, C., 213

modality, 136, 138, 149, 163

monologue, 136, 137, 142, 143, 144. 145, 171, 172, 175

Montgomery, M., 122–3

Mukařovský, J., 120–1, 131, 211

Nash, W., 25, 71, 124

nonrealization, 27–31, 110, 113, 114, 213

normal non-fluency, 24, 34, 137, 146, 148, 169, 174

O'Brien, E.,
    A Pagan Place, 195–6

Oostdijk, N., 88–9

Ovid,
    Metamorphoses, 224

parallelism, 88, 99, 101–3, 108, 112,134, 154

parataxis, 73, 81, 86, 102, 107, 131, 133, 167, 196, 209

phatic language, 137, 168

Pinter, H.,
    A Night Out, 164–5, 174

Pound, E., 215, 216
    The Cantos, 121, 130
    'The Return', 218–19, 222–4

prosodic, 56, 59–60, 63, 149, 154, 156, 158, 164, 165

Proust, M., 196

psycholinguistic, 18, 76, 84, 108, 171, 173

Qian, Z., 130–1

quasi-ellipsis, 13, 17, 19

Quirk, R., 17, 19, 30, 42, 49, 74, 109

radio phone-in, 26, 34, 136
recipe, 40, 179, 180–3, 191
reciprocal, 184, 191, 192
reduced relative clause, 43–4, 52–3, 132, 133, 154, 165, 181
register, 18, 122–3, 124, 136, 150, 167
rejoinder sequence, 33, 36, 39, 51, 142
Rhys, J.,
    Good Morning, Midnight., 196, 198–9, 206–8
    The Wide Sargasso Sea, 85, 87
right node raising, 97
Rimmon-Kenan, S., 199
Ross, J. R., 227

Sadock, J. M., 67
Selders, D., 17
sentence fragments, 11, 14, 21, 45–6, 48, 62, 63, 74, 227
sentence-initial ellipsis, 55–61, 62, 63, 66, 69, 77, 81, 109, 112, 120, 123, 124, 134, 151, 158, 174, 177, 186, 191,192, 204, 209, 216
Shakespeare, W., 171
    Othello, 166, 175–7
Shklovsky, V., 121
Short, M., 29, 117, 126, 134, 169, 200, 201
Simpson, P., 170
Sinclair, J., 15, 21
Sinclair, M.,
    The Life and Death of Harriett Frean, 194–5, 197, 205–6
situational ellipsis, 62–5, 68, 69, 70, 110, 113, 114, 159
Sperber, D., 32, 228
Stacey, D., 25

Stainton, R. J., 16
Stainton-Ellis, K., 107–8, 109
Steinberg, D. D., 76
Steiner, G., 226
Sterne, L.,
    The Life and Opinions of Tristram Shandy, 195, 197–8
stream of consciousness, 78, 171, 173, 207
strict ellipsis, 13
structure words, 70–1, 80, 192
subjectless imperatives, 29–31, 35, 63, 179, 181, 183, 191, 192
subordination reduction, 41–4, 51–3, 85, 107, 112, 133

Tannen, D., 128
Taylor, T. J., 125
telegraphic ellipsis, 16, 68, 71, 72, 74, 76, 77, 79, 109, 113, 131, 134, 135, 152, 153, 154, 157, 161, 164, 177, 191, 196, 201, 204, 206, 207, 217, 224, 227
text convention, 21, 124, 132, 180
Thomas, A. L., 17, 58, 109
Thomas, D., 85
Toolan, M., 40, 125
Townsend, S.,
    The Secret Diary of Adrian Mole, 61, 65–6
Trask, R. L., 39

ungrammatical, 27, 29, 50, 93

van Peer, W., 210
verb phrase deletion, 95, 107–8, 112
Vygotsky, L., 83–4, 173

Wales, K., 82, 117–18, 126
Walker, A.,
    The Color Purple, 120

weak ellipsis, 13, 42, 44, 52, 133
weather forecast, 122 124–6,
    131–2
Whitman, W.,
   Leaves of Grass, 211–12
Wilder, C., 87

Wilson, D., 32, 228
Wilson, P., 130
Woolf, V.,
   The Voyage Out., 42, 43, 44

Yule, G., 182–3